Mastering Software Product Management

Practical Solutions and Expert Tips for Strategy, Decision-Making, and Building & Selling Market-Leading Software Products

Sambit Kumar Dash

www.orangeava.com

Copyright © 2025, Orange Education Pvt Ltd, AVA®

All rights reserved. No part of this book may be reproduced, stored in a retrieval system, or transmitted in any form or by any means, without the prior written permission of the publisher, except in the case of brief quotations embedded in critical articles or reviews.

Every effort has been made in the preparation of this book to ensure the accuracy of the information presented. However, the information contained in this book is sold without warranty, either express or implied. Neither the author nor **Orange Education Pvt Ltd** or its dealers and distributors, will be held liable for any damages caused or alleged to have been caused directly or indirectly by this book.

Orange Education Pvt Ltd has endeavored to provide trademark information about all of the companies and products mentioned in this book by the appropriate use of capital. However, **Orange Education Pvt Ltd** cannot guarantee the accuracy of this information. The use of general descriptive names, registered names, trademarks, service marks, etc. in this publication does not imply, even in the absence of a specific statement, that such names are exempt from the relevant protective laws and regulations and therefore free for general use.

First Published: April 2025
Published By: Orange Education Pvt Ltd, AVA®
Address: 9, Daryaganj, Delhi, 110002, India

275 New North Road Islington Suite 1314 London,
N1 7AA, United Kingdom

ISBN (PBK): 978-93-48107-56-5
ISBN (E-BOOK): 978-93-48107-96-1

Scan the QR code to explore our entire catalogue

www.orangeava.com

Dedicated To

My Beloved Parents

And

My Loving Wife

About the Author

Sambit Kumar Dash is passionate about turning technology product ideas into reality. He has over 25 years of experience in product and business management, architecture, and research and development. His interests in technology expand to document technologies, computer security, artificial intelligence, and natural language processing. Sambit created a PDF reader library in the Julia programming language, which is available on GitHub (https://github.com/sambitdash/PDFIO.jl). He is passionate about developing new technologies and holds eight patents in document technologies, computer security, virtualization, and human-computer interfaces. He has authored two books: *Hand-On Julia Programming* and *Ultimate Web Authentication Handbook*. He also provides product management consultancy to start-ups and early-stage ventures through Lenatics Solutions Private Limited.

About the Technical Reviewers

Shashi is an engineering and product leader in the IT industry with over two decades of experience. He has worked with HP, HPE, Texas Instruments, Motorola, TCS, and MicroFocus in various technical and managerial leadership roles. He is currently working with OpenText.

He holds a Ph.D. in management science from IIT Madras, a Master in Business Law from NLSIU Bangalore, an MBA from IIM Bangalore, and B.Tech. from IIT Bombay. His research interests include decision-making under uncertainty, and entrepreneurial strategy formulation and decision-making.

Bikram Gupta is a product leader with over twenty years of experience at companies such as DigitalOcean, AWS, FireEye, Intel, McAfee, and Cisco. As the Lead Product Manager at DigitalOcean, he focuses on driving Kubernetes and App Platform adoption for SMBs, specializing in cloud-native applications and AI workloads.

Throughout his career, Bikram has transformed ideas into market-ready solutions, developing cloud platforms, security products, and developer ecosystems. His work has spanned from enhancing container infrastructure to advancing network security and simplifying SaaS adoption. Across roles, he has contributed to building scalable systems, improving customer experiences, and driving innovation in evolving technology landscapes.

Bikram excels at translating complex technical concepts into practical insights. Beyond his professional work, he maintains an active interest in emerging technologies, particularly AI, cloud computing, and cybersecurity developments.

Acknowledgements

Product management processes are strategic and require an outside-in view of an organization. Porter's Five Forces framework has aptly identified the factors outside an organization. Over the past several decades, it has remained a foundational framework for sustained competitive advantage (SCA). A big thanks to Dr. Michael E. Porter for this invaluable contribution.

I would like to express my heartfelt gratitude to my teacher and guide, Prof. DVR Seshadri, for his confidence in me to take on the audacious challenge of retelling Software Product Management with a new approach. I sincerely hope I have lived up to his expectations.

I am also deeply thankful to Shashi Bhushan Kumar, Bikram Kumar Gupta, Ranjan Prakash, Charul Sadwelkar, Gajendran Kandasamy, and Aditya Rath, who painstakingly reviewed several chapters and provided invaluable feedback. Their timely suggestions have only made this book better. However, all omissions and errors should only be attributed to me.

I am grateful to my friends, Chittaranjan Jena, Ganesh Sahai, Rajashree Mitra, and my wife Pranati Priyadarshini Mohapatra, who continuously checked on my progress and encouraged me to finish the book. I thank them all for their unofficial project management.

I would also like to thank Shubha, Ritu, Sonali, and Priyanka for their excellent work as editors of this book, as well as Sourabh Dwivedi and the entire team at Orange Education Pvt Ltd for their remarkable support in making this work see the light of day.

Lastly, I thank you for choosing this work for your learning. We hope you enjoy it as much as we did in putting it all together. Please do not forget to provide your comments and suggestions that help us improve the book further.

Foreword

- Prof. DVR Seshadri

(Professor of Practice – Marketing Area, Indian School of Business, Hyderabad)

In the dynamic world of software product management, the complexities and nuances of the role are often misunderstood. This book is a crucial guide for anyone wishing to navigate the intricacies of this vital function, especially within the SaaS landscape. Drawing upon foundational concepts while also addressing contemporary challenges, Sambit adeptly bridges the gap between traditional product management principles and the evolving demands of the software industry.

The insights presented here are not merely theoretical; they reflect a deep understanding cultivated through real-world experiences and challenges that product managers face. The integration of Porter's Five Forces into the framework of product management establishes a robust foundation for strategizing competitive advantage. This book rightly argues that product management extends beyond mere feature management; it is an inclusive discipline that embraces strategic thinking, customer engagement, and cross-functional collaboration.

Readers will find value not only in the structured approach to product management outlined in each chapter but also in the broader discourse about its relevance across varied domains. As emerging professionals and seasoned veterans delve into this work, they will discover tools and perspectives that can transform their thinking and enhance their practice. This is essential reading for anyone dedicated to achieving excellence in the field of product management. It equips them with the frameworks for ensuring sustained success in today's competitive marketplace. I take this opportunity to extend my best wishes to this excellent work as it seeks to inform countless professionals and academics—through valuable insights contained within— on the intricacies of Product Management.

Preface

It all started when I headed the product management function in my last organization. The organization had been in existence for several years but has never had a formal product management function. The CEO was a trained and seasoned manager, worked in several leading MNCs, had started his own IT services startup, and had successfully divested it. This time, he was leading the SaaS-based software product company. He was bemused by the software engineering processes, like agile processes, user stories, etc. He asked me once if there is one book that describes the product management function well enough. During my MBA, I was taught product management from a classic book - Product Management[1], Lehmann and Winer. The book approached product management as a marketing function and added all the relevant topics from strategy and marketing for a marketing professional. However, software product management, agile process models, etc., are not delved into.

In the early days of software product management, I heard senior leadership complaining about product managers (PMs) not presenting the products in large forums and seminars. He had been looking for a product evangelist in the garb of a product manager. An EdTech founder was remarking that hiring product managers is hard because he only gets to meet feature managers and not real product managers. A product head of an organization complains that all of his product managers have an MBA background but lack understanding of technical product development. Another founding CEO of a company with 200-300 employees stated that the product management did not choose the right technology stack. That was the reason they delayed the product release. None of the claims are misplaced, but all these stories highlight how we can be blindfolded in our little definitions of product management while trying to comprehend an elephant by touch alone; a story often told in the context of understanding the complete picture.

I have faced the imposter syndrome. Every organization I have worked for has put forth a new set of challenges as a product manager. I have been instrumental in reengineering the non-engineering technology functions in some, ensuring high-

---

[1] Lehmann, D. R., Winer, R. S. (2005). Product Management. United Kingdom: McGraw-Hill/Irwin.

quality product delivery to revenue protection for products, product expansion to newer domains, streamlining knowledge processes of the organization, etc. All these, alongside the regular day-to-day function of the organization's product definition, customer engagements, better sales, and working with engineering for timely delivery of the product with quality. Some of you must be wondering, where are the user stories or product ownership for agile process management listed? This book is not another one outlining the product management processes or activities. We will ask why product managers do things the way they do. We looked at all the product management functions and stitched them along with Porter's Five Forces[2], a framework for organization strategy for several decades. Thus, our approach is to ensure an organization's product management function is meant for the sustained competitive advantage of the business units. While we will substantiate many of the claims with relevant research or studies conducted by industry experts, academics, and veterans, sometimes we will resort to storytelling when the stories are easier to understand and stick better in the reader's memory. Moreover, where the stories give a general direction to the past events and context, they may be preferred over detailed research data. We outline the chapters along ten significant activities product management organizations undertake while correlating the activities with Porter's Five Forces. Porter's work is associated with industrial economics and is considered an industry analysis framework. However, we choose that as Product Management takes an outside-in view of an organization. The five forces are a great way to represent externalities that affect a business. A product manager who understands these forces and can effectively navigate them has better control over his products. The following are the outlines of the chapters discussed in the book:

Chapter 1. The Practice of Product Management: What is a software product? How can a PM look at the external market conditions and bring them to the organization? We realized that PM activities can be classified into ten broad processes. Aggregated, we call them The Practice of Product Management. By keeping the processes aligned with Michael Porter's Five Forces Framework, PMs achieve Sustained Competitive Advantage for their products.

Chapter 2. Strategy: Organizations are perpetual entities; they will remain in existence for generations. While products have a limited life cycle, there is

---

[2] Dash, Sambit Kumar, Product Management at Crossroads (January 22, 2022). SPM Summit India, IIM Bangalore, 22nd Jan 2022, Available at SSRN: https://ssrn.com/abstract=4195893

inception, growth, and eventual death. Such misunderstandings lead to discussions on strategy, delving into too much implementation or tactical details. Product managers, at least, should have a qualitative understanding of the organization's strategy and leverage the product's strengths to achieve sustained competitive advantages.

Chapter 3. Product Vision: The product vision is the most valuable statement a product management organization owns, probably the only task of the product manager that he cannot delegate. While input from everyone is welcome, if you are a product manager, you should ensure you own the vision and explain it to everyone in the organization or outside. Proper execution of a compelling vision can lead to a successful product in the long run.

Chapter 4. Customer: If you deal with commodities, you face the challenges of an ever-bargaining buyer. You create value drivers with users and influencers to move them away from the buying mindset to a mutual success-oriented customer mindset. For a product manager, there is never one customer. Multiple customers have to be satisfied with the same product. To a Product Manager, a customer is a Trusted Advisor. The idea is to take the input to evaluate against inputs from other customers and come up with a plan to deliver the best solution that gives the maximal value to the overall customer set.

Chapter 5. Pricing: Pricing is not about offering the best discount to the buyer but creating a value perception and taking your rightful share of the perception. Once you move the customer from a buyer mindset to a trusted advisor mindset, it is easy to claim a part of the value added as price. There are only three principles to pricing; the customer should perceive value, the pricing should be competitive, and you should not make losses. When all these factors match, you provide the customer with the best sustainable price in the long run.

Chapter 6. User Experience: Many product managers focus on finding the best interface for better user engagement with the product. While some insist on using design tools, mock-up tools, and prototyping interactions, some insist these must be left to the UX designers to provide the best possible proposals. We take UX to the aspects of functional elements affecting user experience, the tools and frameworks, components of the user interface, and design thinking to achieve a better user experience.

Chapter 7. Contracts: No business operates in isolation. If you are offering a service to your customers, you also need downstream services fulfilled by your vendors. You will need well-defined contracts and service-level agreements for the proper execution. Even contractual relationships are essential for your customer engagements as well. There are various legal interactions among people and institutions that people build. The Govt cannot decide the interaction possibilities among them. The government only defines general guidelines of how they can interact, but keeps the details within the contract to be worked upon by the interacting parties. Parties engage in establishing a legal relationship ahead of time.

Chapter 8. Intellectual Properties: Most organizations are innovative. They try to do things differently from their competition. They have something in them that is core to their DNA and different from others in the same business. How can they identify these core strengths and systematically create distinguishable property elements such as copyrights, patents, trademarks, and so on? In the long run, these will keep new entrants from entering their markets.

Chapter 9. Compliance: Compliance is adherence to rules, regulations, environments, or laws. We have experienced that compliance needs to be analyzed by product managers ahead of time, before other parts of the organization invest any energy in it. In some businesses, compliance is the prime driver, and non-compliance makes the venture a no-go. So, your fundamental need to be in the market is decided by your ability to meet the compliance requirements.

Chapter 10. Agile Process: The agile process framework is an aspect of the product management process. Hence, every product manager should develop a good understanding of it. Certifications and training available today can make one aware of these processes. All agile process frameworks are not alike. Some are useful for individual knowledge workers, some for teams of a project, and some for independent groups. More than learning the nitty-gritty details of the process, product managers should realize the rationale behind the process frameworks. It is often learning from previous mistakes, understanding, and continually improving to do a better job.

Chapter 11. People: Product managers are capable matrix managers competent in operating through unknowns with ease. Hence, communication across the organization is an important aspect. Mostly KPI-driven and numbers-oriented, a few process frameworks like RACI are good for PMs. A person ready to take ownership of a situation can get into such a role. Fearlessness and the ability to deal with all eventualities are the core building blocks in a PM's mindset. The buck stops here is the attitude that PMs need to build.

Chapter 12. Epilogue: A summary of what we discussed in the book. Also, a short discussion on how AI tools are aiding product management functions.

About the Questions

Questions provided at the end of the chapters are for leading you to understand the topic in depth. It is perfectly alright if you cannot answer them satisfactorily in the first reading of the book. Some questions may not have answers in the chapter where they appear. They can create a lingering doubt to be answered in a later chapter. Some of them may need resources outside of the book. As most practitioners' quest, some of the questions may not have a concrete answer or may have different answers based on the situations and life cycles of the product, hence open to discussions and debates.

Colored Images

Please follow the links or scan the QR codes to download the **Images** of the book:

You can find code bundles of our books on our official Github Repository. Go to the following link to and QR code to explore the further:

https://github.com/orgs/ava-orange-education/repositories

Please follow the link to download the Colored Images of the book:
https://rebrand.ly/8c3f8d

In case there's an update to the code, it will be updated on the existing GitHub repository.

Errata

We take immense pride in our work at **Orange Education Pvt Ltd,** and follow best practices to ensure the accuracy of our content to provide an indulging reading experience to our subscribers. Our readers are our mirrors, and we use their inputs to reflect and improve upon human errors, if any, that may have occurred during the publishing processes involved. To let us maintain the quality and help us reach out to any readers who might be having difficulties due to any unforeseen errors, please write to us at :

errata@orangeava.com

Your support, suggestions, and feedback are highly appreciated.

DID YOU KNOW

Did you know that Orange Education Pvt Ltd offers eBook versions of every book published, with PDF and ePub files available? You can upgrade to the eBook version at **www.orangeava.com** and as a print book customer, you are entitled to a discount on the eBook copy. Get in touch with us at: **info@orangeava.com** for more details.

At **www.orangeava.com**, you can also read a collection of free technical articles, sign up for a range of free newsletters, and receive exclusive discounts and offers on Print Books and eBooks.

PIRACY

If you come across any illegal copies of our works in any form on the internet, we would be grateful if you would provide us with the location address or website name. Please contact us at **info@orangeava.com** with a link to the material.

ARE YOU INTERESTED IN AUTHORING WITH US?

If there is a topic that you have expertise in, and you are interested in either writing or contributing to a book, please write to us at **business@orangeava.com**. We are on a journey to help developers and tech professionals to gain insights on the present technological advancements and innovations happening across the globe and build a community that believes Knowledge is best acquired by sharing and learning with others. Please reach out to us to learn what our audience demands and how you can be part of this educational reform. We also welcome ideas from tech experts and help them build learning and development content for their domains.

REVIEWS

Please leave a review. Once you have read and used this book, why not leave a review on the site that you purchased it from? Potential readers can then see and use your unbiased opinion to make purchase decisions. We at Orange Education would love to know what you think about our products, and our authors can learn from your feedback. Thank you!

For more information about Orange Education, please visit **www.orangeava.com**.

Table of Contents

1. **The Practice of Product Management** 1
   - Introduction 1
   - Structure 1
   - Software Product 1
     - *Economics* 3
     - *Sales and Marketing* 3
     - *Engineering* 4
     - *Infrastructure* 5
     - *Technology* 6
   - Product Management Process 7
   - The Framework 10
   - Conclusion 12
   - Questions 12

2. **Strategy** 13
   - Introduction 13
   - Structure 13
   - Strategy and Sustained Competitive Advantage 13
   - Corporate Strategy 19
   - Strategy Tools for Product Managers 20
     - *Porter's Five Forces* 20
     - *Key Factors for Success* 24
     - *BCG Growth-Share Matrix* 26
     - *DuPont Analysis* 27
   - Qualitative and Quantitative Insights 29
   - Conclusion 30
   - Questions 30

3. **Product Vision** 31
   - Introduction 31
   - Structure 31

  The Statement 32
  Competitive Elements of Product Vision 36
  Delivering the Vision 39
   Roadmap 39
   Workflows 42
   Documentation 43
   Product Development 43
  Messaging the Vision 44
   Internal Communication 46
   External Communication 47
  Process to Realization of Product Vision 48
  Conclusion 49
  Questions 50

4. Customer **51**
  Introduction 51
  Structure 51
  Identifying the Customer 51
   The Buying Process 54
   Role of Software Product Management 56
  Buyer to Customer 58
  Mutually Beneficial Relationship 60
  Establishing Value for the Customer 64
  Negotiation 66
  Conclusion 68
  Questions 69

5. Pricing **70**
  Introduction 70
  Structure 70
  Principles of Pricing 70
   Metering and Licensing 74
   Metering for Business 76
   Software License 76

Factors Affecting Pricing	77
Supply	78
Alternative	80
Demand	81
Value-based Pricing	82
From Commodity to Differentiated Offer	84
Pricing Schemes	84
Volume-based Pricing	84
Product Bundles and Suites	86
Tiered Pricing Plans	88
Enterprise Plans	90
Legal Implications of Pricing	90
Conclusion	92
Questions	92
6. User Experience	**94**
Introduction	94
Structure	94
Elements of User Experience	94
Workflow	96
Views	97
Architecture	98
Configuration	99
Permissions and Roles	100
User Persona and Profiles	101
Domains	102
Culture	103
User Interface	104
Screens and Devices	104
Technology	105
Platform and API	106
Knowledge Dissemination	109
Accessibility	109

Tools and Frameworks	110
Ideation and Expression	111
Figma	111
Material Design	112
Delivery	112
Flutter Framework	112
Design Thinking	113
Conclusion	114
Questions	114
7. Contracts	**115**
Introduction	115
Structure	115
Basis of Contract	115
Definition	117
Parties to Contract	117
Sale of Goods	119
Tenders	121
Lawful Subject Matter	121
Implied vs. Express	122
Jurisdiction	124
Enforcement	126
Performance	127
Specific Needs for the Software Industry	128
Licensee's Rights	129
Licensor's Rights	132
Service Provider Rights	134
Conclusion	136
Questions	136
8. Intellectual Properties	**137**
Introduction	137
Structure	137
Basis of Intellectual Property	138

Types of IPRs	141
Copyright	*141*
Trademarks	*145*
Patents	*149*
Patentable Subject Matter	*149*
Industrial Application	*150*
Novelty	*150*
Non-Obvious and Inventive Step	*151*
Complete Disclosure	*151*
Preliminary Application and Continuation	*152*
Infringement	*152*
Design	*153*
Others	*153*
Process of IPR Application	154
Respecting Other's IPRs	155
Open Source	156
Innovation and IPR	157
Incentivizing Innovation	157
Conclusion	158
Questions	159
9. Compliance	**160**
Introduction	160
Structure	160
The Need	160
Penal Provisions of Non-Compliance	163
Gating Criteria and Business Loss	167
Cost of Compliance	168
Messaging	170
Compliance in SaaS Business	171
Operations	*171*
Open Source	*172*
Licensing	*174*

  Conclusion 175
  Questions 175
10. Agile Process 176
  Introduction 176
  Structure 176
  The Need 177
  Components of Agile Process 181
    Requirements 182
    Estimation 188
    Process Model 190
    Scrum 190
    Kanban 190
    SAFe 191
    Iterations 192
    Retrospective 193
  Roles in a Scrum Model 194
    Scrum Teams 194
    Scrum Master 194
    Product Owner 195
    Communication Across Teams 195
  Tools for Product Release 195
    Burndown 196
    Readiness Assessment 197
    Minimal Viable Product 198
    Concept Viability 199
    Competition Viability 199
    Sales Viability 199
    Lifecycle Viability 199
    Go to Market 200
  Working in the Mixed Models 201
  Conclusion 201
  Questions 202

11. People 203
Introduction 203
Structure 203
Internal Organization Interactions 204
Sales 204
Sales Engineering 205
Marketing 206
Support, Customer Success, and Training 206
Architects 207
Engineering and Delivery 209
Senior Management 209
Management in Matrix Organization 210
Managing Product Managers 211
Hiring and Team Composition 212
The Adult Mindset 213
Management by Objective 213
Negotiations 214
Conclusion 215
Questions 215
12. Epilogue 216
Index 220

CHAPTER 1
The Practice of Product Management

Introduction

As seasoned senior management of the organization, you have convinced the investors to embrace digital transformations and are now expanding your team with software professionals. Experienced people have advised you to engage product managers to review your organization's processes to align your digital transformation initiatives with your business goals. An MBA graduate with limited industry experience is hired as a software product manager and is now running from department to department to understand her assignment. Everything she is learning now does not seem to connect to her studies in a two-year MBA program. As a product management leader, you have developed and marketed several products and led product management teams, yet your expertise is only getting highlighted in your functional domain. A cross-functional scope of product management experience is not apparent. If you have dealt with any of these in your career engagements, we try to address some of them in this book.

Structure

In this chapter, we will cover the following topics:

- Software Product
- Product Management Process
- The Framework

Software Product

Every organization delivering software solutions is providing software as a service. Yet, they all talk about software product development and want their development initiatives spearheaded by a product manager. It is the perfect fallacy that every software product manager lives through. Software product managers are engaged in understanding customer requirements. Thus, every product manager has sometimes been questioned why a specific feature requested by a customer could not be delivered exactly as desired. Are business analysts not reviewing customer requirements and helping develop solutions for several decades? Why should the product management function be any different?

As we answer these questions, let us understand what a software product is, why, and what it achieves in the first place. When computers came into existence, they added tools for operating the computer. The computer as a hardware box anyway was irrelevant without the software. Initial computing devices, such as the mainframes, were expensive, and a model would hardly sell in hundreds or thousands of numbers. Suppose a bank needs a mainframe computer for banking operation optimization. It will start negotiating with one of the mainframe providers, such as IBM for the hardware. It will engage Business Analysts (BA) and System Analysts (SA) who will work with IBM on the suitability of the mainframe for the bank's needs. IBM will provide all the tools for the BAs and SAs to outline the specifications for the system. Engineers from IBM or the bank receive training on the system and tools. They will develop software based on the specifications created by the BAs and SAs. Every system was a closed unit with its custom software. The software was a service for a specific hardware. Only an affiliate of IBM or a bank's contractor can provide services in such an environment. One has to develop software specifically for every customer. Being a human-intensive activity, you incur the cost for every customer added.

The advent of Unix was a paradigm shift in computing. A high-level language, C, was used to write the operating system. One can now port code from one system to another system. Unix started running on thousands of mini-computers and workstation class machines. It was not practical for the system providers to support all the custom software development themselves. Workstations started shipping office productivity tools such as word processors, spreadsheets, and presentation tools. With many deployments and varied customer needs, the vendors could no longer meet the needs of all customers. They needed to support the developer ecosystem or community. They also licensed software from some of these third-party developers and included it in their hardware. IBM went a step further. They standardized the hardware specification for the IBM Personal Computer (PC). The vendors who sell PCs for these standards can now bundle the OS from Microsoft. With this PC revolution, Microsoft became the largest software-only vendor. PCs were deployed in millions in several households. Unlike workstations in offices, PCs serve purposes beyond productivity tools. They became tools for education, entertainment, programming, and so on. We are talking about at least a hundred tier-A hardware vendors, tens of thousands of software vendors, and millions of computer users and customers; we have left the closed ecosystem of vendors and customers and moved to an open market. Today, even the mainframe vendors provide open systems tools for developing software for the mainframes. For any vendor to understand the whole market is unthinkable.

However, software services businesses and custom software for specific customers still exist and continue to flourish.

Economics

When developing custom software for your customers as a service, every customer is a unit with its manpower.

```
Revenue (R) = R₁ + R₂ + ... + Rₙ
Cost (C) = C₁ + C₂ + ... + Cₙ
```

R_i and C_i are the revenue and cost, respectively, for the ith customer. Every new customer acquisition incurs additional costs. While the profits are there, they are only nominal. Let us talk about Microsoft. Microsoft sells Windows Home editions for under 100 USD. Can a custom OS be built at that price? It is possible as Microsoft is developing the Windows OS only once and making copies for the customers to deploy. Microsoft has n=500 million active Windows devices. Now, the revenues and costs look as follows:

```
Revenue (R) = n*Price
Cost (C) = C
```

The Cost (C) gets spread over many customers, and thus the price can be lowered drastically. We saw that innovative software products can reach millions of customers and users. Software products companies can grow big and reach billions of dollars in revenues. Similarly, software services companies can reach billions of dollars in revenues. But they target large customers, generating hundreds of millions in revenue from each. We face two challenges with software products:

- How do software product companies ensure that millions, or even billions, of users will use their products?
- How do companies spread the costs across the customer base?

When economies of scale are reached for software development, a software product mindset is in the organization; the costs can be spread across customers. It also means no two customers perceive the same value for the same product they use. For example, Microsoft Word for a lawyer drafting contracts or an author writing a novel is economically more valuable than a householder who types a letter or two sporadically. These create a consistent challenge. Companies are building software solutions for a class of customers, where each customer is seeing differentiated values in the same product. Companies are innovatively spreading their costs across customers in different channels. We will see some of the channels.

Sales and Marketing

Are Microsoft Windows and Office not supposed to be product suites or collections of products? It was the case several years back, not today. Microsoft acquired a few market leaders in the fields of document writing (Word), spreadsheets (Excel), and presentations (PowerPoint). Microsoft would sell Word to the company's secretarial staff, writing official communications. They would type the content in Word, print it, and post it on the notice boards for employee communications. Accounting executives use Excel, and marketing executives use PowerPoint. They were selling three products to the same company in limited numbers. Microsoft has a unique scheme of combining all these products as a suite under Microsoft Office. Office digitally enables a knowledge worker to communicate effectively and should be available on every computer in an office. MS Office is a knowledge worker productivity tool with features of document writing (Word), spreadsheets (Excel), presentations (PowerPoint), databases (Access), email (Outlook), and so on. While Microsoft could only sell ten copies of the individual products, they can sell a hundred copies of the suite. The suite can be priced competitively to the component products, as Microsoft can make more money selling larger volumes. Companies follow such strategies even today.

MS Outlook had two options: MS Outlook shipped as part of MS Office, and MS Outlook Express shipped for free with MS Windows. Today, this free version is Windows Mail and is part of the Windows components. MS Windows as an operating system is no longer just the software to boot a computer. Today, people look at an operating system to provide basic functionalities alongside making the hardware usable. For example, with the operating system, you can connect to the internet and your internet email sites, such as Gmail, Outlook.com, Yahoo.com, and so on. Windows Mail helps you achieve that and is part of the MS Windows product. MS Office Outlook provides connectivity to enterprise email systems and caters to the needs of a different group of users. Microsoft Office Home and Student Edition does not ship with MS Office Outlook. The choice of product bundles in various editions plays a crucial role and can decide the price of a product. We will touch upon this when we discuss pricing. The definition of a product is dynamic. When marketers talk about software products, they use terms such as features, components, products, suites, bundles, and so on. *A group of benefits a customer gets, hence clubbed together as a talking point, are products.*

Engineering

While all the other Microsoft Office products use *Ctrl-F* to search, MS Outlook uses F4 to search emails. It is an inconsistency highlighted by many MS Office users. When you have similar features in a product collection, people will expect them to behave alike. They would like to see tables in MS Word behave similarly to Excel spreadsheet cells. Considering these, Microsoft created engineering components that are across various parts of the products. Microsoft introduced binary components with a Component Object Model (COM) architecture. These could be developed by third parties and used across various products running on a Windows OS, thus achieving economies of scale in engineering endeavors. UI components and REST APIs used across products are similar initiatives engineering organizations use. Another aspect is to use open-source components. Since the company has not developed all the code for the open-source components, there are definite gains in reducing development costs. Some companies use common platforms or core technology components in many products. Again, the engineering gains are shared across products, thus achieving economies of scale. The claim is still hypothetical. While you can share components or platforms across the products, it's essential to ensure the components are capable and built to the needs of the downstream products. Additionally, the component releases must be aligned to the final product releases, avoid conflicting behaviors across the products, and remain resilient to the business agility required in developing products. All these add to engineering and lifecycle process management challenges. Today, most organizations use agile process management frameworks to realize such needs.

Infrastructure

We barely utilize 10% of the CPU, about 50% of the RAM, and hardly any network traffic when we type a document on MS Word. A laptop with an 8-core 1800 MHz processor is beefy hardware for such needs. Processing power, RAM, and even network connectivity costs have gone south as much as hardware prices. However, management of complex hardware, maintenance, and IT resource involvement adds to additional overheads. If we could utilize the hardware to its maximum potential, such additional expenses would be spread over the utilization. While typing this book, the CPU utilization is only 20-30 percent. If we run a test automation task alongside, the utilization will be 70 percent. However, that will not lead to a significant performance overhead for typing. Here are some simplistic anecdotal explanations of cloud computing:

- In an Infrastructure as a Service (IaaS), we manage the laptop and keep usage ready; you can rent it on demand. You do not buy the hardware nor manage and maintain it.
- In the case of a workload management system, we manage the resource availability in virtual or physical machines and place your Docker container. You get the uptime without bothering about the resource utilization concerns.
- In a Platform as a Service (PaaS), you invoke the APIs and get the results. You do not bother about the underlying operating system, hardware, or system management tools.
- In a Software as a Service (SaaS), you access a web page and type in your document without concern about the hardware or software involved.

There is progressively value added as you move from one stage to another. Hence, intuitively, SaaS will be more expensive than PaaS and IaaS. A SaaS vendor may depend on an underlying IaaS or PaaS vendor. For example, Netflix uses AWS extensively for its cloud computing needs.

The cloud reduces the need to stock up on hardware and software assets for peak load.

You can rent as the demand changes. You start incurring revenue expenses and not capital expenses. For a startup, it is easier to justify revenue expenses than holding up funds in capital assets. However, a new customer acquisition adds marginal costs. You run the cloud infrastructure with slightly higher capacity to keep the new customer acquisition agile.

The second issue is with development usage or human interaction with hardware. When developers or authors work on hardware, they take breaks, are interrupted by corridor talks with colleagues, spend time planning or designing the content, and so on. During these periods, the resource is active but not in use. Hardware goes into a low power mode during these periods, but when you reserve a GPU or CPU in the cloud, you incur costs based on the total time you have reserved. In such cases, on-premise hardware may be cheaper for development needs. In the case of production use, you pay for the usage only. With significant revenues, the development overheads are not a concern in most cases, but for a small startup, any saving is welcome.

Working with IaaS, providing service configurations can be complex for most organizations. PaaS may be a quick way to start things. However, a developer may not be knowledgeable in all PaaS environments. They will only use the ones they have experience with. That may lead to vendor lock-in. Any vendor lock-in removes the flexibility of switching to a cheaper option identified later. Hence, SaaS model optimization for economies of scale can be complex, and improper planning may add to overruns.

Technology

The advent of Independent Software Vendors (ISV) in the ecosystem is a reality as the operating system vendors become flexible to enhance interoperability. When Apple decided to move its processors from PowerPC to Intel, they introduced universal binaries. These will run the executables depending on the underlying processor without extra effort from ISVs. Similarly, Google's Flutter Framework can build client binaries and frontends for Windows, Mac OS, Linux, and the Web without significant code changes. Toolsets such as LLVMs can help write compilers and cross-compile code across various operating systems and processor types. Virtual Machine architectures in Java and Python-like environments have made software development OS-agnostic. The internet has made user experience operating systems agnostic, spreading the development costs across larger user populations. These are technological innovations that help the product mindset in software development.

The advent of AI has pushed the limits further. Companies such as Google, Microsoft, Meta, and Amazon provide platforms across products. For example, Google provides Gmail for consumers and enterprises. While developing a Large Language Model (LLM), the emails from Gmail can be used as inputs to the LLM. The prediction hints in a Gmail draft can utilize the LLM as much as Google Docs can to autocomplete sentences. Google Books and News can provide significant data to LLM development. In short, Google has developed a common platform where some of its products supply data. Some products can consume the data and provide insightful products and services. It is not confined to Google only. Every company developing a data platform is trying to reuse the platform across various products. Training an LLM may cost around 5 million USD.[1] A company investing in such a technology will like to reuse it across all its products in due course.

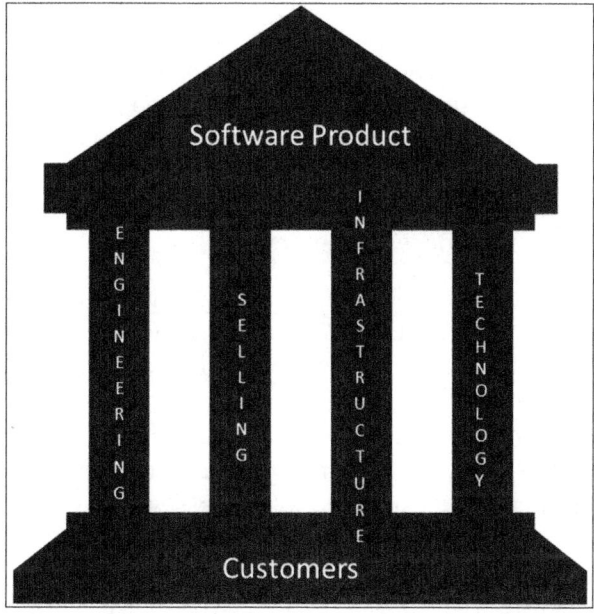

Figure 1.1: *Cost of product spread across all the customers*

We can say the software product is an innovative way to spread your costs across customers who view differentiated value from the similar solution you provide them. For our discussions in this book, this is the definition of a software product where product managers operate. The economies of scale in product development can only be achieved when the processes are managed with clockwork precision. Hence, there is a need for product management to work closely with the processes.

Product Management Process

Software product development and the penetration of PCs went hand in hand. The users were discovering the capability of the PCs and learning how to manage the new beast. The best product development companies employed their best technical minds to create innovative products, and then they were launched in the market. Even with massive launches, the market rejected many products. Marketing departments helped

---

[1] **https://www.newindianexpress.com/cities/chennai/2023/Jun/15/zoho-to-develop-large-language-model-for-generative-ai-2585145.html** accessed 6th March 2025.

identify the target customer and set up price, promotion, and place, but they were not involved significantly in the product development. The void can be seen from the dotcom bubble bust. Every company offered a website-oriented free service to the users while advertisement revenue supported the service. Some companies succeeded using this approach, but large numbers could not survive. These failures made the industry wake up to the new reality and challenges. Some large companies looked at their software development processes and realized from development to launch, it had taken over seven to eight years, only to be rejected by the customers when they were in their 1.0 avatar. Some of the most successful products of our times had delayed launches, quality issues, and bad customer feedback in their first releases. The customer needs may evolve and change, and the product may not remain valid for the market. It led to organizations embracing the agile methodology for software lifecycle management. Agile methods require a product owner to represent the customer in product development; it ensures quick turnaround and market feedback, ensuring product relevance during the development cycle.

To support the product owners, the product managers had to interact with the market and acquire regular feedback. Some product managers played the role of product owners themselves. The e-commerce ventures were popular, targeting the business-to-consumer (B2C) markets. The product managers were data-driven. Since most of these applications ran on the web, they could insert probes to collect user experience statistics for analysis. In some B2C markets, the web-based systems are only digital conduits for other established businesses. For example, Walmart's web storefront is just another channel for their physical stores. The product managers are responsible for the supply chains, existing systems, and processes, not just the web application. Business-to-business (B2B) customers were different. They acted as a conduit between the users and the product manager. The product managers had to engage as business analysts to collect customer feedback. The B2B world of product management involved negotiations, direct interactions, and feedback, while the B2C world relied on automated data collection. By the mid-first decade of the millennium, most client applications had moved to web browsers. Users start comparing websites or applications and expect a better user experience. Mobile devices and social networking websites took user experience to a much higher level of expectation. The scope of traditional UI designing started moving to providing elaborate user experiences, understanding user journeys, and providing the best solution. B2C software vendors focus on UI much more than B2B software vendors. Today, even B2B software vendors are focusing significantly on user experiences.

The need for developing competence in product management is identified in organizations. Organizations wanted the skill enhanced at all levels in product management. Industry consulting and training courses offered by Pragmatic Marketing[2], Blackblot Marketing[3], and the International Software Product Management

---

[2] https://www.pragmaticinstitute.com/
[3] https://www.blackblot.com/

Association (ISPMA)[4] came in handy to meet these needs. All these frameworks are detailed and define twenty or more functional processes for streamlining product management activities. Larger organizations find these frameworks handy as they establish a common understanding across product management organizations. The situation may not be as helpful for smaller organizations as they cannot formally train all the product managers, and there is a management cost associated with strict adherence to processes. ISPMA has introduced a relatively simplified process model defined for startups.

While we took a simple storytelling approach to describe the history of product management, researchers have conducted comprehensive academic studies around 2010 to define software products, the advent of software product management function, roles of software product managers, stakeholder management, the reference models or frameworks currently available in the field, and so on[5]. We suggest discerning readers review these articles for thorough insight into the product management process frameworks. A meta-ethnography study of the product management literature[6] has identified the following core product management functions: product lifecycle management, product requirements engineering, release planning, roadmapping, and vision. It also identifies portfolio management, product analysis, strategic planning, product support, product development, and product launches as supporting activities. While the scope and definitions of product management were a set of discussion topics for the past decade, in the last couple of years, there has been a focus on finding the effectiveness of product management and the challenges the product managers face[7]. Although a small sample size may not be very significant to take a generalized call, the literature reviewed and the diversity of companies from where the samples were collected make the study apt for serious consideration. It may inspire researchers to work on related areas of study. They have identified seven areas where product management is facing the most challenges.

- Requirement Engineering
- Software Development Process
- Team
- Product Knowledge Management
- Organizational - Strategic

---

[4] https://ispma.org/
[5] Samuel A. Fricker, 2012. "Software Product Management," Management for Professionals, in: Alexander Maedche & Achim Botzenhardt & Ludwig Neer (ed.), Software for People, edition 127, pages 53-81, Springer.
[6] Andrey Maglyas & Uolevi Nikula & Kari Smolander & Samuel A. Fricker, 2017. "Core software product management activities," Journal of Advances in Management Research, Emerald Group Publishing Limited, vol. 14(1), pages 23-45, February.
[7] Springer, O., Miler, J. A comprehensive overview of software product management challenges. Empir Software Eng 27, 106 (2022). **https://doi.org/10.1007/s10664-022-10134-5**

- Organizational - Operational
- User Research

They identified 27 issues where three or more product managers raised concerns in an interview. The most frequently identified problem in the interviews was the team's lack of motivation due to a lack of understanding of why they were doing this—resulting in no commitment to achieving goals. Similarly, the problem that got the highest severity and frequency was determining the true value of the product that the customer needs. Both of these raise significant concerns about how effective product management processes are currently. The researchers also worked with several product managers on potential strategies to overcome the challenges[8].

The Framework

A search on LinkedIn showed 5.6 million product management personnel. When there is a surge in a particular discipline, there is pressure to quickly train them and make them aware of the product management function. When enhancing profits from the product is the focus of a product manager, engineering, customer engagement, or user experience are not the qualities for focus in a product management role. While larger organizations look at product management training programs to standardize the product management process, smaller organizations or startups question the very premise of product management processes. In startups, one or more of the founding members conceive the product. The person who has the best understanding of the product plays the role of a Chief Product Officer (CPO). However, the nuances of the product management process may not be there with such a person. The issue surfaces as a challenge in larger organizations as well. Product management is a vast domain. Not all people are well conversant with all aspects of product management. A person focused on sales support or customer evangelizing roles cannot appreciate the need for agile planning, product development, requirements management, and quality management. That is when there is a general tussle within and outside product management functions. Some organizations have junior members serve as product owners in the scrum process while product managers bring in market insights. Organizations that believe in such philosophies will not be successful when product dependency on technology is complex. A product dependent on cryptographic processing or a strong data-oriented focus may need a system architect-level person to drive the product owner role in scrum teams. A mere understanding of the customer's requirements at a high level will do no justice to such a product. Many product managers have shown exemplary technical competence in their careers as

---

[8] O. Springer, J. Miler and M. Wróbel, "Strategies for Dealing With Software Product Management Challenges," in IEEE Access, vol. 11, pp. 55797-55813, 2023, doi: 10.1109/ACCESS.2023.3282605.

The Practice of Product Management

well. Product managers pick up popular books such as Inspired[9] and Empowered[10] to learn nuances of product management and try to incorporate them into their day-to-day activities. Management programs and authors provide the perfect recipe for success when everything is followed in spirit. However, in many cases, the adherence is only ritualistic.

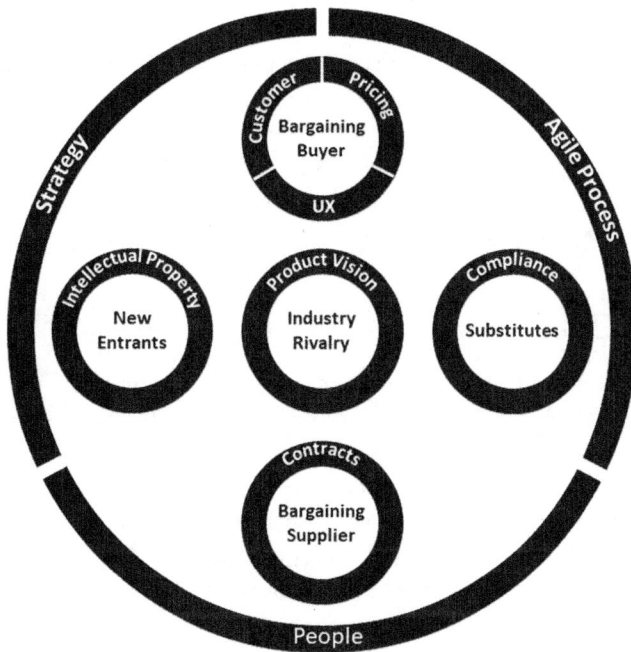

Figure 1.2: *The Practice of Product Management Framework*

Our approach towards product management is to establish a connection from product management functions to the management principles of sustained competitive advantage. The framework is also known as the five forces. We will deep-dive into the framework when we work on strategy. Michael Porter realized and showed with several case studies that an organization is continuously affected by five environmental factors, which he names five forces. They are:

- Industry Rivalry
- Bargaining Power of Buyers
- Bargaining Power of Suppliers
- New Entrants
- Substitutes

---

[9] Cagan, Marty. INSPIRED: How to Create Tech Products Customers Love. Germany: Wiley, 2017.
[10] Cagan, Marty. EMPOWERED: Ordinary People, Extraordinary Products. United States: Wiley, 2020.

Product managers orchestrate their functional skills to tame these forces. These activities are iterative. Product managers continually work with organizational strategy, cross-functional teams of people, and agile management to better these functions. We pick up each function in a chapter and explain how the function helps tame a particular force. For example, a good definition and execution of the Product Vision function can tame the industry rivals effectively. For bargaining buyers, the product management organization can move the buyer to a customer mindset, provide value-driven pricing, and improve the user experience for buying influencers. A well-negotiated contract reviewed in due course can help the bargaining supplier. Intellectual Properties can deter the advancement of innovative new entrants, while higher compliance requirements can affect a substitute taking over the market. An outline of the chapters is provided in the foreword. We call this framework The Practice of Product Management.

Conclusion

In our approach to simplify the product management processes for the experienced and the novice, we introduce The Practice of Product Management Framework. Reducing the overall processes to ten has made the framework lightweight for a practitioner. We add a causality element to the functional activities by associating the functions with the five forces. Lastly, we do not impose a firm process limitation. For example, we insist the organization fulfill the functions with their existing process and metrics if they have worked for them. A continual cycle of reevaluation provides a course correction and a new spin to the wheel. In the following chapters, we will work on these functions and utilize them in product management activities. Our first focus will be how understanding the strategy can help us build a better product.

Questions

1. We have identified four ways to spread the product investments across a large section of customers. Do you realize some other ways to spread the investments?

2. Do you think IaaS can bring in further cost reduction to your product? What will it take to migrate from PaaS to IaaS for your product? Do you think the issue can reduce vendor lock-in and give you flexibility in negotiation?

3. The practice of product management framework identifies ten functions in which the product managers are engaged. What are some of the areas that need immediate attention for your organization?

CHAPTER 2
Strategy

Introduction

Is organization strategy needed for product development? What level of detailed strategic direction do we need to be able to execute a product roadmap? You will find a well-defined strategy document worked out in a large organization. However, BU leaders are reluctant to implement the strategy as it ignores significant gaps or requires changes that will not get the support downstream. The smaller organizations are chasing the next paying customer. While the urgency to convert investments to income is understandable, products cannot be built without a well-planned direction. In this chapter, we intend to encourage product management to develop a strategic outlook in developing and marketing a product.

Structure

In this chapter, we will cover the following topics:

- Strategy and Sustained Competitive Advantage
- Corporate Strategy
- Strategy Tools for Product Managers
    - Porter's Five Forces
    - Key Success Factors
    - BCG Matrix
    - DuPont Analysis
- Qualitative and Quantitative Insights

Strategy and Sustained Competitive Advantage

As per Oxford Languages, strategy is a plan to achieve something. The word something is very open and unclear. However, an organization is set up for a purpose and understanding that may give guidance. Entrepreneurs conceive ideas to solve a business problem. They convince investors to fund their ideas. Let us consider the investors as perfectly rational investors. They would like to get the maximum returns for their investments. Their returns have to be risk-adjusted. Since entrepreneurship is not established, there are significant risks associated with investments. It is a general belief that only 10 percent of new enterprises succeed. So, an investor would expect a much higher rate of return for his investment. An enterprise needs enough profits to keep the investor's interest in mind. The story may not be valid for all enterprises, but for many, maximizing an investor's investment is the primary responsibility of a firm. At this point, some of you may be wondering, a firm is concerned about all the stakeholders and not just the investors. For ease of explanation, we discuss only for-profit economic organizations in the current context. We discuss this as there are theoretical models to explain them in economics.

The economics theory talks about a market. In the market, there are buyers and sellers. Buyers want to buy goods at a price pattern: a demand curve (D). If the price is higher, then there is less demand. It is understandable, as everyone has limited resources. You would not like to spend too much on one need and would want to balance your spending across all your requirements equitably or rationally. In economics, there is no differentiation in goods. All buyers decide based on price only. The sellers will try to maximize their income. The greater the quantity of goods they sell, the higher the price they will demand. Their expectation of the prices can be modeled as a pattern as well. This pattern is called a Supply (S) curve. The sellers are rational as well. They will sell goods based on prices only. While rational pricing-based decisions seem like perfect logic to some, they are unusual, and human purchases are not all that logical. How many of us purchase gadgets, toys, pens, and more from roadside hawkers for compassionate reasons? Coming back to our perfect world of economics, what is the strategy for the buyers and sellers?

It is natural to wonder if the demand or supply curve changes. They do when the buyer preferences change. For example, if the quality of the goods on an overall basis changes, the buyer may want to pay a higher price. So, the demand curve shifts to the right. Similarly, when the goods are used for a while, the buyers expect the product to be available at a cheaper price or almost free. For example, no one is interested in paying for personal email service. So, one can argue the demand curve for that category has moved to the left. Disrupting the demand curves takes some time. While quality is just one of the factors, there are many other factors; disposable income can be one such factor. We leave it to the readers to review a text on economics for the details. Sellers will always like to have the demand curve shift to the right for them to realize a higher price.

Strategy

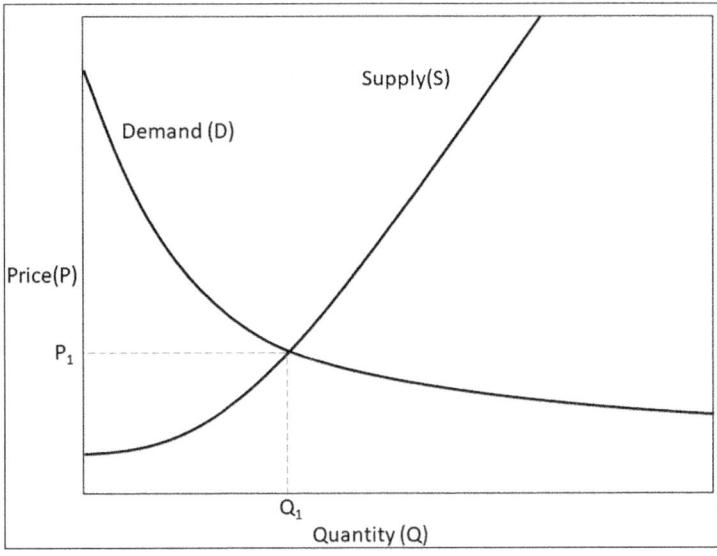

Figure 2.1: *When the demand curve meets the supply curve, transactions occur at the price and quantity in steady state*

Let us assume a simple scenario. In a community, there are 100 children. The community has one school that provides education at Rs. 1000 per month per student to 50 students. We assume only one buyer, the community, and just one seller, the school. A very simple one-buyer and one-seller model. Since the school (school 1) is insufficient for all the children in the community, the community bids for another school. The new school (school 2) agrees to provide education for 80 students at Rs. 800 per student.

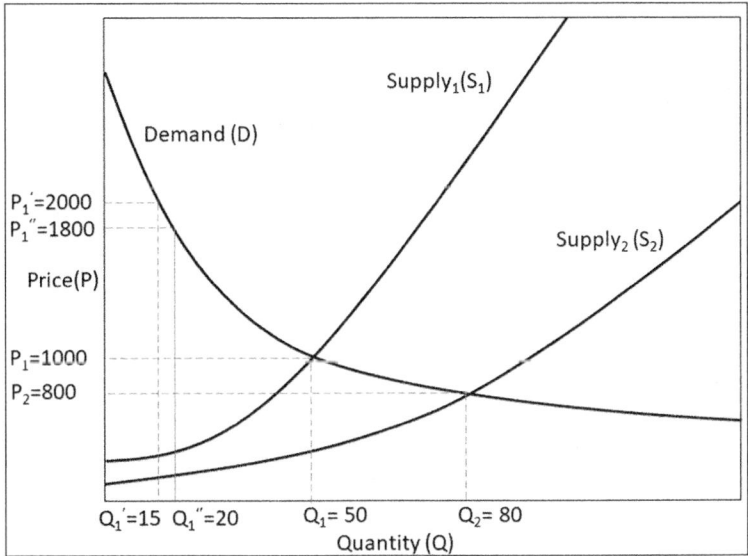

Figure 2.2: *The introduction of a new school changes the quantity each school offers*

Here are a few scenarios that can happen:

- The community will offer 80 students to school 2 and only 20 to school 1. School 1 will get a higher price for each seat, say Rs. 1800. It will cost Rs. 80 × 800 + 20 × 1800 = Rs. 100,000 to the community.
- The community may try to bargain with both schools and offer them 50 seats each at Rs. 1000. This will cost them Rs. 100000. But, school 2 may not accept it as it does not meet their supply expectation. The community may not agree to this as they did not benefit from introducing a new school. They covered all the students but could not get the benefits of breaking the monopoly barrier of one school.
- To be profitable, school 1 may have to let go of its buildings and teaching staff and can accommodate only 15 students at Rs. 2000 per student. It will now cost the community Rs 80 × 800 + 15 × 2000 = Rs. 94,000, but the community cannot accommodate five students.

In an open market, no players can influence the other's decisions. However, none of the players anticipated a disruption to the market was coming. Could it be possible for a supplier to anticipate a disruption can happen? If every supplier maximizes profits, could they have anticipated disruptions and planned for them? These questions led to the development of a firm's generic strategy. Before we discuss generic strategy, let us understand how a firm determines its supply curve.

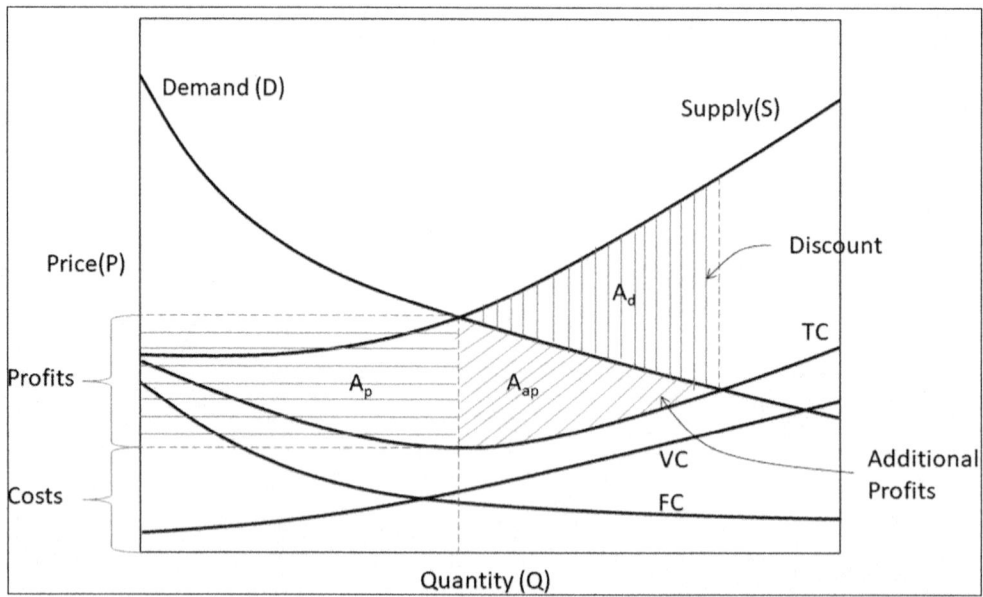

Figure 2.3: *Demand and supply relationship with costs*

To deliver goods and services, a firm needs to incur certain costs. The costs can be of two types: fixed costs and variable costs. The fixed costs do not depend on the quantity or units of goods or services offered, while variable costs depend on the quantum of goods or services. Per unit fixed cost reduces as a firm sells more goods and services. At the same time, variable costs can increase as more goods and services are delivered. For example, in a SaaS product, development costs are fixed. However, the service delivery, such as servers, operational, and support staff expenses, will vary based on the number of customers served. Sometimes, higher capacity is kept for sudden sales expansion or surge load needs. As the number of units increases, these kinds of buffers increase. In all, variable unit cost increases with additional goods sold. A good supply curve should be higher than the average cost curve at all possible delivery quantities such that the firm never incurs any losses in selling goods. All the firms try to optimize the costs to the minimum at the quantity levels where they sell the goods. This way, they maximize their profit potential. The firm gains a total profit of A_p when it sells quantity Q at price P. But there is a profit potential (A_{ap}) it leaves as the goods are priced too high. The firm can dole out some discounts (A_d) and gain access to the additional profits. However, this may not always be practical. Given this possibility, let us look back at some strategies that School 2 can undertake.

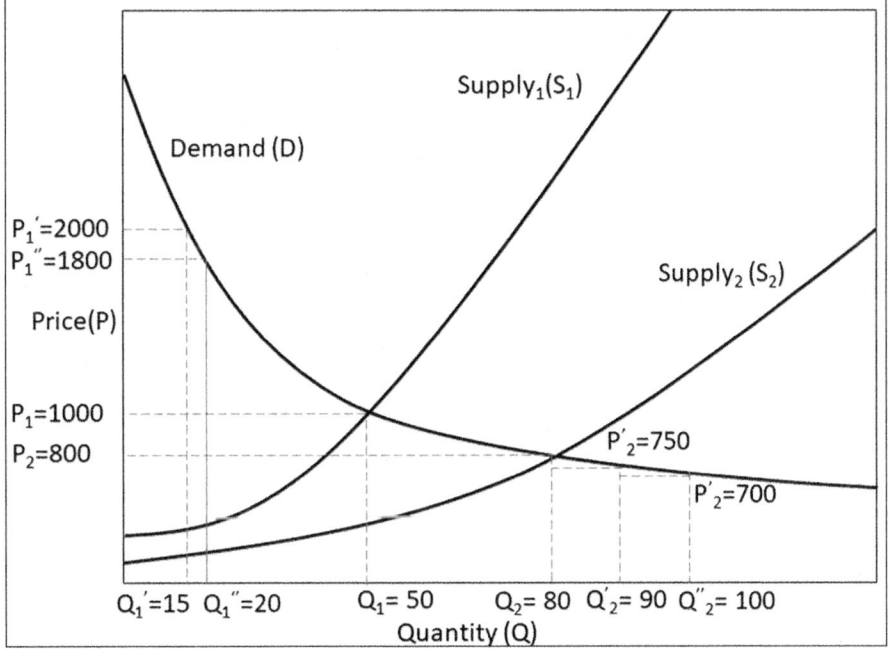

Figure 2.4: *School 2 offers discounts in two tranches*

Suppose School 2 somehow managed higher capacity and convinced the community to offer the first lot at Rs. 750 for ten students and the second at Rs. 700. Effectively, the community will be spending Rs. 80 × 800 + 10 × 750 + 10 × 700 = Rs. 78,500—a spend much less than Rs 100,000 they were spending. School 2 can offer such discounts as their costs are well-optimized to undertake such discounts. They will make suboptimal profits, but they will not incur losses. It will put School 1 out of business. It seems

School 2 is the **cost leader**[1] and is dictating the market; School 1 has to respond to School 2's actions. In short, School 2 has the **dominant strategy**. Whatever it does, School 1 will lose the battle. The generic strategy suggests when a firm cannot compete on costs, it can choose **differentiation** as a strategy. We have oversimplified the problem so far. Education is a complex and subjective field. While the community pays for the education, the students and parents are influencers in choosing the school. The infrastructure, quality of teachers, student-teacher relationships, socialization of students, location, and so on contribute significantly to a school. Mere price leadership is not enough. School 1, being the early mover, has created goodwill in the community that cannot be wished away. It can exploit some of these differentiating factors. What if School 1 focused only on the education of the girl child? Assuming an even sex ratio, the school could have offered its capacity (50) only to girls. The target market would have shrunk, but if they could offer additional differentiating education to girls, it may not lose overall seats. It would have been a **focused strategy** for School 1. Again, a firm can choose between **cost** and **differentiation** strategies in the focus segment.

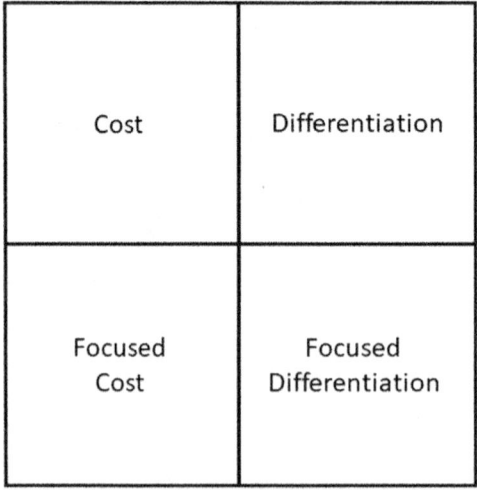

Figure 2.5: *A firm's generic strategy*

Let us look at some questions that come to mind on **generic strategy** with some real-life examples.

- *Can multiple companies in a market vie for a cost leadership strategy?* Yes. They will fiercely fight for market share and try to poach each other's customers with offers, discounts, and so on. The three Indian telecom players, Jio, Airtel, and Vodafone Idea, maintain this posture with competitive pricing plans.
- *Is the differentiation strategy meant for players comfortable with a small market share?* Apple has maintained a differentiation strategy in the mobile market

---

[1]Cost leadership does not always mean low prices. It gives the cost leader the flexibility to sell at any price point and be profitable. We will discuss this further in the chapter on pricing.

and has a significant market share. They are known for their ease of use, aesthetics, and product quality. They get a premium price for the same.

- *Is it possible to have a focused cost and differentiation strategy in the same market?* Apple and Dell in the professional desktop market did the same. Dell showed a low-cost strategy by optimizing ordering, procurement, and supply chain, while Apple focused on better quality, innovation, and differentiation of product features.

A good strategy ensures you have a sustained competitive advantage over the competition. Operational efficiencies of a business are incremental gains. They can be copied by competition over time; competition cannot copy a strategy that easily unless they decide to change their fundamental approach. Secondly, strategy is forward-looking and not a response. For example, to become a cost leader, an organization must keep operational costs to a minimum, optimizing expenses at every level. Doling out one-off discounts cannot put a company at strategic cost leadership.

Corporate Strategy

A corporation is a perpetual entity. It has several business units (BUs). Each of the BUs has its own product and service offerings. The BUs compete in the market for sustained competitive advantage (SCA) of their offerings. While SCA becomes a core guiding principle of strategy for the BUs, a corporation may have different objectives. A corporation must look at various sectors where it must invest. For example, ITC deals in Cigarettes, FMCG, Paper, Agriculture, and Hotels. As a conglomerate, every sector of its business has an independent competitive strategy, which is different from the organization's strategy. Some strategy experts even question if it makes sense for conglomerates to exist in the first place. If survival and giving shareholders value are the goals, conglomerates can register their businesses in the stock markets, and shareholders can directly invest in the portfolio of stocks. Realizing the cigarette sector will have relatively slow growth potential, ITC has invested in and developed other FMCG and Agriculture businesses and has owned leading brands for several decades. Some brands developed organically, and some were acquired and merged into the businesses. Mergers and acquisitions play a significant part in a corporate strategy. While corporate strategy affects everyone in an organization, product managers operate within the boundaries of the BUs developing and launching products. In the day-to-day activity context, sustained competitive advantage becomes the core strategy for most product managers. Some product managers have to make build versus buy decisions and need to look at mergers and acquisitions.

We tried to cover the ground on strategy in a short section. However, readers interested in a deeper understanding of this topic may read the HBR article, *What is Strategy?* by Michael Porter[2].

---
[2] Porter, M.E., What is Strategy? Harvard Business Review, Nov-Dec. 1996.

Strategy Tools for Product Managers

Strategy for SCA requires a product manager to assess the external as well as internal capabilities of an organization. We have decided to discuss four tools for such a discussion. Each of the tools has several decades of use in the management literature. Two help assess the business from an external viewpoint, and the other two help assess the internal processes and performance challenges. We will introduce the concepts and provide references for a detailed study and understanding. Management strategy is replete with frameworks and models. We chose only a few who were time-tested and stood their ground. A practicing professional can use a tool that can provide similar insights, for example, Ohmae's Key Factors of Success (KFS) versus Porter's Value Chain. Ohmae's 3-C model has some overlap with Porter's Five Forces. We have chosen a few as they are popular. For example, a firm's portfolio management has a lot of sophisticated frameworks, but we decided on the BCG Growth-Share matrix as that is taught to most MBA students. More than the specific tools, insights are needed for a product manager. These insights help them assess and be prepared for market dynamics and respond to them rather than reacting to them.

Porter's Five Forces

When we discussed generic strategy, School 1 reacted to the onslaught of School 2's strategy and almost ended up losing ground. Is there a way they could have anticipated the market changes and effectively responded to them? Michael Porter suggested five forces affect every firm in an industry[3]. Hence, a firm should analyze them and respond rather than react. This framework is also considered a core framework for industry analysis.

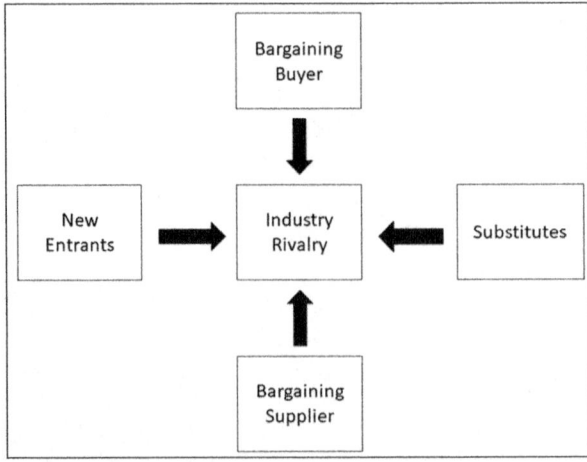

Figure 2.6: *Porter's five forces framework*

---

[3] Porter, Michael E. "The Five Competitive Forces That Shape Strategy." Special Issue on HBS Centennial. Harvard Business Review 86, no. 1 (January 2008): 78–93.

In the hypothetical schools and community case, we had a new entrant. That changed the buyer's behavior as they got better choices. It led to rivalry between players inside the industry. Eventually, School 1 lost the battle. Porter identified the following five factors that every firm faces from its environment. They are:

- Rivalry among the players
- Bargaining Suppliers
- Bargaining Buyers
- New Entrants
- Substitutes

Rather than getting to a detailed analysis of the factors that the readers can find in Porter's original work, we will discuss some past events and the effects of each of the forces seen in the technology sector. For simplicity, we will associate one dominant force to the event, while some events can be attributed to the effects of multiple forces.

- **Rivalry between Competitors:** The technology industry has several examples of these, but here are a few that come to mind.
    - **Microsoft versus Netscape Browser War**[4]**:** When Netscape launched Navigator as the web browser took over a significant market presence, Microsoft retaliated by shipping a free browser in the Windows and Mac OS. This led to Netscape losing its source of revenue from business users and, in the end, filing an anti-trust lawsuit, which Microsoft lost. However, enough water had flown down the drain, and eventually, Netscape open-sourced its browser, Mozilla.
    - **Microsoft versus Sun Microsystems Office War**[5]**:** Sun Microsystems acquired StarOffice from a German company and launched a low-priced alternative to Microsoft Office. However, the product could not compete with Microsoft. Ultimately, Sun Microsystems released the source code under an Open Office open-source license. Today, this source code powers many versions of Office alternates on various Linux and mobile devices.
    - **Adobe versus Macromedia**[6]**:** Adobe and Macromedia were developing products for the media and publishing industries. Adobe was successful in the print media, while Macromedia found its niche in web and server products. The competition was so fierce and skewed on each segment that combined offerings from both complemented like a jigsaw puzzle. For example, to counter Macromedia Flash's dominance in web animation and vector graphics, Adobe promoted the SVG standard with communities.

---

[4] https://www.mozilla.org/en-US/firefox/browsers/browser-history/
[5] https://web.archive.org/web/20150626090829/http://news.cnet.com/Sun-shelled-out-73.5-million-for-Star-Division/2100-1001_3-232561.html
[6] https://www.zdnet.com/article/macromedia-adobe-make-peace-for-bigger-fight/

Finally, Adobe acquired Macromedia in 2005 to end the rivalry.
- **Bargaining Suppliers:** In the technology sector, the suppliers can be ecosystem contributors like independent software vendors.
    - **Adobe and Apple Relationship**[7]: Needless to say, Apple funded Adobe in the initial years for PostScript development, which led to LaserWriter and made Apple Macintosh a publishing powerhouse. Much later in the years, Adobe released the MS Windows-only version of Adobe Premiere and did not adopt the Mac Cocoa platform for the UI of Adobe Photoshop, creating relationship skirmishes between the two companies. In the end, Apple stopped supporting Adobe's flagship Flash on the iPhone mobile platform. One can also attribute the audacious step to the new entrant HTML 5, which substituted Flash eventually. This also outlines the strained supplier relationship as well.
- **Bargaining Buyer:** In technology, buyer and supplier relationship can be complex.
    - **OpenAI and Microsoft**[8]: When OpenAI got rid of its CEO, Sam Altman, Microsoft, which is also a key investor (contract not disclosed) in the company and its largest customer, ensured Sam Altman was restored as the CEO. If OpenAI had not restored the CEO, many key employees would have resigned, and Microsoft would have offered all those employees to join Microsoft in a new AI division. OpenAI buckled to the pressure and took back the CEO. One could also argue that Microsoft was not the only customer of OpenAI. Had Microsoft created a new division with all OpenAI employees, some of the customers would not have worked directly with Microsoft due to their industry rivalry.
- **Effects of Substitutes:** In technology, new entrants and substitutes can be confusing. Most start with a differentiating product and develop a market while not affecting the original market. After some time, the customers reject the old products.
    - **Introduction of Apple iPhone**[9]: The smartphone market was not new. By the time Apple introduced the product, Nokia, Blackberry, Windows Mobile, Sony, Samsung, and so on head phones in the market. Apple introduced the iPhone as a substitute for the iPod, mobile phone, and Internet device. With multitouch and other compelling features of the UI and applications, it created a new category itself. While business users initially took time to move away from email-centric experiences with BlackBerry and Windows Mobile platforms, the iPhone as a consumer phone became so popular

---

[7] https://www.cnet.com/tech/tech-industry/adobe-and-apple-allies-and-rivals-through-the-ages/
[8] **https://edition.cnn.com/2023/11/29/tech/openai-sam-altman-board-microsoft/index.html**
[9] Steve Jobs introduces iPhone, **https://www.youtube.com/watch?v=MnrJzXM7a6o**

that as soon as it started supporting minimal enterprise support, the shift was unstoppable. iPhone and Android in the market consolidated all personal devices and ended the existence of a portable camera as the perfect substitute.

- **New Entrants:** We will call out a new entrant as something that is designed to replace the other with a direct one-on-one competition.
    - **Consortium-based Standards:** Some interesting ones are:
        - **HTML5 and Adobe Flash:** Apple could go head-on with Adobe Flash as the HTML 5 standard has included the SVG feature set. Adobe had itself contributed to SVG to counter Macromedia Flash.
        - **PNG and CompuServe GIF**[10]: GIF became a popular standard for exchanging images but had patented encryption technology. Unisys had licensed the patent and announced they would start enforcing their patents on GIF usage. It did not go well with the web communities, and they developed a consortium-based Portable Network Graphics file format.
        - **Verisign versus RSA**: Verisign was a spinoff of RSA, focused on providing digital certificates using RSA technologies, while RSA focused on the one-time password-related SecurID. Soon, Verisign developed a new one-time password standard as a consortium and proposed new standards, namely, HOTP and TOTP. Then, they introduced new products into the market under Verisign Identity Protection (VIP). RSA had the upper hand on on-premise solutions while VIP was successful as a cloud offering. Later, RSA partnered with VIP for cloud authentication with RSA SecurID tokens branded as GoID[11].
    - **Google Android versus Apple:** Google had no initial plans for developing devices. However, it wanted to dominate the web content. With the closed ecosystem of the Apple iPhone, Google wanted a share of mobile web content. Thus, it acquired the open-source Android platform. Android was licensed to phone manufacturers to develop phones. Although Google did not enter its branded phones till 2015, its promotion of Android OS irked Apple and Steve Jobs[12].

The five forces have affected the technology and management decisions in many cases. Hence, we consider this a significant framework for PMs to focus on. Product Managers take an outside-in view of the business, and Porter's five forces are a great way to classify the externalities that affect a business. Irrespective of using the

---

[10] https://www.adobe.com/in/creativecloud/file-types/image/raster/png-file.html
[11] https://www.computerworld.com/article/2763393/rsa-and-verisign-partner-for-cloud-based-offering.html
[12] https://www.cnet.com/pictures/apple-and-googles-mobile-war-a-photographic-timeline/

detailed industry analysis frameworks developed around five forces, we expect the PMs to identify and monitor the externalities and tame those continually improving their processes. Thus, we propose the Practice of Product Management with the five forces as the backdrop. We believe that if PMs focus on the ten activities described in the book effectively, they can control these external forces.

Key Factors for Success

People aware of the Pepsi Paradox will accept that the taste of soda beverages goes beyond mere taste, and the brand association plays a significant role. The debates on the paradox are among the research communities, and some even question the test methodologies[13]. Whatever the brand of the drink, if the drink has to be sold in India, the brand loyalty will flutter if the drink is not served chilled. Coca-Cola and Pepsi understood the need and provided their branded glass door refrigerators at all the end-distribution points. Coca-Cola also launched an advertisement, *Thanda Matlab Coca Cola* (Cool is synonymous with Coca-Cola), with a superstar of Indian Cinema, Amir Khan, and captured the interest of the masses of rural India[14]. When you make such brand promises, you must ensure they are delivered at the last mile. Irrespective of the taste or brand identity, being served cold is the Key Factor for Success (KFS). Beers follow the same suit. You see Kingfisher or Budweiser branded refrigerators in bars and pubs. A similar question was raised while approving Pfizer's Covid-19 anti-viral injection, Moderna. Moderna required a -20°C storage requirement for several months, while competitors such as Covishield could be stored at 2-8°C, giving a competitive advantage[15].

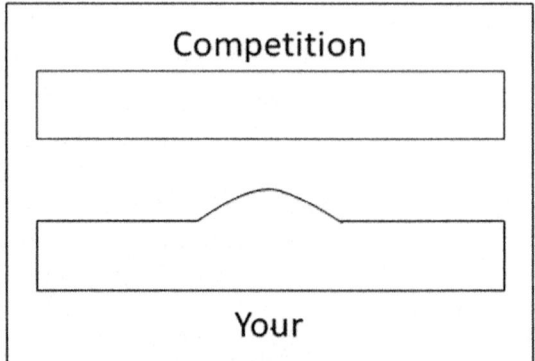

---

[13] George Van Doorn, Beyon Miloyan, The Pepsi Paradox: A review, Food Quality and Preference, Volume 65, 2018, Pages 194-197, ISSN 0950-3293, **https://doi.org/10.1016/j.foodqual.2017.11.007**
[14] How Coca-Cola created a scorching hot campaign with Thanda Matlab **https://brandequity.economictimes.indiatimes.com/news/advertising/how-coca-cola-created-a-scorching-hot-campaign-with-thanda-matlab/95614930**
[15] Moderna Covid vaccine in India: Efficacy, doses, storage, possible 'side effects'. All about it, 1st July 2021, Mint, **https://www.livemint.com/news/india/moderna-covid-vaccine-in-india-efficacy-doses-storage-possible-side-effects-all-about-it-11625103440997.html**

Figure 2.7: *Differentiating KFS from the competition*

Kenichi Ohmae, in his seminal book, *The Mind of the Strategist*[16], explains how to arrive at the KFS using techniques such as value analysis and value engineering. He proposes delving into minute details of features and comparing them with the competitors to realize where the firm is gaining maximum benefits or advantages. He also suggests spotting the segments where the KFS are used maximally and focusing on those segments for maximum value creation. One can use the KFS to develop a focused generic strategy. Michael Porter, in his work on value chains[17], looks into the complete life cycle process of a product and services to determine where the maximum value is added to the product or services. Design Thinking is another way to understand the complete user journey and experiences. The essence of this technique lies in breaking down the business processes to identify the most value-adding factors in the business operations and accentuating them in the product or process. Are KFSs providing strategic benefits, or are they mere operational efficiencies? Once a KFS is recognized, competitors copy it. In the soft drink market, all major brands use the KFS. However, in the case of Moderna, it may not be as simple as it may affect the core manufacturing process of the vaccine technology. Are there any identified KFSs in the technology domain? We can think of the following:

- **Developer tools and core platform tools available on open-source**: The true success of a platform or programming language is achieved when more and more developers start using it. Professional software development happens on such platforms. The market trusts the tools that have the backing of large companies, yet they do not want the control of such companies. They need the tools available to them to review the internal details. Many programming languages and frameworks have been developed in Google, Facebook, Microsoft, and so on. However, the developers prefer when they are available in the open source.

- **Non-market leaders providing their technology to community development as open-source**: When OpenAI kept its large language models (LLM) development closed, consortiums, academic teams, state-sponsored initiatives, and so on, introduced the likes of LLAMA and its derivatives to the open-source. It ensured the monopolistic hegemony of one technology provider was restricted. We have seen this earlier with Netscape opening the source code of the Mozilla browser when it lost the browser war to Microsoft Internet Explorer. This change has led to the development of browsers in community platforms, eventually ending the hegemony of Internet Explorer.

- **Free technology training**: The technology companies create proprietary technologies and create training around those to develop a community of

---

[16] Ohmae, K. (1982). The Mind Of The Strategist: The Art of Japanese Business. United Kingdom: McGraw-Hill Education.
[17] Porter, M., The Value Chain and Competitive Advantage, in Barnes, D., ed (2001), Understanding Business: Processes, p. 52.

developers. However, technology companies such as Google, Microsoft, and so on, are developing training content on Artificial Intelligence and Machine Learning. Since all these provide platforms around AI & ML, adoption around their platforms will improve when a general awareness of AI/ML increases.

BCG Growth-Share Matrix

Boston Consulting Group (BCG) introduced the growth-share matrix in the 1970s to help organizations plan their business portfolio[18]. The intent was to identify the businesses that are doing well to keep them, and those that do not contribute to the firm's long-term profitability should be divested. They looked at how fast a market is growing and what percentage of market share the business holds.

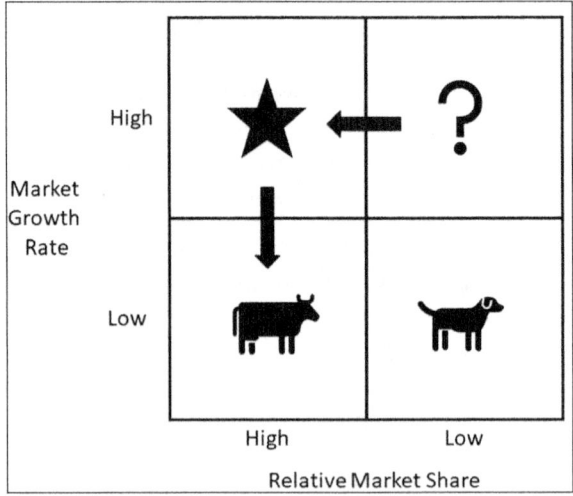

Figure 2.8: BCG growth-share matrix

They classified the products into four categories:

- **Question mark:** A typical business invests in this category. There is strong market growth, but the product is new and has limited market share. The firm should aspire to increase market share and move to the star.
- **Star:** The product has a significant market share in a growth market. Companies will love to have several such products in their portfolio.
- **Cow:** The product was a star, but now the market is shrinking, and the company will milk the cow to fund the next question mark.
- **Pet:** These categories of products do not have high growth potential nor are they in a growth market. They did not do well and should be divested. Most of the time, these have an emotional bias of leaders that makes organizations

---

[18] Armstrong, G., Adam, S., Denize, S., Kotler, P. (2014). Principles of Marketing. United States: Pearson Australia.

lose money for several years.

Only product managers engaged in portfolio planning get to use this framework. However, most product managers face the brunt of this framework in a large organization with multiple products when their investments are taken away, or their BUs are tasked to improve market share. We feel a product manager should use this as a competitive tool. For example, market share discovery is a way to know the market share of competing products. Secondly, it also tells you about adjacent high-growth areas competitors are exploring. It also gives product managers the ability to assess their products realistically and not chase too many products in the pet category.

Being an old framework, BCG reviewed this framework again in 2014 and documented some observations[19]:

- The speed of movement of product categories has changed significantly.
- Companies with the highest market share are not necessarily the most profitable.
- The funding potential of cows in the portfolio is reducing.

BCG recommends the following in the application of the framework:

- Expect the product transition to occur at higher speeds.
- Explore more question marks and quickly decide to pursue or shunt them out. The cows should be milked efficiently.
- With faster movements, pets have increased, and BCG recommends they should be quickly removed from the system.
- A good balance of experiments and market success ensures that future revenues are planned as much as the current revenues.

DuPont Analysis

Financial literacy is critical to the product management functions. The final success of the product is realized by how well it generates profits for an organization. The DuPont method is a good way to understand the financial state of the product and any corrective action to be taken by a company.

---

[19] BCG Classics Revisited: The Growth Share Matrix, June 2014, By Martin Reeves, Sandy Moose, and Thijs Venema.

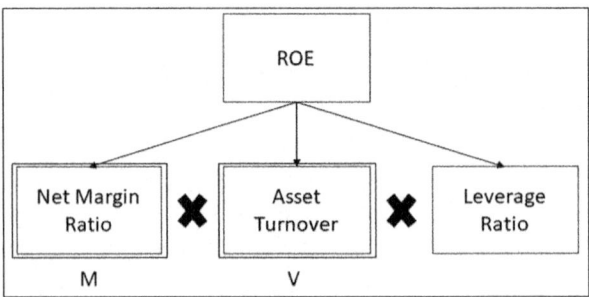

Figure 2.9: *DuPont analysis*

The equation is written as:

$$\frac{Return}{Equity} = \frac{Return}{Sales} \times \frac{Sales}{Assets} \times \frac{Assets}{Equity}$$

Assets over equity is a financial ratio and it considers how a firm has been funded with equity and debt. Hence, it is not so relevant for a product manager. However, the first two ratios are quite useful. Suppose we outsourced the complete development activity for a software product for Rs. 100,000 and developed the product. Now, we are employing another organization to manage and sell the product, and the organization is managing everything and paying us a royalty of 30%.

$$RoS = \frac{Return}{Sales} = 0.3 = Margin$$

If the firm can make Rs. 200,000 worth of sales for us, we will gain asset turnover:

$$SoA = \frac{Sales}{Assets} = \frac{200000}{100000} = 2.0 = Velocity$$

Thus, we will realize RoA = RoS × SoA = Margin × Velocity= 0.6. Effectively, you can do more with the same investment if you can sell more goods. Ram Charan in his book, *What Your CEO Wants You to Know*[20], describes the terms as margin and velocity. The velocity acts as a multiplier for your margin. A profitable firm can multiply its profits significantly by increasing sales. What if you are not tracking the product-level investments? In such cases, engineering or product development headcount can act as a good proxy. A firm should aspire to increase sales to match the engineering strength of the product teams to ensure the revenues for the investments are realized properly. Revenue per employee has also been used as a metric for many IT products and service organizations over the years. In the USA, RPE above a million USD is considered a great number. For Indian product companies, Rupees one crore per employee is a reasonable target. The services organizations achieve half of that number.

---

[20] Charan, R. (2017). What the CEO Wants You to Know: How Your Company Really Works. United Kingdom: Random House.

Qualitative and Quantitative Insights

Most frameworks are as good as the data you provide them. While the guidance is significant, only the relevant inputs lead to assessing meaningful outcomes. Many early-stage entrepreneurs build the product and start competing with the best in the breed, thinking they can take on those. While it could be true, the market may not perceive it that way. Either they have to spend resources messaging through various channels or begin competing with players whom they meet in sales discussions. An early-stage startup may not have the necessary funding for large messaging campaigns. Understanding the competitors should best come from the market perception rather than your aspirations.

In the case of relatively small markets, global research gets to the long tail effect. For example, if a specific country does not have a significant number of customers, they may go with an estimation of market size. In such cases, a better estimate can be arrived at from the pipeline rather than depending on the research data. Some form of qualitative estimation is far more beneficial than exact metrics. For example, Du Pont analysis may not be possible at a product level as many companies do not maintain project or product-based cost allocations. Since product development is an investment for such projects, the product development headcount can be a good proxy for product-level or project-level investment. While many early-stage ventures focus on revenue rather than profits, it is always advisable to track the costs and the ability to compute the costs for a unit of sales. As much as a small profit gets multiplied by a large velocity multiplier, a loss gets badly affected by such large multipliers. Prices and discounts must be computed keeping costs in mind. We will delve deeper into this in the chapter on pricing. If you are operating in a focused market, the market data may not be available as easily in the business press. A periodic web search for news may be ideal for gathering market-specific insight. Sometimes, mere gut instincts provide a much better strategy than significant analysis. Being open to general updates about your industry can benefit you significantly.

Conclusion

We identified the need for a strategy for product management to ensure sustained competitive advantage. Product managers need inward and outward-looking frameworks to understand and develop strategies for their BUs and organizations. We outlined four of them as part of this chapter. However, we encourage the readers to choose suitable frameworks to understand their businesses. We suggest PMs work on a pragmatic level of data and insights to utilize the strategy tools rather than getting overwhelmed by the need for accurate metrics. Once they understand the organization and BU's strategic directions, the next step will be to develop a good product vision and execution plan. We will review this in detail in the next chapter.

Questions

1. Identify the five forces that affect your product. Describe the process you followed to identify the processes.

2. Find out the products that are giving better sales margins in your organization. Why are some products lagging?

3. Identify your product's Key Factors for Success (KFS). What process do you adopt to arrive at the KFSs?

4. Do you have a generic strategy for your Product? If so, what is it, and how did you arrive at it?

CHAPTER 3
Product Vision

Introduction

In the previous chapter, we realized the need for strategy. We chose a battleground and used the relevant strategy tools. The rivalry of players in the industry is one of the forces that affect our business. As product managers, we need to tame this force, yet we are just one of the many organizational entities contributing to the success. We need engineering to build the right product, support teams to address customer issues, sales teams to sell the right solution, and marketing teams to pitch the best value proposition. We need messaging resonating with the customer, a solution approach that makes analysts look at us as a serious contender in the market, and a statement to the market that we have arrived at. If there is a battle, we need a war cry to mobilize the forces in our way. The product vision serves the purpose of mobilizing the organization. In this chapter, we will learn how product managers define a product vision, how the product aligns with the vision, and how the vision is disseminated to the internal and external stakeholders of the organization.

Structure

In this chapter, we will cover the following topics:

- The Statement
- Competitive Elements of Product Vision
- Delivering the Vision
    - Roadmap
    - Workflows
    - Documentation
    - Product Development
- Messaging the Vision
    - Internal
    - External Communication
- Process to Realization of Product Vision

The Statement

In sports, you hear terms like the team played to a plan, they came to the tournament to win, and so on. Cricket has a century-old tradition in India. India's elite picked it up from the British and popularized it in exclusive sports clubs in the metros. But it had not gone to the masses yet. Although India had a long tradition of five-day-long test cricket, the Cricket World Cup[1] was played in English conditions with a limited-overs format completed in a single day. In the previous two editions, the Indian team struggled and performed miserably, registering a victory against a weak side. In 1983, when India started the tournament, no one took the team seriously; the team did not expect to continue beyond the league games to the playoffs. In these conditions, Kapil Dev, the team captain, courageously delivered with both bat and ball and boosted the team morale. However, in the end, the other team members contributed to their potential and delivered India's first World Cup win. These stories are heartwarming and retold in the Hindi movie 83[2].

We are not interested in the 1983 Cricket World Cup but in the next edition of the game in 1987. India was not the winner that year but played exceedingly well and was one of the favorites. Sunil Gavaskar, India's ace batsman of the period, retired from test cricket and focused only on limited-over cricket just for the tournament. Navjot Singh Sidhu and K. Srikanth supported him as specialist one-day batsmen. Kapil Dev, though he had several innings of mention with both bat and ball, was not the only one; he had a team who knew their parts well and delivered on most occasions. The vision to win, which Kapil Dev established in 1983 and walked the path, inspired the team as a unit. That does not mean India had a cakewalk in subsequent editions of the games. India had many ups and downs and won the next Cricket World Cup in 2011. Mahendra Singh Dhoni, the captain, has been credited a lot for applying his cricketing mind, yet the whole team performed when the occasion demanded.

The vision to win has been in the team. It is apparent in all subsequent editions, such as 2015, 2019, and 2023. India has not won these games but has always been among the favorites. Most importantly, the success or failure of these matches cannot be attributed to one player but has been a collective effort of the team. The 1983 World Cup Indian contingent included 14 players and 1 team manager. But in 2019, the contingent had 15 players, almost the same number of support staff. IT experts travel with the teams, analyze ball-by-ball details, and update the team about the strengths and weaknesses of their own and opposition players.

The game is far more complex and performance-driven than it was in 1983. The same applies to the software industry as well. Building a software product involves efforts and contributions from a team of experts. Coordination across the team to achieve the eventual goal is a necessity. We mention sports in a business context. Yet, there

---

[1] **https://www.espncricinfo.com/series/prudential-world-cup-1983-60832**
[2] 83 (Hindi Movie), **https://www.imdb.com/title/tt7518786/**

are some significant differences. There is no clear winner or loser in a business. While financial gains can be stated as primary reasons for business, a company does not need to win over another for its economic success. The competition is rather subtle. Every company needs to reach out to all potential customers with similar needs. The potential customers need to choose one of the companies that provide them with the best value for the price. There are only a finite number of potential customers with the needs. A company will try to reach every one of them. It is this limited supply that leads to competitive rivals in the industry. To counter these rivals, companies build product visions that benefit the customers or the target audience and compel them to choose the companies over their competitors. We will produce the best product for the market, but that is not a good enough vision.

A good vision should have three crisp statements answering the following questions:

1. Who is the target audience for your solution and what problems are you solving for them?
2. How are you achieving this?
3. Why can your competition not achieve the same?

Think of a cost differentiator in the generic strategy. Assuming we do not consider any industry-specific attributes, the following can be a good product vision statement.

We shall provide

the best value to our customers

by

systematically optimizing costs

unlike competition,

who are indifferent to the customer's cause.

The low-cost players price their products the cheapest—it is a misconception. They can price their product for multiple demand price points. The customers will pay for the value they perceive for the product; they are not interested in the cost of production. Similarly, low-cost players optimize their operations and become the cost leaders in the market. Low-cost players can challenge that the competition is indifferent to the customer's value perception. They sign up for the cheapest price point in every deal. Many sales teams love to dole out such discounts for aggressive customer acquisition. Is your product vision equipped to handle such situations? Desktop or on-premise server products can be priced with significant discounts, as the product development costs are sunk. Any additional sale is a revenue without a significant operational cost. However, for SaaS products, there are operational costs. You cannot discount them beyond the variable costs. We will discuss some of these aspects when we discuss pricing in a later chapter.

A discounting mindset without operational efficiency can push you into a red zone. We all have seen companies publishing corporate visions, but do product visions exist? If so, why don't we see them? Product vision existed before product management processes were formally introduced in organizations in their modern incarnations.

The quotation from Walt Disney, "*If you can dream it, you can do it*[3]," was often mentioned in various Adobe software installers and campaigns over decades[4], particularly in Adobe Photoshop[5]. The essence of this visionary statement is an appeal to say Adobe is about innovations that can bring human dreams and thoughts into reality. It sells well with audiences such as graphics artists and desktop publishers. When Adobe entered enterprise markets with Adobe Acrobat and its revolutionary Portable Document Format (PDF), Adobe had to fight a different battle. Adobe had to create an association of the Adobe brand with PDF documents so that the brand would get visibility[6]. Here are some changes Adobe brought about in 2003:

- Adobe Acrobat Reader, the free reader to read PDF files, was renamed Adobe Reader.
- Adobe Reader was available on all mobile devices such as Windows Pocket PC, Palm OS, or Nokia Symbian devices.
- One could annotate PDF files in Adobe Reader without a full version of Adobe Acrobat, a technology internally code-named ubiquity.
- Adobe integrated its PDF generation technologies with workflow providers such as SAP.

Adobe Acrobat and PDF took on a new tagline *Everywhere You Look*. While started as simple product launches and messaging taglines, these have been in corporate-level marketing messages. It is hard to ascertain if an Adobe Acrobat Product Manager wrote a vision statement, but Adobe wanted to make PDF files ubiquitous or a synonym for *Everywhere You Look*. Many subsequent actions from Adobe and the ecosystem responses only supported this initiative. Many players started providing PDF creators and tools. Microsoft provided a default PDF printer as part of the Windows OS. Adobe released the PDF specification as an ISO standard ISO-32000-1[7]. All these ascertained,

---

[3] **https://magicmadebydisney.com/2021/04/27/finally-the-origin-of-if-you-can-dream-it-you-can-do-it/** accessed 8th May 2024
[4] **https://twitter.com/NadCee/status/1782872642237673892** accessed 8th May 2024.
[5] **https://www.facebook.com/100064958611068/posts/10157128170269685/** accessed 8th May 2024.
[6] Adobe marketing collaterals from Computer History Museum, **https://archive.computerhistory.org/resources/access/text/2019/04/102780010-05-01-acc.pdf** accessed 8th May 2024
[7] ISO 32000-1:2008 Document management Portable document format Part 1: PDF 1.7 **https://www.iso.org/standard/51502.html** accessed 8th May 2024.

Product Vision

PDF is now *Everywhere You Look*. A consistent vision gets operationalized and realized in the long run.

The proof of a product created with a vision is the launch of the iPhone by Steve Jobs[8]. He introduces a device that replaces three devices—a music player, a phone, and an internet device. It essentially packs all these features into one device—provides internet access as capable as a desktop or laptop with a fully capable browser, unlike competition that just provided email and limited low-fidelity browsers such as Blackberry and Windows Mobile platforms. The iPhone had no stylus and supported multitouch with fingers, which was different from the devices of the period. Did Apple have a plan B? As much as the iPhone was a killer product, Apple also introduced the iPod Touch the same year. A device that did not have a phone but only had a unified music player and internet experience.

Early Google products were all aligned with the corporate mission of organizing all the world's information[9]. It meant Google would control how data gets created, consumed, stored, or even delivered. It gave the flexibility to scan books, organize photographs, encourage blog writing, embed advertising monetization in promoting search analytics, and create browsers and mobile devices. Organization of the world's information also led Google to invest in Artificial Intelligence (AI) early. AI scientists such as Peter Norvig have been working for Google since 2001. However, very few companies create such a compelling mission that all the products they build can derive their vision from. It also came with challenges when Google could not dominate the phone market, although it owned the Android platform. Google Pixel was an outsourced afterthought for the initial years, looked as a good reference for Android implementation and not a mass player. One can also argue that Google never understood social networking, although it tried hard with Orkut and Google Plus.

While the market appreciated Apple's unification strategy of mobile devices, Microsoft launched Windows 8 to unify usage experience across devices. Microsoft tried campaigns like I Want to Be Everything at Once[10], though catchy with Lenka's music did not get the user connected. So much so that within a few months of a lackluster response from the market, the Indian launch chose the catchy Bollywood number, asking young people to give Windows 8 a try[11]. Unlike desktops or laptops, where the users tend to be tech-savvy and understand the need for an operating system, phones and tablets are just off-the-shelf working devices. Running the same OS as a Windows desktop was not appealing. People looked at the gadgets as a different beast. Windows

---

[8] Steve Jobs unveils the iPhone, CNET channel on YouTube, **https://www.youtube.com/watch?v=LOb3FJhDbYs**
[9] Google Founder's IPO Letter, **https://abc.xyz/investor/founders-letters/ipo-letter/** accessed 9th May 2024
[10] Windows 8 reklama, YouTube Channel: MicrosoftPLVideo, **https://www.youtube.com/watch?v=AkfPdrHVHkY**
[11] Microsoft Windows 8 Commercial "You And Me Together" Long Version, YouTube Channel: KunduDance, **https://www.youtube.com/watch?v=UZF9cZJUl7k**

8 UI supporting non-touch and touch device experience was not as seamless, leading to an overall loss for Windows 8. Eventually, Microsoft exited the mobile phone market, giving a complete free hand to Google Android.

When diverse sets of people come to one consolidated outcome, a vision must exist. Whether explicitly communicated or realized over the interaction with the product and the team can be debated. We saw examples of product vision that later became corporate messages (Adobe), a corporate mission that swept the product vision across the product lines (Google), a product launch that looked like someone reading out a product vision statement (Apple iPhone), or a product vision that did not connect to the users (MS Windows 8). These are experiences of several decades. Today, product managers build products that attract audiences from various domains. There is external venture funding that needs a crisp understanding of their investment. A clear vision statement is a compelling start to bring people together.

A product vision has a limited time horizon. However, predicting how long the product vision will be relevant to the market is difficult. Hence, companies prefer defining an end-of-life plan at a fixed timeline. For example, Microsoft gives a five-year mainstream support to its operating system products. The lifecycle allows the organization to review the product vision and launch a new version of the product with an expanded scope to the existing vision or a fresh vision. The vision leads to many requirements captured as a roadmap. In a release, only a part of the roadmap gets implemented. When the product vision changes completely, the roadmap items can become irrelevant. For example, when you launch a SaaS-based product, the need to deploy a license key may not be relevant. If you are developing a cross-version migration utility, the life of the utility is about one or two years and not the product life cycle of five years. Every time you work on a new product version, review the product vision and the requirements in the roadmap. Remove the requirements that are not aligned with the new vision from the roadmap.

Competitive Elements of Product Vision

Let us write a hypothetical product vision for the Apple iPhone 1.0 product:

- We offer our consumers a device that has a music player, an internet device, and a phone.
- We offer a capable browser, a large display, and a multi-touch-capable screen that the users can navigate using their fingers.

Unlike the competition that uses an arcane keyboard or a stylus to navigate, failing on user experience, Apple was already a leader in the iPod music player market. To some, it may sound like, here is the new iPod with internet and phone. Apple also launched an iPod touch device with just the additional internet feature to the iPod with a touch screen but no phone. In short, Apple was still targeting its base, not coming after the phone market. iPhone did not have email sync and some basic features needed for enterprise users. Windows Phone and Blackberry targeted that market a lot more. Consumer phones were a focus for Nokia, Samsung, and so on. But they had limited capabilities. Here is the Apple iPhone, a consumer phone with smartphone features. One can call iPhone 1.0 a minimum viable product (MVP) that connected to the users very well. The next version of the iPhone, iPhone 3G, came with some enterprise features such as email sync. The rest is history.

How did competitors react? They ignored the iPhone as a serious product to start with. Their focus was enterprise, so they were selling newer phones, enterprise messaging servers, and so on to enterprises. iPhone tied up with SIM-locked plans with telecom providers. It made the pricey iPhone cheaper on an EMI scheme with the plans. Nokia focused on selling phones through telecom providers. However, they had limited capabilities called feature phones. Apple was developing a closed ecosystem for its apps, music, and developer environment. While Google signed a deal with Apple to include search and maps, they were skeptical about their plans in the long run. While they had no control over Apple, they did not want others to come with similar closed ecosystems. They started an open-source consortium with Android and tied it with several hardware manufacturers, such as HTC, Samsung, Motorola, Dell, Lenovo, and so on. In many ways, Android had a similar user experience as the iPhone, such as multi-touch support, an app ecosystem to create any software, even a music player, and a native browser. Since Eric Schmidt was part of the Apple board, Steve Jobs felt he had access to Apple's plans and replicated them in Android[12].

When you let your vision be known to the world, competitors will respond. However, not in the same way as your vision. Android feature-wise was iPhone-like, developed a multi-profile OS like Microsoft Windows CE and Windows Phone, and depended on an ecosystem of vendors to deliver its vision, yet ensuring their company mission of organizing the world's information is still intact in their Android plans. Android ships with a collection of Google apps and features that a vendor cannot override; for example, a search bar is native to the Android UI. Google did not replicate Apple's vision; they were influenced by Apple but developed their product. Eventually, Android killed the Microsoft Phone.

A product vision is an internal document. How does the competition come to know of it? The expression of the vision is visible in the product design, product documentation, advertisements, marketing campaigns, and so on. However much you try, your competitors will come to know of your product vision and respond to it. In the chapter on Strategy, we discussed Key Factors of Success (KFS) proposed by Kenichi Ohmae. He proposed a value engineering and value analysis framework to identify the features in the product that differentiate it from the competition significantly and accentuate them. However, as soon as a KFS is known, the competitors will replicate it. It now depends on how strong your KFS is. Apple iPhone used software and hardware

---

[12] Walter Isaacson, Steve Jobs: The Exclusive Biography, 2011, Hachette, UK.

to provide a compelling user experience that the competition could not replicate. Rivals fight with each other. They try to show their upmanship over the others in the market; there is so much spending on advertisement and media management, one would wonder who is this good for anyway? In an open market, competition leads to consumer choice. As long as there is ethical treatment of media and advertisements, even the government will create a healthy atmosphere for competition. Here are a few advantages of competition in the market.

- **Development of Categories:** When similar products in the market interact and compete in a similar marketplace, they create a category. For example, the iPhone, Samsung, Google Pixel, and so on compete in the high-end smartphone market. Oppo and Vivo have a unique presence in the phone camera segment. Xiaomi is popular in the value-for-money segment. As a consumer, when you decide to buy a phone, you directly focus on the category you are interested in. As a vendor, you should focus only on 3-5 competitors. However, many early-stage organizations do not want to define that target set. When they do not define their category right, they are pitted against everyone in the market. With limited resources, they cannot compete with everyone in the market and eventually lose out.

- **Analysts, Influencers, and Reviewers:** As products become sophisticated, it requires skill to analyze products and inform them to the audience. In the tech sector, Gartner and Forrester are well-known analysts. They suggest IT strategy to many top organizations in the world. In doing so, they review many enterprise software vendors and release comparative studies across these vendors. For example, the Gartner Magic Quadrant compares vendors according to the completeness of their vision and their ability to execute and categorizes vendors as leaders, visionaries, niche players, and challengers.

    Forrester releases a vendor comparison report called Forrester Wave for various enterprise software categories. Companies work hard to be part of the Gartner Magic Quadrant[13] or Forrester Wave[14] every year. Companies such as G2.com analyze business software products and services and report their benefits and efficacy. Several business publications on technology report on consumer gadgets. TV news channels have specific hours dedicated to the analysis of upcoming technology gadgets. Social media has several influencers who have dedicated videos on the unboxing and teardown of various technology hardware and software. The whole industry has come up to help customers understand the complexity of the technology world.

- **Evaluation Guides and Battle Cards:** Every product vendor provides product evaluation guides to help potential customers choose their product over the

---
[13] Gartner Magic Quadrant - **https://www.gartner.com/en/research/methodologies/magic-quadrants-research**
[14] Forrester Wave Methodology - **https://www.forrester.com/policies/forrester-wave-methodology/**

competition. Vendors would highlight their features and entice potential customers by showing significant value added. Another document that vendors share with their potential customers is a battle card. The battle cards come in various formats. The commonest is a table of features versus competitors with qualitative comparison across; Harvey balls are a common visualization for such charts. There are descriptive battle cards as well. Vendors publish such documents. So, they are almost always biased. However, the critical analysis of competitors is quite detailed. One can get good information about a market by evaluating the battle cards and evaluation guides from various vendors.

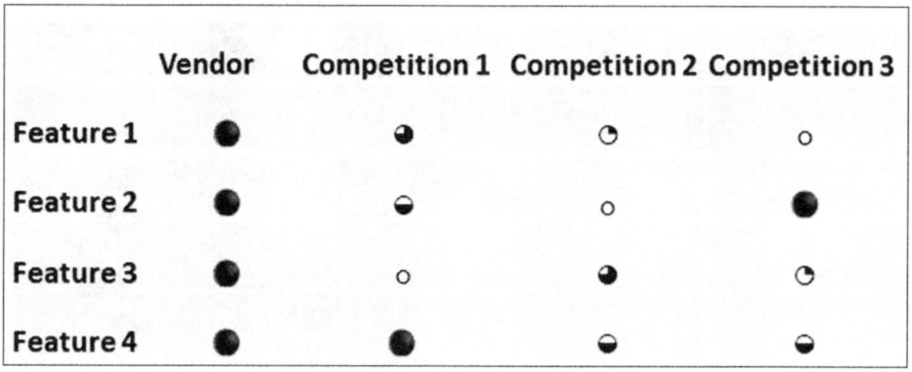

	Vendor	Competition 1	Competition 2	Competition 3
Feature 1	●	◕	◔	○
Feature 2	●	◑	○	●
Feature 3	●	○	◕	◔
Feature 4	●	●	◑	◑

Figure 3.1: *Battle card with Harvey balls*

Competition helps customers get the best value for their money. However, it creates significant overheads for the product teams. As long as you develop a product, you will always have to keep in mind how the product performs vis-a-vis competition, not just in terms of functionalities but also in terms of mindshare. Will the customer recommend the products to others? Can the customer become a reference customer and provide testimonials?

Delivering the Vision

We have the product vision. To deliver the vision, we develop the product and ensure it meets the customer's needs. It generates revenues and meets the profitability requirements set forth for the product. While those are the eventual goals for a product, there are a few intermediate steps a product manager should keep in mind. The intermediate steps help product managers assess progress, take corrective actions, and ensure the product is delivered on time with the right quality.

Roadmap

Let us go back to the Apple iPhone example again. What does it mean to deliver on the vision? Is it possible to decide on a product with three statements? We create a simple mind map of what it means to provide a phone, music player, and internet device on a handheld gadget.

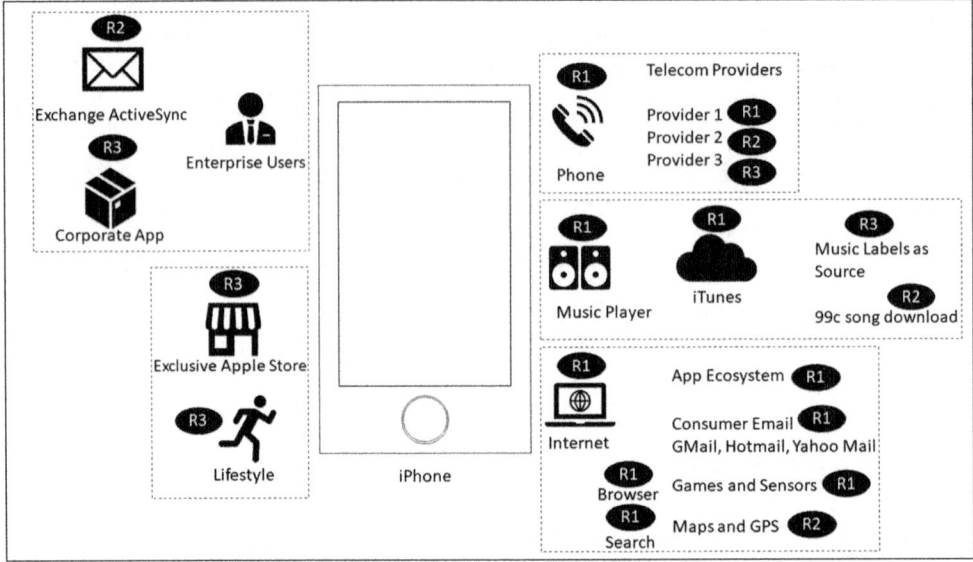

Figure 3.2: Apple iPhone features; a mind map

Apple needs to partner with telecom providers so that they can sell mobile devices with monthly subscription plans. Such devices are to be SIM-locked to the telecom vendors, while non-locked devices are popular in Asia and Europe. Apple cannot partner with every telecom provider in one go. They will move steadily with one partner at a time. We presume they develop one partnership for each release. That's the reason you see release milestones R1, R2, and R3 against each provider. As a music player, iPhone users have experienced the iPod. They know they can download music from iTunes. Can iTunes partner with other music labels to download their music? Instead of downloading complete albums, can we cost-effectively download a specific song? While launching iPhone 1.0, Apple did not have answers to these, but they had it in their minds to address in R2 and R3 releases.

The internet readiness requires a lot of features in the R1 release itself. For example, you will need a browser and search interfaces working. Native application experience that utilizes a mobile form factor needs to be better. Handheld gadgets are used as gaming consoles by many. So, sensors such as an accelerometer or a compass can show better value to a person. People will connect to consumer emails such as Gmail, Hotmail, or Yahoo Mail. Similarly, phones can have GPS and provide an accurate position on the map based on the satellite positioning data.

When Apple launched the iPhone, they knew they could not be blind to enterprise customer needs. The enterprise customer needs connectivity to corporate email systems such as Microsoft Exchange. Corporate IT would like to provision and manage applications on the user's devices. They should be able to wipe application data when the user leaves the organization. Apple also wanted to associate an element of lifestyle with the iPhone brand. Apple and Nike collaborated to send workout data to nikeplus.com. Apple also launched exclusive stores to sell its goods, adding a lifestyle element. Neither the enterprise functionalities nor the lifestyle associations were available with the first version of the iPhone. Yet they would all be in the mind map with a reasonable sense of release milestones. While we showed a simple mind map, some would create a formal marketecture showing how various subsystems interact with each other and associate releases to the subsystems. However, the most common means of representation is a timeline-based roadmap. Given our oversimplified iPhone example, here is the roadmap on a timescale.

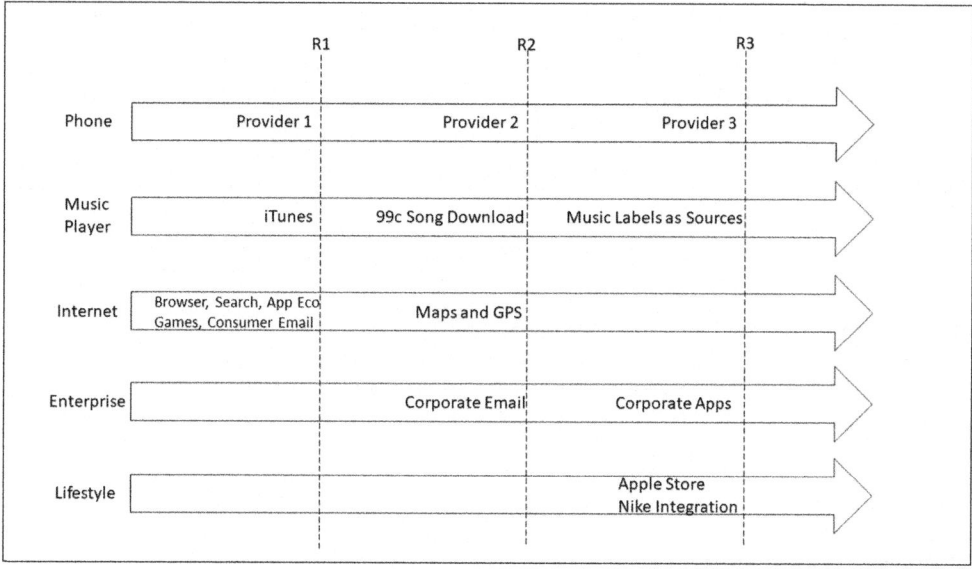

Figure 3.3: *A sample iPhone roadmap on a timescale*

Should you use the mind map view or the timescale view for roadmaps? Both have their advantages. The mind map or marketecture view gives a quick way to explain the product and its subsystems. The timeline view lets you understand what gets released in every milestone. Sales teams prefer the timeline view as they can discuss with the customers easily. The mind map and marketecture are a great way to explain your vision. However, when it comes to engineering, these roadmaps are much higher level. Engineering would like to understand what specific features they would implement in every release. If you were to break a complex system like an iPhone into granular-level details for engineering requirements, it would fill up several hundred pages.

Roadmaps are great visualization tools for associating functionalities with the final deliverable. However, the closer the timelines are, the better the predictions are.

When a timeline of a release is too far ahead, the chances of meeting the timelines are only tentative. Many product managers prefer to commit to a roadmap just six months to a year ahead. How detailed should roadmaps be? Some would like to see granular details, including bugs on a roadmap. Too many details make the roadmap confusing. We will recommend a roadmap item as a user benefit that the customer can correlate.

Can a roadmap be a deliverable for a product vision? A roadmap is not good enough to sell or earn revenues for the organization; yet, for a product manager, it begins as a talking point to various stakeholders. There is some form of concreteness to a roadmap. The product manager can discuss with an early-stage customer and convey how they perceive the product and how they plan to develop it over time. A customer planning to use the specific product features can provide immediate feedback. And the product manager can realign the roadmap to consider the customer's needs. The customer is aware that the organization is developing the product based on their direct feedback and is open about it. While this is easily possible for a business-to-business (B2B) market, taking consumer feedback at an individual level may not always be possible.

In a business-to-consumer (B2C) market, the number of consumers to interact with can be large, and maintaining confidentiality is hard if you interact with a large number of consumers. However, product managers discuss with consumers in focused groups. From the focused group discussions, the PMs can associate certain features or workflows the customers are interested in. With the help of designers and software developers, they can develop prototypes for further feedback. These prototypes are not built into the product, keeping product confidentiality. We will discuss further on these in the chapter on Agile methodology.

Workflows

Every customer interacts with the product in a well-defined process. Let us take the example of a user booking an airline ticket. She decides the places, the dates, the time most convenient, and the most reasonable price. She can select all these from a collection of options presented to her. The process she utilizes to select her travel plans is called a workflow. Product managers discuss with the customers and bring up the common workflows. Simple workflows that cater to a larger pool of customers are preferred over complex ones. Workflows also depend on the user interface decided for the application. A web workflow will focus on selection from wizard elements, while a chat interface will capture data from a conversational context as in a chatbot. Many AI chatbots capture workflow context from previous conversations, emails, and more. While product managers engage with customers in defining the workflows, they involve the UX engineers and designers to fine-tune the workflow requirements. With user experience becoming a focus for many products today, product workflows need further focus for every product manager. We will delve further into this aspect in the chapter involving user experience.

Documentation

Information developers or document writers often write product documentation. They often write the documentation after the product development is complete. Why should product documentation be looked at along with the product vision? Two aspects majorly drive product documentation—a conceptual outline of the product that explains the product rationale, the workflows, and user benefits. The second aspect is the specific function of a product, such as the interaction of the user interface and the users. The first part remains almost static from the beginning of the product. Some of the concepts can even remain valid across product releases. More than information developers, product managers have better control and understanding of these aspects of the product. We suggest the product managers incorporate these aspects of the product. Secondly, these aspects of the products can be shared with potential customers, sales, and marketing teams so that they get a conceptual view of the product. These sections contain historical perspectives, product use cases, and concepts and rationale behind the development of the product. Documenting these early as part of the product vision makes it easier for engineering teams to develop the product or quality assurance teams to test the product features. It also reduces clutter when the concepts are involved.

Product Development

The proof of the pudding is in the eating. For a software product, it is ultimately the product development where we realize the application of all the vision, planning, and execution. Hence, it is the step where all the hard work comes to fruition. The product managers ensure the vision is translated correctly to every person in the product development process, and they build the right product. As with the product vision, the product managers define the product requirements. With agile practices in software development, most product managers define the requirements as user stories. While the user stories are granular, they inherently talk about a specific value-add for an end customer. At the level of the product vision, a user story is too granular. It may be ideal to speak of a higher-level abstraction of a user story. These kinds of abstractions are called epics.

Let us go back to the same iPhone example. As we build the latest iPhone product, we require 5G capabilities in the telephony elements of the product. For the iPhone we conceptualize, we want the gadget to connect to a 5G network if it is available. At the conceptualization phase, we need not know the exact specification of the network. We may not even build the network capability in the chipset. We can outsource that element to a third-party provider. Instead of a product manager building the detailed chipset for 5G connectivity, we may engage a program manager to interact with various network vendors and work on outsourcing plans. As a product manager, we still need to understand the interface of the interaction of the 5G components with our phones.

We should know the size of the components, where the components should fit in, the system bus where the components will interface with, and so on.

An epic is abstract and conceptual yet has enough placeholder presence for planning the product. Epics also play a significant role in transitioning responsibilities across teams. In our iPhone example, one of the teams is developing the native app experience, while another is trying to build the browser. Both are substantial requirements. They need large teams with one or more product managers in each of them. We conceive two epics. The first epic is about developing a capable browser similar to a desktop browser. The second epic is developing an app ecosystem that can be in the form factors of a mobile screen. Each epic gets developed by independent teams. However, we will coordinate intermittently to ensure both requirements are on time and ship in the iPhone. Epics are at a high level of abstraction. They are broken down into detailed stories so engineers can work on them. In the chapter on agile methodologies, we will discuss further on this topic.

Messaging the Vision

A good product takes time to build; you need to market the product. Communication must reach the influencers and analysts to attract interest in the market. As much as it is important to build a great product, communication of the vision to the stakeholders is crucial for product managers. The strategy and product vision processes ensure a good demand prediction and forecast. However, the realization of the vision lies in the supply side, where the right product is built and delivered to the right customer. Its success lies in a good go-to-market (GTM) strategy. However, the GTM can depend on internal as well as external stakeholders. We discuss the GTM requirements from internal stakeholders. A good GTM requires the marketing mix of:

- Product
- Price
- Place
- Promotion

While we have discussed the product, let's focus on the other marketing mix attributes. Price is a critical attribute in a GTM strategy. Price represents the value a customer attributes to the product. A high-value solution for the customer can demand high involvement from the customer and a different sales approach. We will discuss the rationale for pricing in detail in a later chapter. A good GTM is about providing visibility to the product. Hence, the place for launch can add to this visibility. The place in marketing does not mean a physical location but how and where a product reaches the customer. Some of the larger organizations focus on a solution marketing approach to GTM. For example, Microsoft may propose a GTM for IT administrators of large organizations. In proposing this solution, Microsoft may include Azure Services,

Identity and Access Management Products such as Microsoft Entra, Configuration Manager, and so on. All these are independent products, with their product teams delivering several parts. However, the impact is most significant when all the product teams can interact with the customers and present in an aggregated manner. The solution marketing team focused on IT administrators would like to bring several products to one platform. All these product releases may have happened in different timelines. When all the products are part of a single solution-oriented GTM, they should be interoperable. These plans do not limit themselves to an organization only. Azure Monitoring services integrate with IT Service Management connectors from BMC or ServiceNow. Such solution marketing initiatives can benefit these vendors to talk about their product offerings in a Microsoft forum. Every large organization offering platforms has its developer or user conferences. Some notable ones are Google IO, Apple WWDC, Adobe Max, AWS Global Summit, Microsoft Ignite, RSA Conference, and so on. Large ISVs and partners look forward to sponsoring events or being invitees to such prestigious conferences. Similarly, analyst firms and industry groups conduct conferences. These places bring in a focused audience to pitch one's product. However, these are expensive events and need proper planning and a clear execution plan to make the best impact. Good communication is one of the most important aspects of a GTM process.

While we discussed the importance of place for launching the product, promotion is also an equally important aspect. Promotion is a conscious effort to attract buyers. The offers during a promotion are not considered as a part of a pricing strategy. During a solution marketing event for IT Administrators, Microsoft may offer 100 licenses of the Microsoft Entra ID platform as a promotional event. A hundred licenses for free are for the IT Administrators to test the product on a small scale or departmental deployment to try the product and not a realistic deployment. Sometimes, vendors may want to launch a new product by bundling it with adjacent products. Here, one needs to observe the intent of the vendor. During data center migration from on-premise to virtual environments, many IT Operations Management vendors offered data center sizing tools for free. These sizing or measurement tools improved the sales of operations management tools. Although given out for free, the assessment tools were part of the pricing strategy and not a mere promotion. We will consider the following as the difference between pricing and promotion.

- Discounted pricing is a strategy extended to multiple customers. An organization can do so when it is operationally efficient to keep costs low. However, there are costs involved in a promotion. These costs incurred are with a clear intention to further sales.
- A pricing scheme must meet the variable costs of operations. We will discuss some of the legal pricing aspects later in the book. Promotions are expenses, and firms make conscious choices for such decisions. Such expenses ideally should be captured in the marketing expenses or costs of goods sold (COGS). Price discounts are captured only in the revenues.

- Promotions are limited-time or event-based. However, pricing is repeatable. Always low-price or discounted price match schemes by some of the retail stores are actual pricing strategies and not mere promotional offers[15]. Large discounted retailers can introduce such policies as they maintain their cost of operations to a limit.

Internal Communication

The expression of a compelling vision is in its realization. However, it takes a village to raise a child or realize a vision, in this case. While the vision emanates from the strategy, the senior management should sign up to the product vision. However, there are two distinctive operational challenges seen at this level. In large organizations, strategic initiatives can be strong. However, the business unit (BU) leadership may not like to implement the strategic initiatives so that immediate operational gains are not affected. In relatively small organizations, the senior leadership may prefer opportunistic gains in the business to a strategic focus. For example, realizing a product vision may derail immediate business deals. Striking a balance is crucial in such cases. A product vision is a relatively long-term commitment. A product team needs to give six months to a year of commitment.

The second challenge one may face is in deciding on the Minimum Viable Product (MVP). The departmental focus can be different for various aspects of the product. Sales teams will focus on easier demonstrability, marketing teams on elaborate competitive feature sets, engineering and support teams on product stability, and so on. As a product manager, deciding on an MVP is a significant challenge in a new product launch. Once the MVP gets market acceptance, incremental additions become easy. We will discuss the product prioritization process in the agile process later in the book.

The GTM process often brings significant interaction between product management, sales and marketing, and operations teams. Deciding on the place and promotion for the GTM may involve regular interaction with the marketing teams. Developing the collaterals for GTM is another significant part. In larger organizations, product teams look at the solution marketing calendars to ensure they get a portion of the marketing budget. Aligning the product releases to solution launch events is a great way to be part of organizational initiatives. In collateral development, a product with better revenue share may take a significant mindshare. The product teams should own the product content to ensure the solution papers have the right level of exposure for the products.

The challenges in smaller organizations are different. The product management becomes the pivot for all product content. In such cases, maintaining consistent

---

[15] Walmart Price Match Policy, USA, **https://www.walmartcontacts.com/price-match-policy** (accessed 30th May 2024)

messaging can be a concern. Since the sales focus is on potential opportunities rather than a consistent product plan, one may see product comparison requests for any vendor that comes into a sales discussion. Not having a clearly defined vision for a product in such circumstances makes the product teams chase after deals rather than focusing on product development. Almost all product managers take pride in closing sales deals for the organizations. However, there is a balance that needs to be understood here. If a product sales process requires product management with no additional product features, the manpower requirement in solution selling and product knowledge in the field teams should be a focus. There could be a need to hire more solution engineers, better training for the field, and so on, while PMs should plan for this as part of the GTM plans.

The same applies to product operations and support as well. The engineers developing a product should not be involved in managing and operating the SaaS-based systems for two reasons. Production systems are not for debugging. Secondly, the persons knowing the internal workings of the product should not access the customer data. Most data center or cybersecurity-related standards discourage such practices. When a customer faces issues with a system, she contacts a product support team to report. Support engineers who are well-acquainted with the product can address these issues with ease. Good product training with a proper understanding of product vision can help support teams in decision-making. In larger organizations, support teams are shared resources across products. The better the focus given to them by the product teams, the lower the product support costs. The support organizations are ranked L1 to L3 based on their product and knowledge skills. A resolution at a lower level reduces the cost of support. Product engineering involvement in the support process reduces the team's focus on engineering newer product versions and may lead to addressing quality issues and rework. A product can only be supported well when the quality metrics are met.

External Communication

The product vision needs a communication outlet in the external audience as well. The most significant external audience is the customer. The customer would want to know how the product can help them realize their needs. Is the product built to solve the issues they face? A product should address the problems faced by a customer. Only then does the customer see a value-added product; thus, they pay for it. It is the premise for building a product or solution. The solutions papers or product collaterals keep this goal in mind. While direct customer communication is important for product teams, it is not always practical. The product teams reach out to selected customer sets like lighthouse customers. These are a small set of customers who are early adopters of the product. They work through the product development process and provide feedback along the release. Some are part of product beta programs. Some of these customers are active in multiple forums and can provide references for the product.

In the section on GTM, we discussed conferences and showcase events. PMs make presentations and showcase the product on the stage. These evangelization activities ensure enough interest and mindshare in the people's minds. Not all the participants are necessarily customers in such events. Some are significant influencers. For example, an IT administrator attending an event may influence the CIO of the organization to look out for a new capability that can improve employee productivity. Some of the products can be technical. The influencer's knowledge, in such cases, is trusted by the organization's management in decision-making. Product evangelization requires a specific skill set to be developed in people. Some people act as user forum managers and reply to product queries raised in such groups. In the open-source communities, freelance evangelists are sponsored by organizations to keep the group alive and discussions focused.

While there can be several external communication channels for product managers, our last discussion will be on industry analysts. Industry analysts generally provide consulting services to organizations in a focused IT area. Due to the very nature of engagements, they interact with the market and influence opinions in the market. Their solutions involve software products, and in recommending those solutions, they analyze many software products. Hence, the analysts work as a great intermediary for buyers and sellers. Both sides trust their industry understanding and expect them to provide insights that can make their offerings attractive to buyers. The product teams want the analysts to be mindful of their products and recommend them in their solutions. Some analysts provide solutions for the software vendors as well. For example, they can offer pricing insights in various geographies, the trends in the market, and adoptions of better technologies in the market. Some offer synergetic insights for partnerships and buy versus build decisions. Product teams often discuss their vision with analysts to vet it with market insight and ensure the vision gets better coverage and acceptance in the analyst's mind. Organizations take vendor briefs seriously and want measured communication passed to the analysts for better impact.

Process to Realization of Product Vision

Successful delivery is the way to realize a good product vision. A complex product can involve hundreds of people working for several departments. Some of the people engaged may not even belong to the organization. All these people are expected to have their focus intact all through the delivery of the product. They know what is expected of them and what they expect from the other people involved. The progress of the teams is well understood. When some teams are not meeting their timelines, their limitations are visible with utmost precision. There is a culture of openness that makes progress apparent to the organization. If any intervention is needed, people in other groups or divisions can proactively help the people meet their timelines. If delays affect the other teams, they are prepared and able to share their status on time. The lack of transparency in a project creates concerns for project delivery. At every level, people like to add buffers to hide the delays in the project. We recommend using Agile Methodologies to bring transparency to the project and enhance visibility in the operations. In the chapter on the agile processes, we will evaluate these aspects in greater detail.

Figure 3.4: *Product vision to realization*

At the core, we perceive the product vision. The vision leads to delivering a compelling roadmap, workflows that make meaningful contributions to the customer needs, and documents that explain the rationale of the product conceptualization. In the end, we deliver the product, realizing the product vision. The vision also needs to be communicated to the internal and external audiences. Communication creates awareness and helps in the demand generation of the product. All these activities require a consistent project management process using agile methodologies.

Conclusion

Industry rivals are the first of the forces that affect a business. In the product management process, we delved into a product vision to address this force. While the product vision is just three statements, the realization of the vision requires processes for building and communicating the vision. In this chapter, we identified some approaches for delivering and disseminating the vision.

As we proceed to subsequent chapters, we will see how the elements of the vision are reflected in other processes. The people and agile management processes we discuss in the later chapters will bring further strength to realizing the vision. However, the next force we will be discussing is a bargaining buyer. We will study the change from a bargaining buyer to a customer mindset to add value.

Questions

1. What is the product vision of your product? How is it different from the vision stated by your BU head?

2. Discuss with others in your product group and understand their understanding of the product vision. Is your understanding the same as theirs?

3. Has the business press reported about your product? Is their understanding the same as the vision you have set forth inside the organization?

4. Has your BU set up a consistent product vision inside and outside the organization? What can be done to set the process right?

CHAPTER 4
Customer

Introduction

When we decided to model our product management framework around Porter's Five Forces, some management professionals objected to the choice of framework. They argued that Porter's Five Forces is more aligned with an economist's view of a firm. They are right. However, even with this economic lens, one force within the model—the Bargaining Buyer—is particularly relevant to product management. The world of economics deals with commodities. Commodities are alike, and the only differentiating factor is price. In most sales discussions, we dole out discounts before signing the contract. As product managers, we want to change the buying behavior. We want our products to add value to our customers' cause. Products are not commodities. We want the customer to communicate with us and not a buyer to bargain with us on price alone. In this chapter, we will understand the sales process and focus on delivering value to the customer.

Structure

In this chapter, we will cover the following topics:

- Identifying the Customer
- Buyer to Customer
- Mutually Beneficial Relationship
- Establishing Value for the Customer
- Negotiation

Identifying the Customer

In most goods and services, the buyer and seller relationships are straightforward. Buyers obtain the goods and services from a seller for financial consideration. Buyers pay a price, and the sellers accept to provide the goods and services. In most cases, we colloquially call the buyer a customer and the seller a service provider or a vendor. When it comes to software, the relationship gets complex. There are multiple layers of customer and vendor relationships here. In the simplest form, let us think of Microsoft Office 365 as a service. As a consumer, you pay Microsoft an annual license fee to use the service on one of your personal computers. Microsoft is the software vendor. You become a Microsoft customer and pay a yearly subscription fee to use the software. It is called a business-to-consumer (B2C) relationship. An individual consumer becomes a customer of a business.

A company like Acme Corporation wants its employees to use Microsoft Office 365. In doing so, it wants to ensure its employees become more productive and use standardized office practices across the organization. Microsoft will sell a solution to a company or business. These relationships are known as business-to-business (B2B) relationships. However, B2B relationships lead to more complexity. In this case, the employees of Acme Corporations are using the software. We call this a business-to-employee (B2E) relationship. Let us think of a net banking application. Hypothetically, Citibank licenses core banking applications from Oracle Financials to provide net banking operations to its customers. It can be called a business-to-business-to-consumer (B2B2C) relationship. Similarly, Microsoft can provide Microsoft Office 365 to a government entity, leading to a business-to-government (B2G) relationship, or an educational institution, making it a business-to-education (B2Ed) relationship. The colloquial business relationship terminologies are not as relevant, but the awareness that different dynamics between the buyers and the sellers exist in such relationships.

Identifying the customer in these cases is crucial. Let us think of an individual purchasing a Microsoft Office 365 license from Microsoft and using it on her laptop. The individual is the buyer as well as the customer. She decided to use Microsoft Office 365 and bought it for herself. Of her free will, she uses Microsoft Office. In the case of an employee of Acme Corporation, our employee is using Microsoft Office. But she is not doing so of her free will. She needs to fulfill her employment objective. She is a **user** but not a customer in the true sense. Technically, a purchasing department may have paid for the software as a **buyer**. The IT department assesses the suitability of Microsoft Office and can be an **influencer**. In a small organization, the founder or CEO may have gotten MS Office as part of some new PC purchases. Since the CEO has affected the decision, we can consider her the customer. Yet, she may not sign the final sale contract with Microsoft; the purchasing or IT departments may have signed the purchase documents. We discussed this case in some detail to highlight that a customer is not necessarily the buyer, the user, or even a documented person on sales contracts. The customers are distributed entities. Their roles are spread across buyers, users, and influencers. Hence, in B2B sales, it is crucial to understand the business processes involved in a purchase decision.

We, as citizens, pay taxes to the government in exchange for various benefits such as roads, infrastructure, schools, and hospitals. Some may argue that we are customers of the government, but this is not entirely accurate. In a typical buyer-seller relationship, both parties engage based on free will and through a contractual agreement. We will discuss this aspect further in a later chapter. However, the relationship between the government and its citizens is not based on a contract; it is governed by the laws of the land. Citizens have specific rights and duties, as does the government. These rights and responsibilities are not transactional, unlike a buyer purchasing a product with a monetary consideration. Taxes paid to the government are not monetary considerations for the government services. A government has regal duties towards the citizens, for example, population census, governance, tax collection, and so on. Then, there are government services such as schools, hospitals, and so on. The services in the second category are industry-like, and a citizen is a customer in such cases. Why is this distinction important for a software product manager? As governments consume more digital services, we need to understand if the services are part of the regal duties of the government. For example, a tax collection portal will follow the IT Acts and Rules to the last tees and dots. However, the hospital management product for a government hospital can be more flexible. Even a commercial general-purpose hospital management product can be used in a government-run hospital.

A common indirect taxation was introduced in India in 2017 under the Goods and Services Tax (GST), a significant change for businesses, particularly Small and Medium Enterprises (SMEs). To help them file taxes, the government provided free software packages for accounting. Six[1] software vendors offer these packages to interested registered SMEs whose annual revenues do not exceed 15 million Indian Rupees. The government wanted the vendors to provide these services free for at least two years. However, the vendor and the beneficiary company can extend the contract based on a mutually agreed price and time. A customer and vendor relationship exists between the accounting package vendor and the beneficiary SME. However, is the government a vendor or a customer in this relationship? The government offered the **channel**, which the vendor exploited to reach a set of customers. Although the government expected the vendor to provide the service for two years for free, it is still beneficial for the vendor. The SME will start paying when they complete two years of enrollment or earn revenues exceeding 15 million INR in a year. Both conditions are not hard for the vendor to track. The lead is qualified. The SME needs to manage her accounts in some accounting package—an example of a promotion we discussed in the previous chapter.

All businesses in India need to file for compliance with applicable government laws. The businesses appoint auditors or compliance officers to file such compliance documents. These auditors are independent entities and are not employees of the businesses they audit. While filing the compliance documents, the company directors or managers sign the document using digital signatures. Only a handful of certifying authorities (CAs) approved by the government can issue digital certificates to an organization. These

---

[1] uBooks (Adaequare Info Pvt. Ltd.), Cygnet FACE (Cygnet Infotech Private Limited), FocusLyte (Focus Softnet Pvt Ltd), CaptainBiz (IRIS Business Services Limited), Saral Accounts (Relyon Softech Limited), Zoho Books (Zoho Corporation Private Limited)

CAs have their portals or websites through which they sell certificates to the business directors. The certificate issuance process is technically complex and is always issued by the CAs to the end user using an electronic device or USB token. No intermediary is allowed in the issuance process. With all these limitations, the CAs use the auditors as a channel to reach the directors of businesses. Purchasing certificates through auditor services is far cheaper than directly from the CA. We will discuss the pricing aspects and rationale in the next chapter. Why would a CA reach the businesses through the auditors and not directly to the businesses? In the last chapter, we discussed the role of place in marketing. Reaching out to a potential buyer when she is looking for something increases the possibility of a sale. For example, a company secretary (compliance officer) can register a new company for the directors of the company. It is the perfect place to issue digital certificates to business directors, as the registration of a company means filing additional compliance documents periodically, and the need for the digital certificates will be felt immediately. However, the certificates are issued directly from the CA to the business directors using an infrastructure provided by the CA. The compliance officers act as **resellers** and normally do not modify the software provided by the CA. However, the CA can make minor customizations for the compliance officers to enable them to highlight their brands.

Let us get back to SaaS-based software products. Amazon AWS, Microsoft Azure, and Google Cloud are the most used SaaS platforms. Independent Software Vendors (ISVs) would like their software to be used by customers of such platforms. All these platforms have created marketplaces through which the ISVs can deploy their solutions. The solutions are customized and aligned to the infrastructure of platform providers. One can think of this as developing for iOS or Android mobile devices. With closed ecosystems of **platforms**, they also act as channels to deliver products and process payments. In short, a product reaches its intended audience through buyers, users, influencers, channels, resellers, and so on. All of these can affect your product's effective buying process. As a product manager, you need an understanding of their influence on your product. Anyone who can influence the economic distribution of your product can be a customer, not directly, but this broadest definition helps product managers design the product better.

The Buying Process

A typical buyer with a **buying orientation** will focus on looking at all the possibilities of reducing the cost and try to choose a cost-effective solution. An influential buyer in an organization will have the final say in the buying process and gravitate to the product or solution available at the cheapest price. Buyer tools have been developed in the past few decades. These tools help in engaging and debating with other buyers in other organizations and developing consensus among buyers for consortium buying. They help establish common criteria across the vendors with requests for proposals (RFPs) or requests for quotes (RFQs). Maintaining vendor databases is also a feature of such tools. We will discuss pricing in a subsequent chapter. Our focus here is to understand the customer better, beyond discounts and prices. To a buyer with a buying orientation, the price is the most important factor. Such buyers would prefer standardized products across all the vendors. The vendors offering products at the least cost of ownership are preferred. Moreover, the buyers would depend on third-party tools, analyst reports, and so on, rather than investing in an internal evaluation team. To attract these customers, you offer the most competitive pricing, register with all significant product catalogs relevant to the industry, and make your solutions available on standard marketplaces such as Google Play Store, AWS/Azure Marketplaces, and so on. Moreover, you should participate in product comparison websites such as G2 Crowd, Gartner Peer Insights, and other industry-specific websites. If you are a well-known vendor in the market, most analysts will mention your products and solutions in their reports. You must engage and aid the evaluation process to avoid unnecessary biases against your solution.

There are buyers with a **procurement orientation**. In the traditional B2B markets, they were concerned with the supply chain alignment for streamlined delivery of products and solutions. While supply-chain alignment is not the most crucial aspect of the procurement process of software services, these buyers set up a procurement team of experts. The experts can be users, consulting analysts, procurement advisers, and so on. They analyze their requirements and propose a feature list needed for their applications. These kinds of buyers float RFPs specifically designed for their requirements. As a vendor, you would respond to the RFP questionnaire. If your product meets the expectations of the RFP, the bid is approved, and the sales activity proceeds. The composition of the procurement team puts the vendors in a tricky position. Software products are essentially complex. Software products are very different, even though they solve similar problems. So, comparing them with datasheets does not say much. The experts would raise objections through RFPs or create Proof-of-Concepts (PoC) scenarios. The vendor's sales or system engineering teams will implement the PoC and showcase it through demos. On a general notion of seeing is believing, such demos and PoCs establish confidence in the product. If the technology is complex and the procurement team does not understand it, demos and PoCs establish confidence. Sales Ready Products (SRP)[2] is a process model for decreasing sales timelines. A Minimal Viable Product (MVP), just enough product features to meet a customer's needs, is something we will discuss in the context of the **Agile Process** in the later chapter of the book. While experts and senior management are interested in demos and PoCs, a user would prefer a trial software and would like to explore the product herself. They appreciate the software installed and configured for a reasonable number of use cases.

Lastly, there are buyers with **Supply Management** Orientation. They establish strategic partnerships with vendors and use the vendor's expertise to address the end-user needs. With the advent of AI, many classic traditional businesses have started their

---

[2] https://www.sequoiacap.com/article/the-templeton-compression/ accessed 18th Feb 2025

digital journey. For example, a bank would like to complete a Know Your Customer (KYC) activity using a user's biometry. While banks know financial management and operations, they are relatively novices in face recognition, biometric scanning, and authentication. They depend on a third-party Identity and Verification (IDV) partner to provide such capabilities. These IDVs address the needs of varied industries, including the financial domains. Even in the domain, banks will have custom workflows that vary from bank to bank. The banks employing an IDV can express their requirements. The IDV can propose integration solutions based on their experiences with other customers from the financial or any other domains. The bank and the IDV can learn from each other and make their solution robust. The supply management orientation of a buyer develops an inherent trust with the vendor. A trust that enables them to discuss their future business needs with their vendors. While we applied the buyer orientation to the software industry, a detailed analysis can be found in the book Business Marketing Management[3].

Role of Software Product Management

Software products are inherently complex. No two software are the same, even if they solve similar problems for the customer. So, one cannot apply a commodity mindset to software purchases. A buying orientation does not work effectively. Here are some of the reasons for the complexities:

- **Workflows:** Every software product has certain assumptions of the environment. When such assumptions are standard through business practices or regulations, the software tools will adhere to those. However, in cases where such assumptions are non-standard, there are variations. Let us think of an accounting package. Since there is a practice of using the double book-entry system for accounting packages, most software on accounting will adhere to it. The laws of accounting and taxation will direct them to use similar ledgers. However, approval workflows, vendor management, or inventory management can be the prerogative of every vendor.

- **Operative Environment:** Every software product is designed to work in a specific environment. In pure SaaS-based software, the environment dependencies do not affect the end users. When we use an ERP package from the cloud, it does not matter if the package is available from a Linux or Windows Server. What if the web pages are incompatible with the Microsoft Edge browser or Apple Mac OS Safari browsers? In such conditions, product managers resort to statistics. We developed the applications for the most used end-user devices. Thus, Google Chrome is the browser of choice. What if an important customer has standardized on using Microsoft tools and Microsoft Edge as the browser on the employee desktops?

---

[3] James C. Anderson, D.V.R. Seshadri, James A. Narus, and Das Narayandas, Chapter-3, Business Market Management (B2B): Understanding, Creating, and Delivering Value, 3/e

- **User Sophistication:** Users vary in the level of sophistication. Accounting software meant for professional chartered accountants requires a different level of detail from a wallet application among friends sharing day-to-day expenses. Let us think of an IT Service Management application. An employee reporting a laptop issue would like a simple form and description of the problem. An IT staff addressing the issue would like to know the employee's department, if the department has the budget, if the laptop is within warranty, and most importantly, which IT staff should be working on the issue, and so on. Can the same software have different user-centric views? We will discuss this further in the chapter on User Experience.

- **Delivery Channels:** Most startups deliver minimal features to the initial customers, addressing their immediate needs. They engage with other potential customers and realize the missing features. However, the customer support requirements have not been enhanced. The CXOs were attending to the requests of initial customers. As soon as a customer reports issues, the vendor adds them. Every new customer looks like a project for the whole organization. The product's configuration or customization needs are significantly higher for customers to handle themselves. Suppose such a vendor has decided to release their product on the AWS marketplace. The expectations change overnight. The customers on the AWS channel would prefer a base pre-configured system with minimal need to contact any professional service or support. For the small organization in the current state, it is a significant change.

When we say understanding the domain, we expect the product manager to know these aspects of the product and the market. Understanding the market means understanding the customer. How do you relate to a customer in the first place? Interestingly, it is far easier to interact with the buyers when they are in supply management orientation. They have organized experts to engage with vendors, ready to discuss their strategy and plans. They expect the vendor to engage with them regularly. These customer sets are the best for the product managers to engage with. They use the product most effectively and provide the necessary insights into the vertical integrations in the industry. They allocate vendor management experts who would engage with the vendor to verify their use cases. They are the ideal customers for early access programs, perfect beta testers, and references for subsequent sales initiatives. You do not get many of these customers, unfortunately. A product manager should spot such customers and interact with them regularly. Unfortunately, most buyers fall into the buying or procurement orientation. When pricing becomes the most significant criterion for sale, it gets to deep discounting. We will look at these aspects in the chapter on pricing. However, there are external websites, industry advisors, and experts buyers trust. Product managers may engage in analyst relationships. They would need to participate in third-party evaluations of the products vis-à-vis competition. Product managers present their solutions and vision to analysts and explain how they have solved various industry-specific issues. The company must engage in industry forums and professional networking sites for potential customers. These advertising and PR activities ensure there is enough visibility of the product in the market. While some organizations induct marketing teams to address these needs, the product-related content requires the attention of the product managers for accuracy.

Buyer to Customer

We saw from the transaction mindset of a buyer in the buying orientation to the consultative mindset of a supply management orientation. It is natural to ask if we could change a customer's buying orientation from buying to supply management. The customer orientation develops over several years of engagement in the process; one vendor cannot change an organization's orientation. Even organizations with a consultative mindset cannot engage with all the vendors at similar levels. The customer's involvement with every purchase is not the same. Let us think of a laptop purchase for the employees and operating systems for the desktop. Laptop purchases will involve much more than operating systems. There are more brands; they have several distributors. There is only one operating system for office desktops—Microsoft Windows. Apple Mac OS X ships with the hardware. So, you have fewer options to choose from. Price also plays a significant role in deciding the level of involvement. The same organization investing in Enterprise Resource Planning (ERP) will take several months of evaluation involving every department. Here are some of the aspects product managers should know about their customers:

- **Purchase Involvement:** An organization would like to reduce search costs and minimize purchase frequency for products that need high involvement. Moreover, they would like to coordinate with the vendor to ensure future versions of the products are addressing their needs.

- **Strategic Alignment:** A product strategically aligned to an organization's business will get the focus. The organization will consider such vendors critical to their success and ensure their delivery schedules and timelines are aligned effectively. In these cases, the customer would get involved in early access programs, beta testing, and so on, to cut down integration efforts. With such customers, product managers should highlight their vision to ensure mutual synergy. More importantly, some of these customers can be potential targets for vertical integration.

- **Value Perception:** A customer who sees value in the vendor and her products will maintain the relationship. The perceived value of a customer is beyond just the total cost of ownership of products they purchased. An organization with a strong focus on corporate branding will consider the vendor maintaining their website of high value. An e-commerce site that attracts customers to its portal will value a lot on the landing page of its website.

A buyer-to-customer transition indicates how much we understand the customer's internal systems and processes. How can we align our product to the customer's needs for strategic synergy? The vendor organization should connect to all levels of the customer organization and maintain two-way communication. Sales should be in touch with the buyers and keep track of the changes in the organization. The support teams should engage with the users and address their needs. They should spot new use cases the user is anticipating and provide feedback to product management for enhancement or suggest potential cross-selling opportunities. In an IT service management product, the support person realizes the IT admin of the customer encounters a repeating task. However, the customer has not licensed the automation module. Here, the support executive can highlight the importance of such a component and impress upon the IT admin to ask the management to license that component. The IT admin, an influencer, can engage with the management and impress upon them. Customer support is considered an overhead. Organizations try to minimize such expenses. With Tier-1 and Tier-2 support handled by chatbots, human engagement is getting minimized. However, customer support is a great place to discover and understand the customer needs.

When a customer purchases a product off the shelf, she will not tell where and how she will use it. As product managers, we optimize products to the needs of the customers in our knowledge. What if the customer finds a different use altogether? In India, this concept is called jugaad. Here are a few examples: using a kitchen knife as a screwdriver, a mobile phone as a timekeeper or the backlight as a torchlight, and a washing machine to churn yogurt for large-scale lassi production for the public. Some of these have seen new products, such as the Swiss army knife. Before smartphones became popular, Nokia launched the Nokia 1100[4] model that had a torchlight in the phone. It was an innovative product, considering developing countries had regular power failures. When smartphones became handy, the flash used for the camera was repurposed to work as a torchlight. Portable cameras with flashlights have been there for much longer than mobile phones. Why were they not repurposed to work as torchlights? Unlike the mobile phone, the camera was not always available to the user. Today, the mobile phone has replaced the consumer-grade digital camera and the torchlight. Both these use cases are due to companies observing gadget buyers and studying the usage pattern carefully.

Let us work on an example of a company trying to run a certifying authority business in a country like India. Here are some things we know about the certificates:

1. Certificates are a secure way to authenticate a user.

---

[4] Nokia 1100 was the most popular mobile phone as well. **https://web.archive.org/web/20120924175238/http://conversations.nokia.com/2011/02/15/7-nokia-world-records-that-will-blow-your-mind/** accessed 13th August 2024

2. The government of India has passed laws[5] that make signing by digital certificates equivalent to signing with ink, but only when the CA is approved by the government.

3. These changes in law can make many paper-based processes electronic.

4. The Ministry of Corporate Affairs (MCA)[6], which manages the companies in India, mandates all submissions to be electronic only.

5. Taxation for corporates in India is mandated to be carried out by digital signatures only.

As a product manager of the CA business, we must design our products for the right market. If we look at the aforementioned first statement, we will establish a technically sound platform for verifying a user and issuing certificates for him. We will go from business to business, convincing them how a certificate is a secured authentication process. However, no regulations or legal requirements exist for such companies to buy our product. Now, we look at the second and third events from the market—these open new avenues for us to convince businesses. We can convince organizations to buy certificates from us, as they will help them submit electronic tender responses instead of physical documents. However, with user authentication, they needed certificates for all the employees. E-tenders are to be submitted by only a handful of corporate employees. The event four makes it mandatory. All corporates now need digital signatures. Documents can be submitted to MCA only after an auditor's approval. As much as electronic signing is critical for MCA submission by the corporation, an auditor must approve the document again with a digital certificate. Hence, auditors are the best channel partners to sell digital certificates. However, they are not technically savvy. So, all the software and technology needed for them to promote the certificate selling must be supplied by the CA. An overall review of the certificate issuance and review process added newer software for the end users and channels and introduced new compliance needs for the CA. Moreover, the CA can provide digital signing workflows for documents. Expanding the horizon from a simple end-user certificate buying workflow to a corporation meeting its compliance or legal needs added more business avenues for a CA. The government's approval of electronic workflows has made the remote Know Your Customer (e-KYC) and its associated Identity Verification (IDV) market a reality.

Mutually Beneficial Relationship

Issuing and using digital signatures is technically complex for directors and business managers of a company, although they are the users and beneficiaries. Audit intermediaries such as Chartered Accountants, Company Secretaries, and so on

---

[5] Chapter VI, Information Technology Act, 2000, Union of India

[6] **https://www.mca.gov.in/MinistryV2/digitalsignaturecertificate.html**

support all government-related filings. For a CA business, focusing on this community is good enough to target the mandatory certificate-related legal business. The CAs provide discounted prices for certificates purchased from audit intermediaries. They provide the necessary software and training to the audit intermediaries. The example we chose is complex, but it shows a case where the customer who pays for the service does not connect with the vendor, but the vendor and channel relationship is strong. Can you think of another example? Where you, a software product vendor, keep the interests of end customers, channel partners, or distributors in mind.

A few companies have created mindshare in consumer and enterprise businesses with the same sets of products, for example, Adobe, Apple, Google, and Microsoft. It is easier for a company to engage with a few hundred large organizations, showcase the product or solution, and sell the products. Once you have an entry point, you expand more and more adjacent use cases for the same businesses and increase your revenues. Google started the enterprise business as a follow-up from the consumer business. Gmail was a popular free consumer email with better search features than other free emails. It provided better storage. Google wanted the consumer to look at Gmail for their small office and home office (SOHO) purposes. Start small with a few accounts and add more employee accounts as you grow kind of models. Today, Zoho[7] uses the same strategy to attract SOHO users to its platforms. Microsoft used its enterprise success to sell into the consumer domain with personal and family editions of its office products. Now, you can use the same office experience as home users. Apple stated that you can use the same privacy and security on your iPhone for your office emails and other communications. There is an inherent perception of the brands by the users at the workplace or home, and the same trust is projected across. It is a powerful way to build relationships with your customers.

These are all massive brands. How do you reach your customers and tell them about your brand? Most of these companies run worldwide events and try to deliver their vision regularly. Today, social networking and videos can reach each customer. Customer data collection and profiling can provide targeted messaging about your products, including personalized videos with generative AI[8]. While corporate-to-end-user communication has been established, there is a need to receive feedback promptly. There has to be a two-way communication. The larger organizations engage support forums, chatbots, and social networking listeners to collect feedback and aggregate and record it for analysis. Sometimes, direct human interaction is needed as well. They would sponsor individuals or small business users to reach the user conferences on discounted tickets. It helps the product teams to interact with individuals and gather feedback. Even the channel partner and distributor networks are sources for collecting

---

[7] Zoho – Cloud Software Solutions for Businesses, **https://www.zoho.com**, accessed on 13th August 2024.

[8] Collins Ayuya, How Generative AI Personalization Transforms Marketing, June 3, 2024, eWeek, **https://www.eweek.com/artificial-intelligence/generative-ai-personalization/** accessed 13th August 2024.

data from the ground levels. Product demand is an indicator of the consumer adoption of a product in the B2C markets.

Sometimes, it takes more than one company to generate consumer interest. Let us talk about consumer email services. One of the earliest email services was Hotmail. Microsoft acquired the company and later rebranded it as Outlook.com. Yahoo launched Yahoo Mail. When Google launched Gmail, consumers were aware of free email services. The extra storage space Google offered made the transition to Gmail rather quickly. While Hotmail and Yahoo Mail familiarized emails among internet consumers, Google reaped the benefits with Gmail. Platform vendors, such as Google and Microsoft, are creating ecosystem enablers rather than directly providing consumer solutions. Let us talk about passwordless authentication. With the web becoming ubiquitous, it is cumbersome for users to remember the passwords for every site. Microsoft dominates the desktop client market, and Google the mobile and browser markets. Both companies decided to introduce hardware-based and biometric authentication schemes for the users. You can authenticate to a website by validating your fingerprint on a mobile phone or special-purpose hardware. This technology is called Passkey. Google and Microsoft pushed several standards over a decade called FIDO and implemented the WebAuthn[9] standards in their browsers. Hardware vendors such as Yubico[10] and mobile platforms such as Android and Apple iPhone integrated these authentication standards. If Microsoft and Google had not made an authentication platform and had decided to sell the authentication hardware themselves, the users would not have had confidence in the technologies. The ecosystem led hardware vendors such as Yubico to develop the hardware tokens. Google enables passkey authentication on its websites. However, it does not provide the hardware authenticators and leaves that space for other players such as Yubico. The same applies to Artificial Intelligence and Machine Learning technologies. The big tech firms are releasing research reports in regular publications so that technologies are reviewed, adapted, and enhanced by communities. These create confidence in the platforms such firms are offering. An open ecosystem platform for many software vendors can sometimes make the industry grow through a network effect of many vendors joining the bandwagon.

How are consumers reciprocating to such brands and platforms? Consumers respond by adopting, evangelizing, or merely reporting on the technology. The technologies or companies we state in this book are reports about them and tell an audience educational story without any direct commercial gains for the author from the vendors. Some consumers vouch for specific brands and technologies; they promote them in various forums, creating value for the vendors. Thus, mutual trust develops among the consumers and the brands. User advocacy is considered genuine in the communities and creates better responses than advertisements or other forms of

---

[9] An authentication standard developed by the World Wide Web Consortium (W3C)
[10] Yubico is just one of the many vendors offering FIDO-enabled hardware under the brand: YubiKey **https://www.yubico.com/products/yubikey-5-overview/** accessed 13th August 2024

promotions. Unlike the B2C market, in the B2B market, trust establishment is far more direct.

For ease of explanation, we will choose direct sales scenarios. A sales leader approaches a senior member of an organization, a typical CXO of a specific department of interest. If you sell a product related to Information Technology or IT security, you would approach the Chief Information Officer (CIO); for HR products, you would approach the Chief Human Resources Officer (CHRO), and so on. A vendor may hire a domain-centric senior sales executive, for he is well-connected in that market. Some companies sell updated directories of CXOs and all their reporting hierarchy for the marketing teams to enable the sales organization. In a large organization, a CRM or ERP system takes several years for deployment and employee adoption. Choosing the right tools is a Damocles sword hanging on every CXO. The impact is organization-wide. An improper implementation can lead to a fallout in the careers of the CXOs. CXOs prefer a conservative position, epitomized in statements such as Nobody Gets Fired For Buying IBM[11]. At the peak of the career, a wrong decision can lead to eventual downfall. While interpersonal trust can open the gate, there is very little you as a vendor can achieve in product sales. The CXO sets up an evaluation committee or a buyer forum consisting of users, information architects, purchase executives, and so on. These influencers have a say in the final sales of the product. The sales leader per se cannot connect to these people. The users and analysts are closest to the product workflows. They would look at the Proof-of-Concept (PoC) and comment on how their existing workflow addresses the scenario—a competitive input. Information architects can review the product architecture and security limitations. Purchase executives will question the pricing rationale and comment on discounted prices from other vendors. The fact that the customer is discussing means the alternatives are not ideal for them. Every choice is a bargain—there is no perfect product or solution. Marketers and product managers can review these inputs and ensure the customer's viewpoints are resolved in the selling process by improving upon the pitch deck, documentation, brochures, and other marketing collaterals or product features. There is a consistent demo script for the audience to present the demo scenarios. All the objections raised must be addressed. A good win-loss report should address all these finer points. However, in reality, they are less than perfect.

In most product organizations, sales teams try to engage the product manager in the early sales process for large customer accounts. Senior management staff in a revenue growth phase of the product think this is a customer-focused approach. A product manager in this role is an extension of the sales team. He is trying to pursue the customer or claiming that their product is the right choice, rather than selling the solution the customer needs. The product manager is also a seller in the customer's mind. In the SaaS world, selling is a continuous process. You will reach the customer every year or

---

[11] Duena Blomstrom - "Nobody Gets Fired For Buying IBM". But They Should., Forbes, 30 November 2018, **https://www.forbes.com/sites/duenablomstrom1/2018/11/30/nobody-gets-fired-for-buying-ibm-but-they-should/** accessed 15th August 2024

even every month sometimes, depending on the license model. The customer needs a trustworthy partner to discuss her issues. Some organizations identified this need and introduced the concept of a client or a customer success manager. A client manager is technically a support executive tied to specific named customer accounts. Anytime the customer needs something related to product support, new use cases to discuss, a negotiation on purchase, and so on, they reach out to the client manager. The client manager would work through the vendor organization hierarchies to provide the client with what they need. When the customer needs it, a client manager will invite the product manager to the customer site or call for a discussion on the product. Sometimes, the product managers involve such customers directly for discussion on a feature they are introducing or a beta testing of the product, and so on. These kinds of associations with the customers are product-centric, and the association is of trust in knowledge. We want product managers to engage with these kinds of relationships. Will your customer ask you for your insights in the domain but not connected to your product? These discussions lead to the development of new features in the product that the customer already needs. You have a market without the need for explicit selling.

Establishing Value for the Customer

Why does someone need a racetrack-ready sports car on the road? With an 800-HP engine[12], the Ford Mustang GTD will be the ultimate Mustang that will make Porsche, Mercedes, and Aston Martin sweat[13]. The Mustang has been the ultimate American muscle car for six decades. Every generation of the Mustang is a cut above the previous and has its die-hard followers. Buying pricey cars is generally considered a bad investment by most financially sound minds[14]. Yet, cars do sell. People often buy beyond their means, and brands stay for several decades. Brands such as FCUK or WROGN would never gain a market share had they not appealed to an audience that represents defiance of social norms, the younger generations. A customer pays the price as a consideration for the value she gets. Some of the B2C purchases are neither economical nor rational. Behavioral psychology plays a significant role in many of such decisions. We will keep that from our discussions and focus on the value that economics can ascertain.

Business purchases roughly fall into such categories. There are occasional decisions such as spending at corporate and marketing events, yet most purchase decisions for

---

[12] A typical F1 car has an overall 1000-HP engine.
[13] Making Mustang® History, Ford Motor Company - YouTube Channel, **https://www.youtube.com/watch?v=fMGhaAfCnIY** accessed 15th August 2024
[14] Warren Buffett Shares 12 Things You Are Wasting Money On, Here's All You Need To Know, India Times, Vanya Gautam, 18th September 2023, **https://www.indiatimes.com/worth/news/all-you-need-to-know-12-things-people-waste-money-on-615332.html** accessed 15th August 2024.

business consumption go through some stringent economic justifications. Here are some reasons for the business decisions being rational:

- A relatively large number of people are involved in the decision-making.
- The decision-makers are not necessarily the direct users or shareholders of the business.
- There is no disposable income in business. Any savings is a direct profit to the stakeholder in the business.
- The businesses are under financial audits for their spending.

B2B marketers consider these aspects meticulously and are often obsessed with value for the customer. The product manager must understand customer value. The customer value is tied to the customer's internal process metrics and industry structures; thus, the product manager focuses on the customer's business. Let us talk about the banks and their need for IT security. Per government regulations, banks should diligently protect the customer's private data. All the banks are bound to comply with these norms. Their IT management would analyze and find several systems where customer data is stored. If such systems increase and have significant exposure possibility to an external hacker, their loss of revenue due to a data breach may increase. Suppose they estimate the revenue loss from such a data breach to about 100 million USD for the ten systems they have. A bank would manage the risk by buying the insurance policy from an IT cybersecurity insurance provider for a million USD, roughly one percent of the revenue loss due to the data breach. A vendor of an e-KYC solution proposes the following:

- The customer data shall be localized with the eKYC platform in the private cloud.
- The other systems can access the customer information on a need-to-know basis. They will not cache this information.
- The e-KYC platform shall encrypt all the customer's data at all times—in rest or motion.

The overall exposure surface of the data was reduced. The bank still needs protection for the e-KYC system but just one system instead of ten earlier. The overall exposure possibility is reduced to 10 million USD. They can manage the risk with insurance of 100,000 USD. There is a direct value add for the customer of 900,000 USD. The challenge in all this lies in how far you understand the customer's organization and their customer workflows. Many organizations engage with their customers to evaluate real gains from deploying their solutions. When evaluated meticulously, they can act as reference material to discuss. Some larger organizations review their best practices in operations and bring up new products around those. Google BeyondCorp is one such case in point. Google published the idea[15] of BeyondCorp as a potential IT infrastructure protection in distributed office environments. Later, the company launched it as a formal product[16]. An internal process that turned in a Zero Trust Enterprise Security product to an external audience. Since it was a transition from an internal process to a product, Google knew the nuances of the workflows. While products are for many customers for scalability, it helps to develop them as a service offered to a few key early adopters to understand the domain and use cases. Secondly, such early adopters can become early investors in the product. Better understanding can improve the value for the customer.

We used some examples from regulations-driven industries to showcase value. They are simple to explain the customer value, so we used them in the examples. As one e-KYC provider, you could reduce the private data exposure area, hence the insurance premium, and add value to the customer. Any other e-KYC provider can tell the same story. For the regulation-driven customer, the provider at the cheapest price wins. Let us relook at the Certificate Authority (CA) and business users market. The user does not interact with the CA, only pays for the charges, and does so only to overcome a government regulation. The audit intermediary is not the most technically savvy person to understand the effect of a certificate product. She is interested in a discounted price from the CA. In such cases, large organizations introduce the brand to differentiate themselves. A technical product that is difficult to explain is a good candidate to partner with a known brand for better visibility. Commercial fonts are a good example. For the end-users, they are sold either through operating systems or with editing applications. However, professional publishers buy them from the font vendors.

Negotiation

The Spanish word for business is Negocio. Every business involves a give-and-take relationship that needs some form of negotiation. Most discussions end in some form of positional bargain. Here are some of the approaches organizations take with customers:

- The customer is the King; as long as we have committed, we deliver it somehow.
- Customers are not aware of what they need. They do not understand the value associated with the product.

The believers of the first aspect will never say no to a customer. Moreover, saying no becomes exceedingly difficult in societies with high power distance. The problem is you never understand what the customer needs and depend on proxies to ascertain

---

[15] Rory Ward, Betsy Beyer; BeyondCorp: A New Approach to Enterprise Security ;login:, Vol. 39, No. 6(2014), pp. 6-11, **https://research.google/pubs/beyondcorp-a-new-approach-to-enterprise-security/** accessed 15th August 2024.
[16] BeyondCorp, **https://cloud.google.com/beyondcorp** accessed 15th August 2024.

the requirement. With complex requirements as IT products lead, you end up over-committing for a paltry sum and eventually do not deliver as there is no business viability. The second category never listens to the customer. The vendor has developed a product strategy and vision and got the relevant funding; now they are building the product. They want to focus on what they are doing or only focus on the market they have traditionally sold into. Both of these are hard positions to take. Somewhere the minds must meet for the customers and the business or the product managers to be successful.

Requirement elicitation is a well-understood science. Yet, as soon as the problem is stated, we jump into finding solutions to the problem. Let us understand it through a parable. A long auto-tunnel has a signboard—please turn on your lights. In broad daylight, people enter the tunnel and forget to switch off the lights as they exit. The light remains switched on when they reach their destination. It drains their batteries eventually in a few hours of leaving lights on in the daylight. As soon as the problem is known, people suggest solutions that should be at the end of the tunnel. Most of them ask the drivers to switch off the lights. What if it is dark outside? Asking the driver, Are Your Lights On?[17] at the end of the tunnel is good enough for the driver to take the right action. In some sense, the product management requirement elicitation falls into the same category. Most customers may present their requirements as solutions—I need these UI elements that can trigger a push notification on my phone. People with a "*Customer is the King*" mindset may follow up with an argument: What is the issue in providing the customer with what they need? To a product manager, the challenge is finding out what other customers would feel about such a feature. When you get to the root cause of the customer request, you realize the same problem exists for other users as well. When you have problem-based requirements elicitations, it becomes easier to negotiate on the customer's needs.

We improve our listening skills by separating the problem from the solution. Product managers are in a precarious position in negotiation situations. They are defending someone who is not there to support them. When a customer requirement has genuine technical limitations, the PM starts defending the engineers on the project in front of the customer. Engineering does not agree with the workflow stated by the customer. The customer has to be defended by the PM in front of engineering. The sales team is asking for a discount for the customer so that they can win the deal. PM is justifying why the customer should be paying the price quoted. When you fight a battle as an advocate, you justify your position on the principles of the game. The grounds of the negotiation strengthen as you have visibility right through. Positional bargaining begins when each party does not try to understand the other party's viewpoint. Every negotiation situation is due to information asymmetry. As a PM, it is crucial to understand the other party's viewpoint.

---

[17] Donald C. Gause and Gerald M. Weinberg, Are Your Lights On? 1990, Dorset House Pub.

We look at the pricing negotiation for the e-KYC vendor. The customer is getting a straight profit of 900,000 USD on insurance premiums. Technically, vendor A can ask for the whole amount as a cost of ownership for the e-KYC solution or can provide a discount of 50% and agree to a price of 450,000 USD per year. The customer will commit as the Best Alternative to the Negotiated Agreement (BATNA)[18] is an additional 900,000 USD of insurance premiums. Vendor B, who has better knowledge of A's bid from past experiences, bids at 300,000 USD per year. The customer gets a better alternative, and the BATNA drops to 300,000 USD. A can no longer win unless she drops the price further. When closed envelope bids are invited from vendors, the buyers are essentially looking to arrive at a BATNA quickly. A vendor can break out of the price bargain by introducing a compelling value differentiator that the competition cannot offer within the same price range, yet is crucial for the customer. You know it only when you have understood the customer's value metrics. Feature-to-feature comparisons do not give good mileage in negotiations unless backed by a strong ground for negotiation.

Conclusion

We have buyers, users, influencers, channels, and so on, all contributing to the customer. The effective execution must cater to all the constituents of the customer organization. Focusing on only one constituent can make value gaps for others. Moreover, there is a need and interest to negotiate for better value realization from both sides. There is a need to be conscious of the complete user journeys across various functions of the customer organization. While we focused on an aggregated view of the customer, we cannot ignore the buyer by not giving her a rational pricing basis. That will be the subject matter of our next chapter.

---

[18] BATNA and other principles of negotiations have been extensively discussed in the seminal book, Getting to Yes by Roger Fisher and William Ury, 1981.

Questions

1. Analyze your product and identify the customers for your product.

2. Present your product's vision to your customer. Is the customer aligned with the vision? What are some of the suggestions they are looking for in the product?

3. For your product, write a value proposition statement. Discuss it with the customer. Will the value proposition change for each customer?

4. Spend a day in the customer environment to identify and understand how the customer uses the product. Update your product with additional features expected from the customer.

5. Create a checklist that helps you map out key stakeholders (buyers, users, influencers, channels, and so on) and outline negotiation strategies for each. How will following this checklist improve your product's value delivery and customer relationships?

CHAPTER 5
Pricing

Introduction

Product management is not solely about building the right product; ensuring market acceptance is equally crucial. Market acceptance is often demonstrated when customers are willing to purchase the product at the desired price. How does the seller know the price in the first place–a dilemma that keeps a product manager occupied in every sales deal? We will look at what a business knows about the buyer to be able to price their products. As much as the process of product development drives the price of a product, the eventual application of the product also determines the price. We will discuss some of the methods used to price a product. It will help the readers to understand the rationale of pricing decisions taken in their organizations and modify them if some of these ideas resonate with their needs. Moreover, we will discuss how an organization can price products based on a customer's value perception and engage with them to price the product right for the market.

Structure

In this chapter, we will cover the following topics:

- Principles of Pricing
- Value-Based Pricing
- From Commodity to Differentiated Offer
- Pricing Schemes
- Legal Implications of Pricing

Principles of Pricing

We cannot discuss pricing without focusing on the economic theories behind it. When we deal with economics, there are some inherent assumptions.

- We deal with commodities. They are alike and do not depend on who is buying or selling. This is not quite true for software products as there is never a perfect match between two software products.

Pricing

- Buyers and sellers have limited resources.
- They are rational people who would transact purely on their gains in the current transactions.
- There is no hysteresis in the transactions. Only the current price determines the fate of the sales.

While we enumerate some, there is more one can add to the list[1] here. In *Figure 2.1*, we have discussed the demand and supply concept from economics. However, we assumed demand and supply curves exist in the market. How do we arrive at a demand-supply curve in the first place? It is difficult to find the price and quantity relationship between the buyer and seller independently. Since the buyer and seller are interacting and bidding, we can arrive at a price. A place where you see this happening is the stock market. The buyers and sellers keep bidding for stocks. They specify their intended buying and selling prices; the sales happen based on the bid price.

Orders	Buy Quantity	Buy Price	Sell Quantity	Sell Price	Fulfilled	Pending	Transactions Quantity	Transactions Price
1	150	11.00				Order 1 (150)		
2			100	10.00	Order 2	Order 1 (50)	100	10.00
3			50	12.00		Order 1 (50) Order 3 (50)		
4	100	12.00			Order 3	Order 1 (50) Order 4 (50)	50	12.00
5			200	11.50	Order 4	Order 1 (50) Order 5 (150)	50	11.50
							VWAP	10.88
							Average Price	11.17

Table 5.1: A sample bidding system

In a hypothetical stock bidding system, we have five orders placed by buyers and sellers. Let us evaluate how the system records the transactions.

- As the market opens, a buyer has placed Order 1, and a seller has subsequently put in her sell Order 2. They are not aware of each other's price. Order 1 is fulfilled partly at ₹10.00 for only 100 nos.
- Next, another seller places Order 3 at ₹12.00. Order 3 cannot fulfill Order 1.
- When Order 4 is placed, Order 3 is fulfilled. Order 4 is pending.
- Looking at it, a seller will try to place an Order 5. He would also like to entice the Order 1 buyer to update his bid by giving a mid-way price option of ₹11.50.

---

[1] Thanos Skouras, George J. Avlonitis and Kostis A. Indounas, Economics and marketing on pricing: how and why do they differ? Journal of Product and Brand Management, Volume 14, Number 6, 2005, pp.362-374

- Three transactions could materialize from the five orders placed. The average price of the transactions is ₹11.17. The volume-weighted average price (VWAP) is ₹10.88.

A typical auction system may consider these as the market price. Interestingly, not a single transaction happened at the market price. Some auction systems use the term last transaction price (LTP) to highlight the price of the last executed transaction. While auction-based pricing is common in commodities such as stocks and agricultural communities, is it a viable purchase model even for software licenses?

The RFP and RFQ-based systems are essentially reverse auction systems. The buyer solicits the price for her requirements, and the sellers offer their price to comply with the requirements placed. However, this is not practical for all purchases. Let us consider housing. Houses get bought and sold only sparingly. A person may purchase or sell one or two in a lifetime. People customize houses to their needs. Finding one in a locality that is almost identical to another will be hard. Yet, there is an average housing price. Then, there are builders. They sell several houses of similar kinds to various customers. While there are customizations, one can get a close estimate for houses of similar types. An analyst from a market research company reaches these builders and collects data about dwellings sold. Since housing choices can depend on people's income, they focus only on the mid-income group for two-bedroom houses. The prices where we recorded the transactions are points on the demand curve.

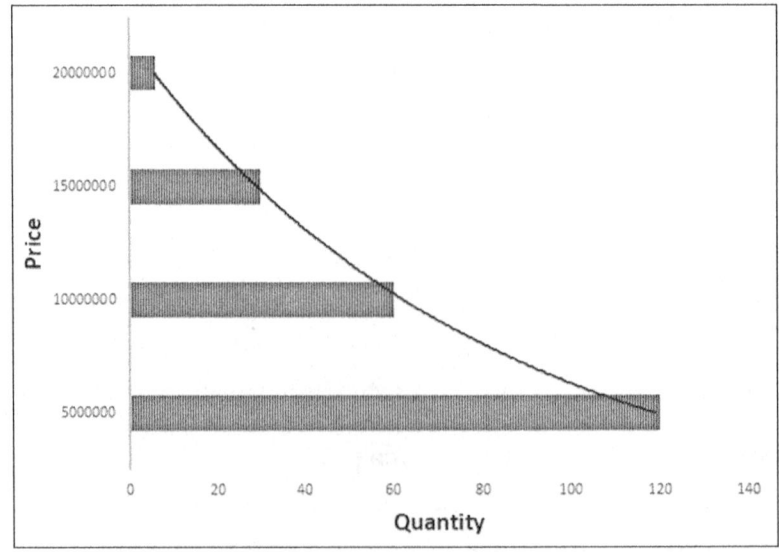

Figure 5.1: *A sample demand curve*

When you take the histogram[2] of the prices and plot the price on the Y-axis and the quantity on the X-axis, you will see a plot as shown in *Figure 5.1*. However, these kinds

---

[2] In a histogram, the quantity is shown in the Y-axis. **https://www.techtarget.com/searchsoftwarequality/definition/histogram** accessed 25th August 2024.

of statistical estimates of the demand curves have their limitations. A sale of a house can take several months of negotiation. In a volatile market, housing pricing can vary significantly. If the sales materialize in a long time, you will have inaccuracies due to price variations. Similarly, if you consider a small-time duration, you may not get a statistically significant population size to estimate the histogram. Since housing prices are regional, the prices collected must be in a geographic region with a minimum price variation. The methodology approached sellers for data collection. These sellers are only dealing with new houses. It did not take the impact of the resale market and how the older properties are priced. Builders give discounts on early bookings. Properties of a similar nature may be priced differently based on when they were booked. In the preceding example, we used a market survey with the suppliers to estimate a demand curve. All survey-based experiments need a controlled environment and have a few assumptions. Can a survey be conducted on buyers directly? Most e-commerce companies can do these experiments very easily. The seller can discount a category of products over a reasonable period and study the buying patterns. Those patterns can translate into a demand curve. However, the demand curves are only based on their customers and cannot be attributed to the complete market for the product with all buyers and sellers. The Indian government mandates retail products to provide a Maximum Retail Price (MRP). The sellers can sell their goods at a price lower than MRP.

One can argue that a product's price is due to its features. There exists a part worth for each of these features in isolation. Can those be estimated somehow? For example, a car model has four possible colors—red, blue, black, and white. We survey and find if customers will pay additional for these colors. We introduce a new front grill and want to see customer response and the possibility of its drawing additional revenues. Let us assume we have three such features in a product. Each feature can have four possible variations. If we could find the prices of each combination, we would reach the price of the isolated features. Our example has 4 × 4 × 4 = 64 combinations. Since each combination must be tested in the market for its price with surveys, it can be daunting. Techniques such as **conjoint analysis**[3] can reduce the combination requirement to 4 + 4 + 4 = 12. With smaller retail products with limited feature states, the part worth can be estimated. Extending this to software products for complex, business-centric applications can be difficult. Microsoft Windows can have **4400+** configurations[4] on a group policy. Creating surveys for customer feedback on such large configurations is impractical. Business users may be using a small subset of features of a product. A few people can provide meaningful input, as no individual understands all the features.

---

[3] Tim Stobierski, What Is Conjoint Analysis & How Can You Use It? Harvard Business School Online (2020) **https://online.hbs.edu/blog/post/what-is-conjoint-analysis** accessed on 24th August 2024.

[4] Group Policy Settings Reference Spreadsheet for Windows 10 2022 Update (22H2) **https://www.microsoft.com/en-us/download/details.aspx?id=104678** accessed 21st August 2024.

Metering and Licensing

Before we discuss licensing, let us understand how we interact with software systems. End-users use software directly, or their usage information is available with the system, and an analyst or agent extracts that information for further processing or action. For example, in the case of a health application, the patient information (end-user) is used by a doctor (agent) for treatment. The user or agent will interact with the system using an end-computing device. The device can be a web browser, a mobile or desktop app, or an Internet of Things (IoT) device mounted on her vehicle. The information can be processed in the end-computing device as edge computing or passed on to a server. The server can be in an organization or from a public cloud infrastructure such as Amazon Web Services (AWS), Microsoft Azure, or Google Cloud Platform (GCP).

About two decades back, edge devices did most end-user computations. A user would install the necessary applications on her laptop or desktop and work. Some examples are Microsoft Office, Adobe Acrobat and Reader, AVG Antivirus, and so on. Any application needing immediate user response or user interactions needed a native presence on a desktop. The desktop applications were independent and needed intermittent connectivity to upload or download data from the internet. For example, email clients contacted the servers only once every 10-15 minutes to download or upload messages. Since the user installed software on the machine, one could meter licenses based on the machines. A person could be using multiple machines. So, he was permitted to install the software on several machines with a per-user license. However, these user metering techniques were extensions of machine-based or per-installation metering.

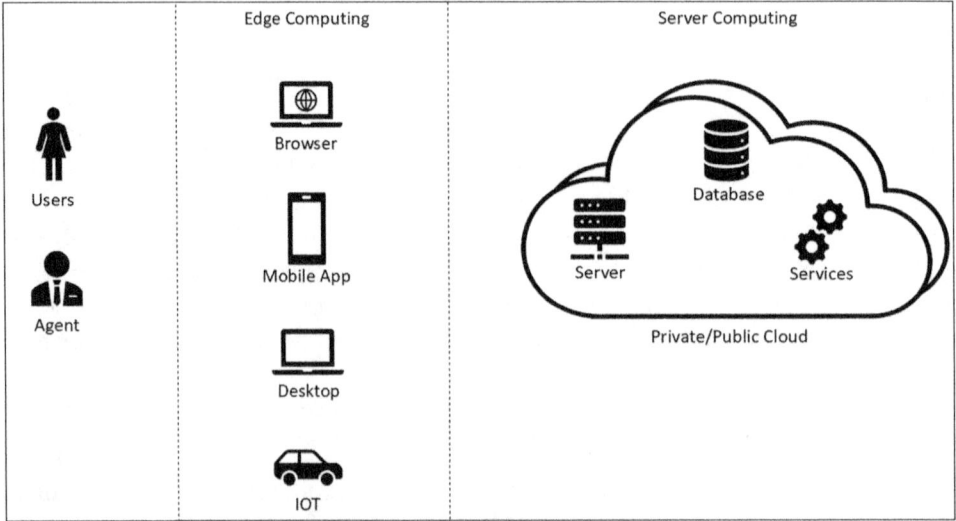

Figure 5.2: An outline of software interactions

While single end-points enabled end-user computing, there was a need to collaborate with organization users. Client-server systems helped collaborate better. An email server could manage and route emails to relevant persons, while an employee could type emails with email clients. Email clients were free, while email servers were to be licensed. Technologically, every email on the server is a transaction and can be considered a metering unit. However, businesses prefer metering schemes based on their functional needs. An organization primarily looking for an email system for employee communications will prefer pricing based on the number of users. However, an organization using the email system to send bulk posts for marketing campaigns will utilize the system differently. Could the email server vendors not charge based on the copies of the server software they installed? With advances in web architectures and browser technologies, vendors built interactive applications for the browsers and served the relevant data from the servers. With browsers as the clients, the need for application-specific clients disappeared. We had to only think of licensing the server software.

The server hardware went through a significant transition during these times. Processors can have multiple cores[5] that parallelize instruction processing. With hardware virtualization, a server can host hundreds of OSes with varying virtual CPUs, disk space, and network configurations. Cloud orchestration platforms provide a means to slice and dice high-performance hardware (HPC) into smaller computation units. Infrastructure software providers started metering the number of CPU cores[6,7] to license. With cloud computing, the servers can be custom-sized to customer needs with virtual CPUs (vCPUs), custom disk storage, and network throughputs. Initially, server licensing was a complex phenomenon. Per-installation licensing had its limitations. While hardware processors can have hundreds of cores, some software editions cannot use[8] them. So, partitioning the servers into smaller virtual machines is the only option. Secondly, is the database installed on bare metal with 32-core different from four installed on 8-cores each? While technically they can be, it became hard to explain to procurement teams. Metering to be successful should be:

- Easy to explain
- Easy to measure

---

[5] Intel® Xeon® 6 Processors with Efficient-Cores (E-Cores) **https://www.intel.com/content/www/us/en/products/details/processors/xeon/xeon6-e-cores.html** accessed 24th August 2024.
[6] Microsoft SQL includes a core-based license. **https://www.microsoft.com/en-us/licensing/product-licensing/sql-server** accessed 23rd August 2024
[7] Pricing and licensing for Windows Server 2022, **https://www.microsoft.com/en-in/windows-server/pricing#layout-container-uida3b9** accessed 23rd August 2024.
[8] SQL Server – Scale Limits, **https://learn.microsoft.com/en-us/sql/sql-server/editions-and-components-of-sql-server-2022?view=sql-server-ver16#scale-limits** accessed 23rd August 2024

- Easy to enforce
- Easy to demonstrate in action

Cores are easy to count. As an explanation, the software does twice more with a 2-core system; the price must be twice[9]. Counting cores is easy, and operating systems have APIs for the applications. An application can report anomalies easily through logs, installers, and so on.

Metering for Business

Metering should have a meaning in a business context. An Infrastructure as a Service (IaaS) vendor will provide machine specifications like real-life hardware. They will have CPUs, memory, disk space and speed, network speeds, and so on[10]. Platform as a Service (PaaS) vendors will talk about transactions. For example, AWS Lambda is priced at the amount of memory consumed per millisecond[11]. Software as a Service (SaaS) vendors would prefer users or transactions as a measure based on the customer needs. Let us talk about authentication. A SaaS-based authentication vendor typically registers the users on its servers. When a user tries to access a service such as the HR portal, the portal redirects her to the authentication server. She authenticates with the authentication server. She is issued an access token on her browser, which the HR portal accepts and authorizes the user. If she now tries to access an IT portal, she does not have to authenticate again. These are single sign-on systems. Most vendors license single sign-on systems to enterprises on a per-user/employee basis. For the banks, the use case is B2C, and the user is external. There is a significant difference in pricing[12]. Some B2C customers are licensed for active users or even per transaction. Due to the nature of business, SaaS vendors may use different metering for their customers rather than offering the metrics their vendors use. While estimating the operations cost, these aspects must be kept in mind.

Software License

Software is copyrighted intellectual property. They are intangible assets with ownership maintained by the creators or the publishers. They are in the same light as other copyrighted materials such as books, literary works, music, and so on. They are not sold like goods with unlimited rights. We will discuss the IP aspects of software

---

[9] This is a poor explanation. It will depend a lot on the parallel nature of the software.
[10] Amazon EC2, machine sizing, **https://aws.amazon.com/ec2/instance-types/** accessed on 25th August 2024.
[11] AWS Lambda Pricing, **https://aws.amazon.com/lambda/pricing/** accessed on 25th August 2024.
[12] Okta prices enterprise authentication for USD 2 per user. For B2C, they charge USD 70 per 1000 active users per month. There is an inherent assumption that an enterprise user authenticates 30 times a month while B2C users are infrequent users and only seen once a month. **https://www.okta.com/pricing/** and **https://auth0.com/pricing** accessed 25th August 2024.

in a later chapter along with the contractual implications. A software license is a right given to use within certain permissible guidelines. We highlight some examples.

- **Redistribution of runtime libraries:** When you build an application using a software development kit (SDK), the SDK may permit you to bundle a runtime library to be installed along with the software.
- **Attribution:** An open-source license may require you to state in your product documentation, mentioning the open-source product as a building block.
- **No warranties:** Some libraries will not take the liability of any nature due to imperfections or bugs.
- **Source disclosure:** Some open-source licenses may enforce disclosure of derivative work to the public.
- **Source code escrow:** In case of a business failure, the licensee may demand the source code be given to them to ensure their business is not impacted.
- **Restrictions on reverse-engineer:** A license does not permit the customer to reverse engineer a product and understand its internal workings to develop her competing product.

We state only a few commonly seen in practice but they can be quite elaborate.

Factors Affecting Pricing

The price depends on three factors, which are demand, supply, and alternatives to the product. The alternative can be offered by a competitor or by a custom solution worked out from existing infrastructure. Let us say an organization has a security guard at the entrance. The organization moved to a biometric authentication system and aggregated all the security staff to a central hall with security cameras. If you provide digital security systems, one obvious challenge is being competitive with the other vendors in the digital security systems space. You would also have to consider the manual security system. If there is an alternative to your product, a customer can choose it over your product. When we price a product, we consider all these factors. We state this with a framework as shown.

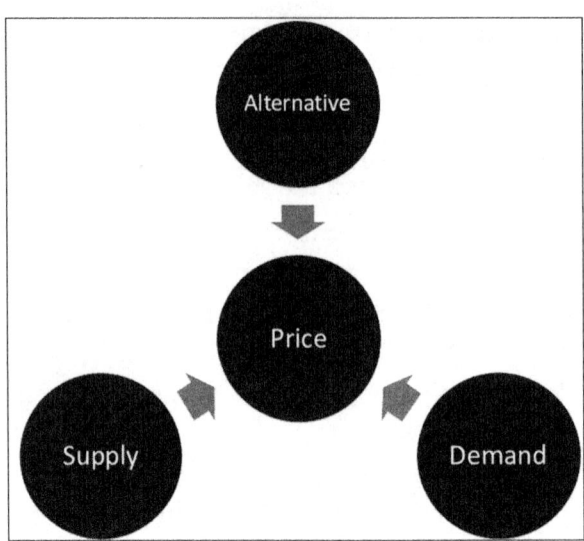

Figure 5.3: *Dependency of price on other factors*

We evaluate each of the factors and see how they affect the pricing.

Supply

A supplier will be careful not to price her products below the cost of production. We discussed these at some length in *Chapter 2, Strategy*. In *Figure 2.3: Demand and supply relationship with costs*, we stated that when a supplier can manage her costs, she can sell at varying prices over the complete demand curve. While that is an audacious goal for market leaders, it is not entirely untrue in the software engineering market. Microsoft sells the Windows Home Edition operating system for under 100 USD, while the Windows Server Editions sell for tens of thousands of dollars. Software companies can do so as their development costs spread over large sales volumes. We have discussed this as part of the definition of a software product in *Chapter 1, The Practice of Product Management*.

Another challenge we will realize is recording the costs—most smaller organizations record costs at the organizational level. The budget is estimated and maintained with the executives. Expenses are not attributed to the products properly. Hirings are not tracked based on products. People may move around from project to project, making cost tracking hard. Larger organizations assign cost management to the business unit (BU) level. Some BUs are as big as a small company. They do not have clarity across product expenses. They may all share the resources, for example, employees, servers, and software. Lack of knowledge of costs makes it hard to price. If you have a decent customer base, the firm can spread the cost of software development over all the customers. People were not concerned about sales volumes with on-premise or desktop software products. The same is not valid for SaaS-based products. There is a running expense associated with them. There are also customer support expenses.

Sometimes, governments buy software products for employee use or pass them to their citizens. Because there are only a few similar projects and volumes can be very high, it may not be practical to find proper pricing for such products. The same applies to utilities such as electricity, ports, airports, road constructions, and so on. Because of the heavy investments needed, only one or two vendors can service such needs. The government issues contracts for such projects using a bidding process. These regulated monopolies need to report their audited costs to revise pricing. Cost-based pricing is the preferred approach to these kinds of products and services. There are guidelines from the Federal Acquisition Regulations (FAR) and Defense on cost-based pricing[13]. Most welfare states cannot accept the government is generating profits from services provided to the citizens or letting a private entity make super-economic profits in partnership. Hence, private-public-partnership (PPP) projects are audited for their costs. Understanding the guidelines is important, as it can help us identify the costs of product development, delivery, and operations.

- **Work Breakdown Structure:** A good cost estimation or reporting requires a breakdown of the activities involved. A notional sizing and quantification of efforts help estimate the budget better. The breakdown or a derivative can maintain the actual costs in the product development for such activities.
- **Direct Labor:** The people working on the product directly for its development and operations can be assigned to this bucket. Expenses on employees should be recorded as a cost to the company to account for all benefits provided to the employees.
- **Direct Material:** It includes all the equipment used for a specific product. For software development, it includes all the machines used, licensed software, and maintenance of equipment utilized for the project.
- **Indirect Costs:** It can be due to shared pooled resources such as general and administrative expenses, operational costs, building rents, utility bills such as water, electricity, and so on. If the activities are well organized with a proper work breakdown, then it is possible to capture activity-based costing (ABC). Project management tools with financial management capabilities can capture the ABCs. However, without such tools, attribution over various direct metrics can be a good placeholder. For example, office rent can be proportionately distributed over the number of direct labor per product.
- **Profit Margin:** When cost-based pricing is used even for governments, normal profit margins are permitted over the costs. However, governments do not

---

[13] Darrell J. Oyer CPA. Cost-Based Pricing: A Guide for Government Contractors. Berrett-Koehler Publishers, 2012. While the guidelines are for the US organizations, the other governments are not entirely different from these approaches.

allow firms to make supernormal profits when operating regulated monopolies under a license. The riskier the project, the higher the profit potential. US Federal Acquisition Regulations (FAR) recommends[14] the following margin or fees:

- Experimental or Research: up to 15% of costs
- Architectural or Design Work: up to 6% of costs
- Costs + Fees based work: up to 10% of costs

- **Inflation and Currency Effects:** Software products may involve inputs from international markets. For example, you may import third-party software, foreign vendors may provide product development and consulting services, your local currency may be volatile, the investors may be funding in a foreign currency, and so on. It is best to maintain the account in the most stable currency and adjust for inflation intermittently.

Product cost estimations and accounting are separate from organization accounting practices for statutory compliance. For example, statutory compliance may not permit capitalization of salaries. You may capitalize product development costs over 3 to 5 years and record it as a fixed cost. Similarly, you can estimate the operational and support costs over 3 to 5 years. As your customers or users increase, your operational, support, and delivery expenses, such as the costs of cloud servers, may vary. These operational costs are variable. You will also need to arrive at the volumes of service you will deliver in the meter we have discussed in the section Meters and Licenses. This way, you can arrive at a per-transaction meter cost. Using that information, you can estimate pricing for each licensing scheme you plan to use.

Alternative

Whenever you launch a product, you know some competitors provide similar services. It may be worthwhile to find the prices for which they are offering their products. With the right market intelligence, it is the easiest way to discover the product's price. Sometimes, the process is called competitive pricing. Here are a few ways to understand competitors' price insight:

- Price is on the websites of most competitors. However, actual deals may see significant discounts.
- Gather price knowledge while bidding to the potential customer. The customer is not bound to share price information of other bidders, yet while bargaining, information sometimes escapes.
- Analysts provide product market insights for a fee that you can subscribe to.
- Some analysts provide competitive insights about a group of products on their websites. Prices are one of the comparison metrics.

---

[14] ibid

- A simple web search can provide project costs, contracts, and so on. One can estimate the prices from that.
- Purchase inquiry about a competitor's products.

However, collecting such data from ex-employees or distributors can be a breach of trust and is unethical and illegal. While gaining pricing insights from the competition is the easiest, they have their fair share of downsides.

- There is an assumption that the competitor is providing a similar function as yours.
- Buyers assume pricing is the common factor across competitors and start comparing feature-to-feature offerings, even for features they would never use. However well you try, pricing becomes the most important consideration in the solution choice.
- The analysts comparing the product features may not understand the relative strengths of the functionalities in the context of a real problem. The exercise may be a datasheet comparison or pure academic pursuit.
- Improper product vision may put your product in competition in several adjacent markets and drain energy documenting competitive positioning. The direct competition for a product should be kept to 3 to 5 by the right level of targeting.

Customers can address their needs using alternative solutions rather than looking for a competitive solution. For example, an IT department can record the IT assets in an Excel spreadsheet. They do not need a formal IT Asset Management (ITAM) solution. The process has limitations and is not cost-effective for a large organization. For a small office home office (SOHO), it may be a reasonable solution. If you are a supplier of an ITAM solution, you need to be aware such alternative options may exist. Such customers may not agree to the need for an explicit ITAM solution. However, if you plan to target such markets, the competitive pricing should look at the spreadsheet as a competition.

Demand

Every customer has limited resources. They may **want** some goods or services, but there is no specific problem those goods or services can address. The **want** translates to a **need** when they can associate a problem that the goods or services can address in their lives. The need transitions to a **demand** when the customer wants to address it by paying for the goods and services. A demand is there when the customer sees an economic value. We will understand the want-to-need-to-demand transition with an example. Suppose three or four professionals, such as lawyers and accountants, quit their jobs in large organizations and start something of their own. In their previous organization, they had case management systems—the tool used to maintain a case for a client. The professionals would contribute their part of the activity in the tool and pass it on to the next person downstream. They would get notifications when they have to complete their tasks. They would update the time spent on the task and the actions taken. The case updates were recorded as part of the logs. Finally, a billing module aggregated the time and effort spent on such a case and billed the client every month. The organization had over a hundred professionals working on around five hundred active cases. In the new startup, the professionals had hardly ten to fifteen active cases. They do not have a dedicated accounting team or a client management team. They interact with the clients at a personal level and reach out to them for cases, relationship management, or even billing. The professionals understand case management and want it. But they do not have the budget for it. They may start with personal email, calendar, or WhatsApp to maintain their case management process.

To these startup founders, the demand for enterprise case management software does not exist. But they need a team-level case management system. Someone identifies these needs. She takes open-source components and sets up a SaaS-based offering for these small-scale case management needs. Such a product can be popular in the market and get acceptance. The enterprise vendors look at the competitive product and make a functional comparison. They end up stating how great their product is; the market does not understand the real needs. Features do not drive the demand in the market. Understanding the customer's needs adds definite value.

What is the price of the team-level case management product? The founders are industry veterans and are aware of a case management solution. However, they cannot pay for an enterprise product. They are looking at a less feature-rich product. But the price they want to pay does not quite depend on the features but on how much the founders can spare from their income for such a need. Notionally, they have a number in mind. They will only buy the product at that price point.

Value-based Pricing

The product helps the customer achieve some business objectives. Can those business objectives be quantified? The customer has a notional idea of how much she can pay for the product. Let us say without a team case management product with the office productivity tools, the following problems are observed:

- The partners have to manage calendars in their personal Gmail accounts.
- Delay in client response time due to improper coordination with individual tools.
- They have to individually record the cases in a Word document and send the document to the next person for updates. The updates may not get tracked properly.
- They spend more time coordinating, recording, or managing their activities.

- They have to track time for client tasks and manually enter it into a spreadsheet. Loss in recording will lead to unbilled hours.
- And so on.

If those problems are analyzed, we can fully understand some areas of improvement in using a case management tool. Case management tools can mitigate the earlier inconveniences and improve upon them. However, they cannot eliminate them. Now, we can estimate the actual gains resulting from using a case management tool. That is the economic value added to the customer. As a vendor, you can showcase this added value and take a percentage of the value added as the product price. That is the principle of value-based pricing. Using our tools, you saved X dollars over a year.

Since value perception is the customer's prerogative, there is an information asymmetry acting against the vendor. The only way the vendor will understand the customer's environment is when the customer shares her workflows and processes with the vendor or the vendor understands the customer's environment based on her previous experiences. The whole process is meaningful when the seller is in a consultative mode. She understands the buyer's processes and enhances them by providing tools.

In the last chapter, we discussed Google's BeyondCorp product for Zero Trust Networks. Google conceptualized the idea, ran an internal prototype and adoption campaign, understood the various use cases, and conceived a saleable product. The first iteration of BeyondCorp Remote Access, or saleable offering on the platform, was launched in 2020[15]. Sometimes, in-house solutions can take that long, as the initiative started in 2011. However, smaller organizations can look at building consultative engagements with customers and build components that can be productized or bundled later into a proper solution.

For consultative selling, the following ecosystem must exist.
- The need or problem you are trying to address has to be a high-value and high-involvement task for the buyer.
- The buyer and seller must establish a professional trust in their approach.
- The buyer and seller develop a coordinated solution to reduce discovery costs. The buyer engages with the vendor as she saves a lot more than bidding for competitive products.
- A low-value and involvement product will not fit into this selling.

At some point, even high-involvement products give way to standardized offerings. Insurance selling was almost always agent-driven and consultative about a decade ago. Today, insurance aggregators try to push standard products through a website. When a standard product sale does not work out, an insurance agent intervenes. While

---

[15] **https://cloud.google.com/blog/products/identity-security/keep-your-teams-working-safely-with-beyondcorp-remote-access** accessed 20th September 2024

developing a product, engage with early adopters to identify the real value drivers and engage with them to include them in the product.

From Commodity to Differentiated Offer

The goal of selling a product is to ensure a customer realizes the value and pays the right price. The competitor is an intruder in this discussion. Engage with the customer and ensure that your solution addresses the customer's needs. However, most sales discussions lead to a discussion on how the proposed solution is better than anything in the market. It is an analyst's approach to evaluating a product. They are looking at a group of vendors and proposing value-for-money options to their clients. The sales approach should focus on the customer's problem and how your solution can address the customer's needs. A customer evaluating your product wants her needs met at the least cost over time. They are not keen if you are leaders or laggards in the market if you cannot meet their needs. The leaders in the market only ratify the ability to execute and deliver value over a time horizon. The more your solution looks like another one in the market, the more your product becomes a commodity. A commodity is purchased only on price. The better value you deliver, specific to a customer, the more differentiated your offer becomes. Since none match your capabilities, you get to derive a price as a percentage of value added to the customer. Can you sell a product without invoking the competition during the discussion or unnecessarily showing off all the cool features you have and focus only on the use cases the customer is evaluating a solution for? Let the customer talk about competition and then apply all the ammo you have against the competition. The more you discuss competition, the more you move to a commoditized offering.

Pricing Schemes

We looked at three principles of pricing a product. They are demand, value, or competition-driven. In real life, you face challenges of pricing for volumes, bundling and unbundling of products into and out of suites, enterprise pricing with unrelated organization products, captive product pricing, and so on. All pricing schemes adhere to the principles of pricing. We will study a few pricing schemes.

Volume-based Pricing

You are a small entrepreneur who has started a business and is reaching out to companies with 1000 to 5000 employees. In a business discussion, you realize a company is considering packaging your service for its retail users. The retail users can be a hundred thousand to a million or even more. If the customer base increases over the year, they will like to avail price discounts for that expanded plan. They are asking for pricing in three ranges: 100,000, 1 million, and 10 million user bases. The product price should be just for your existing customer base. Yet, it should accommodate large

Pricing

expansion plans. In *Chapter 2, Strategy*, we discussed a firm's generic strategy of being a cost leader and deciding to honor the entire demand curve. A good volume discount pricing plan should mimic the demand curve. We assume you have the technology and resources to support such a large customer. It is unlikely you have the industry demand curve with you. How will you come up with a reasonable volume discount plan?

Interestingly, economics has tools to address this. If there is a reduction in product prices, does the demand increase for such action? A reduction of price or discount is proportional to the product price. Similarly, the increase in the demand would be proportionate to the quantity sold. The economists considered these factors and developed a ratio called elasticity. Mathematically, elasticity (ϵ) is defined as shown.

$$\frac{\Delta Q/Q}{\Delta P/P} = \epsilon$$

Assuming constant elasticity, the equation can be written as:

$$\frac{\Delta Q}{Q} = \epsilon \frac{\Delta P}{P}$$

Using calculus, the equation can be solved to:

$$\log Q = \epsilon \log P + C, \text{ where C is a constant.}$$

We take exponentiation on both sides and get the equation:

$$Q = KP^\epsilon \text{ or } P = kQ^{1/\epsilon}, \text{ where } k = K^{-1/\epsilon}$$

K is again a constant with a value of 10^C. We applied the aforementioned principle and created a volume-based pricing curve for 10 to 100,000 users. We exaggerate the prices a bit so that the representation looks prominent while plotting.

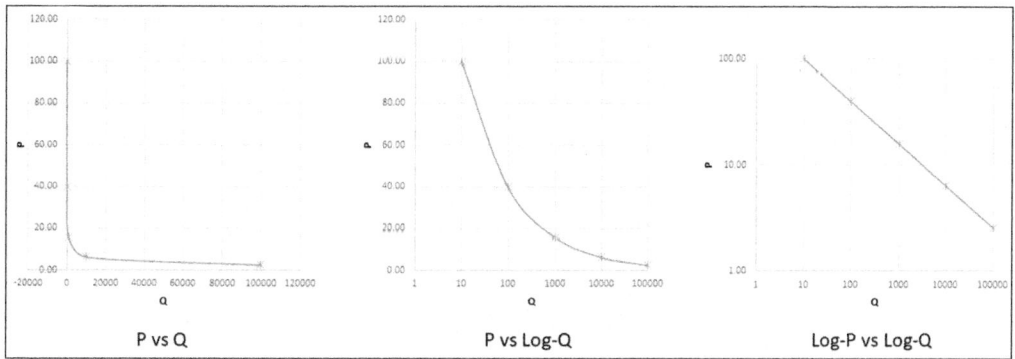

Figure 5.4: *Representative volumetric price curve in normal, semi-logarithm, and logarithm scales*

The P vs Q curve has a sharp slope for smaller Q, while the curve is almost flat for larger Q values. The log-P vs log-Q is a straight line as discussed in the preceding equations. We have a reasonable model to fit data to finalize the curves. We can suggest the following as some data points:

- Estimate the unit cost of delivery at the highest delivery volume possible and add a profit margin to it. Add a margin to incorporate deal-specific discounts, as they are not uncommon in large deals.
- The pricing for normal operations, such as the 3000-5000 user range.
- List price of the product, which is typically quoted for 1-10 users.

A curve fitting along these data points can provide a consistent volume-based price curve. It may not be the industry demand curve but it is close. Your estimates will improve as you engage with further larger deals.

Product Bundles and Suites

Can the demand for one product be used to drive demand for another? It probably can if the following characteristics exist:

- The products cater to almost similar audiences.
- The demand for one is relatively low, but the need is in the market. The product is substantially elastic to price.
- The other product is relatively inelastic in pricing and has substantial demand.

Bundling both together can potentially drive the sales of the product selling less in numbers. We present this with a diagram.

Pricing

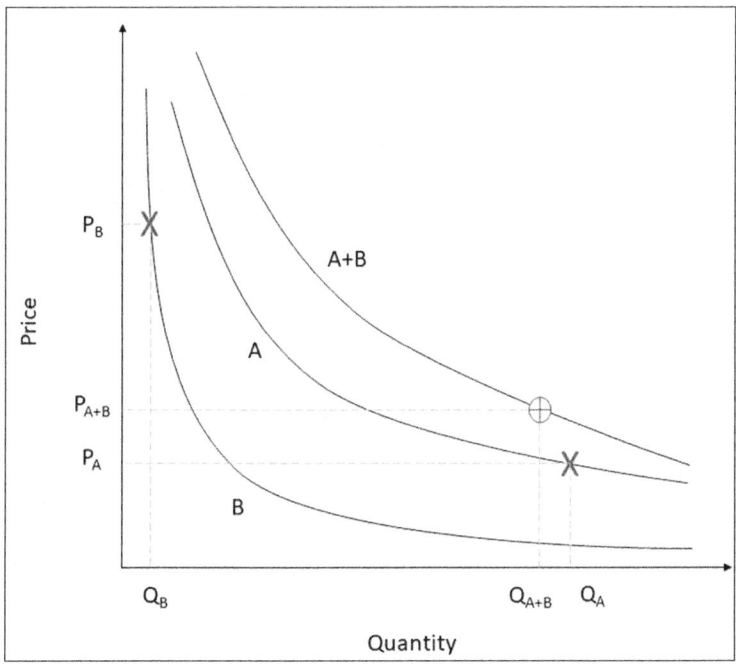

Figure 5.5: *Rationale for bundling A and B*

In *Figure* 5.5, product A has higher demand and a relatively inelastic price curve. Product B is selling a lot less into the same user population. So, the company combines both and launches a combo offer of A with B. There will be fewer sales of the combo or suite as people who are price-sensitive and do not see much value in product B will feel they are paying a higher price for A. The buyer behavior for a suite can be explained by using price elasticity.

However, the market messaging for combos or suites of products is quite different. The markets present the case of buying two products at the price of one–a showcase of product B being discounted significantly in the offer adds to significant customer value. Creating a product suite is not the same as providing promotional tag-along offers. Here, we are considering launching A+B as one product offer. We may stop selling A and B independently altogether. In *Chapter 1, The Practice of Product Management*, while defining software products, we discussed Microsoft Office replacing the point products, Word, Excel, PowerPoint, and so on. These are conscious product decisions. The perceived discounts are not due to promotion but a shift in demand, thus the price.

We will take a few cues from the Fast-Moving Consumer Goods (FMCG) or Fast-Moving Consumer Fashion (FMCF) industries. These will distinguish the role of promotion from creating a product bundle.

- Discounts on clothing, such as buy 2, get 2 free: Clearly, a promotional offer on old stock or factory seconds.

- Selling a matchbox with a pack of incense sticks: With cooking gas and spark lighters, the role of a matchstick is almost gone in households. A matchstick is relevant for lighting a slow-burning flame such as an incense stick. Even for smokers, a gas lighter helps light up the cigarette. However, using petroleum-based products to light up incense sticks is not acceptable to religious sentiments in India. So, selling a matchbox with incense sticks is a natural choice of product bundling.
- Include a toothbrush with a large pack of toothpaste: A promotional offer during a price hike. Once the batch is over, the subsequent batches have no toothbrush in them.

There are varieties of use cases and examples of product bundling. Before closing, we will discuss captive product pricing. Think of a shaving razor. The razor blade is the active component, while the razor device only holds the blade safely and securely. A razor manufacturer can sell the razor at a discounted price while selling the blade at a premium. In technology products, a printer is another such product. While the printer is sold cheap, the cartridge carries a part of the printer's price. In health care, the same is true with blood sugar measurement units. The price of the test strip can cover the discounts on the glucometer. In software, we see it in platforms. The spoke-like products built on the platform hub can act as captive pricing models. Captive products have a level of stickiness with the customer. Once sold and liked by the customer, it is far easier to sell add-ons and additional products around the platform. A slight premium can be charged as switching out from the platform has some limitations and associated costs.

Tiered Pricing Plans

With many products developed as platforms, pricing structuring has become standard across organizations. Each product group has three to four categories. You will see the segregations, termed silver, gold, and platinum tiers, or base, standard, and premium. This practice is the three-tier or good, better, and best (GBB) pricing model. Here are some examples. Microsoft Office 365 products for business[16] organized as:

- Microsoft 365 Business Basic
- Microsoft 365 Business Standard
- Microsoft 365 Business Premium

Figma[17] provides creative tools for UI/UX that are licensed as:

- Professional Team

---

[16] **https://www.microsoft.com/en-US/microsoft-365/business/compare-all-microsoft-365-business-products-b** accessed 17th September 2024

[17] **https://www.figma.com/pricing/** accessed 17th September 2024

- Organization
- Enterprise

GitHub[18], a Microsoft company, provides CI/CD infrastructure for most software companies today with plans such as:

- Free (Individuals)
- Teams
- Enterprise

Atlassian[19], another market leader in project management tools, licenses its products as:

- Standard
- Premium
- Enterprise

The on-premise products installed in the customer infrastructure had capabilities based on the hardware provided by the customer. It is no longer relevant in the SaaS model. Moreover, the customer is interested in a final pricing based on per-user or transaction meters. Instance, core, or installation-based licenses are becoming a thing of the past. In a Good-Better-Best (GBB) license[20], the vendors are interested in the **better** tier of the product. The intent is to sell a maximum number of copies of that tier. They display a feature-wise comparison of a **good** and the **best** option to entice the customer. The best tier is expensive and includes large enterprise features such as user management, administrative features, directory integration, private cloud migration, and so on, which matter to large enterprises only. The good version is the trial pack for budget-sensitive users. Sometimes, the good version is for free without product support. Very few organizations will run a production system on a free system without an SLA. While GBB is great, vendors also use innovative license schemes based on the customer and the use cases. Microsoft licenses the retail version of Office 365 for individuals or the complete family[21]. In business tiers, they also have an app version[22] that uses desktop software for Word, Excel, and PowerPoint installed on the end-user machine.

---

[18] **https://github.com/pricing** accessed 17th September 2024
[19] Atlassian Jira Pricing, **https://www.atlassian.com/software/jira/pricing** accessed 18th September 2024
[20] Rafi Mohammed, The Good-Better-Best Approach to Pricing, HBR September-October 2018, **https://hbr.org/2018/09/the-good-better-best-approach-to-pricing** accessed 17th September 2024.
[21] Microsoft 365 Home Edition Pricing, **https://www.microsoft.com/en-us/microsoft-365/buy/compare-all-microsoft-365-products-b#For%20home** accessed 18th September 2024.
[22] Supra. 16

Enterprise Plans

In the previous section, we discussed the pricing schemes of a single product. Organizations with many products would like to entice their customer base to use more of their products–think of them like buffets in a restaurant. Adobe has a tier dedicated to such customers[23]. Libraries or publishers[24] provide annual subscription plans for all their publications. Many organizations have special discounts for the education markets. Exposure to these tools early in life can eventually help the students ask for the tools when they become industry leaders, leading to future sales. Organizations have special pricing for the public sector price list. When deployed in one state, the product acts as a reference implementation to the next state. There is an element of promotion built into these pricing schemes. But the promotions are perpetual. Hence, they should be part of the pricing exercise. Some organizations provide discounts to large customers based on the combined dollar spending on all products. When the sales process starts, the first business unit that sells the product may not have to discount. At some point, when the billing exceeds a threshold, the subsequent products sold are with discounts. If a product is already on a volume discount or contains several commercial third-party components, additional discounts based on overall sales volumes across products can be a costly mistake. The PMs should ensure the pricing can address these complex situations. Since these pricing plans are designed at the organizational level, the PM has to keep the discount in mind while pricing the product. Tweaking them to the right levels is of definite value.

Every business works on its pricing continually, improving in each iteration. They introduce new pricing schemes to meet the needs of their industry at a specific time. We touched upon only a few schemes here to sensitize the PMs. Every pricing scheme needs to meet the pricing principles of cost, competition, and value, driven by supply, alternatives, and demand. These principles ensure business viability. Next, we will see if there can be legal ramifications for not following these pricing principles.

Legal Implications of Pricing

Competition is core to an open market economy. Competition among market rivals ensures demand and supply determine the prices. However, organizations with dominant positions[25] in the market can favor specific suppliers and arm-twist others to comply with their terms and conditions. E-retailers are known to woo customers by providing substantial discounts. The discounts can be so high that one can say the

---

[23] Creative Cloud All Apps for teams, Adobe Creative Cloud Pricing Plans, **https://www.adobe.com/creativecloud/business/teams/plans.html** accessed 18th September 2024

[24] O'Reilly Learning Platform Pricing, **https://www.oreilly.com/online-learning/pricing.html** accessed 18th September 2024.

[25] Section 4, Explanation a, The Competition Act, 2002, Union of India

deals are with predatory pricing. Predatory pricing[26] means the products are priced below the cost of production. The dominant players can weed away competition and establish a monopoly. The Competition Act 2002[27] provides the legal framework under which businesses should operate. Attaining a dominant position through normal business operations is perfectly legal. However, abuse of the same is not permitted and is categorically outlined in the act. The provisions are typically known as antitrust protection. Almost all countries have some form of antitrust protection in their legal systems. We will discuss this further in a subsequent chapter. Here, we will focus only on antitrust measures related to pricing. In India, the Competition Commission of India (CCI) is the apex governing body for issues related to antitrust. We will discuss two cases related to antitrust that have been of importance in the Indian market.

- **Bharti Airtel Limited vs Reliance Industries Limited & Other on 9 June 2017**[28]: Bharti Airtel (Airtel), the informant, claimed Reliance Jio (RJIL) had abused its dominant position and engaged in predatory pricing by providing a free 4G connection to its initial users. Reliance Industries (RIL) had a dominant position in the petrochemical market. Being a promoter of Jio Infocom, it can use that dominant position to influence the market. However, the CCI found Airtel had a 23.5% market share over Reliance Jio's 6.4%. It also held that RIL, though a large company, did not directly engage in the telecom market. The business was confined to RJIL only. RJIL did not have enough market muscle to command a dominant position. Thus, the order was passed in favor of RJIL, and the case was closed.

- **Cases involving Amazon and Flipkart in various courts and tribunals in India**: Delhi Vyapar Mahasang, a member of the Confederation of All India Traders (CAIT) that represents 80 million traders in India, filed a complaint with CCI stating Amazon and Flipkart have indulged in antitrust trade practices[29] by giving preferential treatment to sellers, deep discounts on mobile phones sales including selling below the cost, providing some sellers priority listing in search results, and so on. CCI got into action, conducted several surveys, and submitted a report that considers both Amazon and Flipkart guilty of such practices. Earlier, Amazon had divested its subsidiaries, such as Cloudtail and Appario Retail, to avert the possibility of its investment in sellers that

---

[26] Section 4, Explanation b, The Competition Act, 2002, Union of India
[27] The Competition Act, 2002, **https://www.indiacode.nic.in/handle/123456789/2010** accessed 19th September 2024
[28] CCI Case No: 3 of 2017, **https://www.cci.gov.in/antitrust/orders/details/335/0** accessed 19th September 2024
[29] Amazon and Flipkart Breached Antitrust Laws: CCI, The Hindu, 13th September 2024, **https://www.thehindu.com/sci-tech/technology/amazon-flipkart-breached-antitrust-laws-cci/article68637232.ece** accessed 22nd September 2024

can attract unnecessary attention to antitrust provisions[30]. CCI can penalize Amazon and Flipkart up to 10 percent of their revenues. They have asked both organizations to furnish their financial details[31]. Such cases take a long time to decide with appeals in higher courts.

We discussed these cases to sensitize the PMs to the legal ramifications of aggressive pricing to penetrate the market and establish leadership. Amazon and Flipkart may successfully justify their actions, just like Reliance Jio managed to convince the courts and could overcome antitrust actions. However, these compliance measures are expensive. Businesses must provision for legal expenses while planning such drastic pricing goals.

Conclusion

We started understanding the principle of pricing and realized how supply, demand, and alternatives in the market affect the pricing. We showed that value-based pricing can provide better margins. When a customer realizes the value, goods and services are well-differentiated from the competition. We looked at pricing schemes that help enterprises show value to their customers, for example, volume-based pricing, bundling of various products, GBB pricing, and enterprise plans. A company's objective should be to earn profits legally. We highlighted that aspect with some recent legal decisions on antitrust laws in India. In taming a bargaining buyer, we realized the need to move the buyer to a customer and looked at the pricing as a tool to improve our bargaining potential. The next chapter will focus on the User Experience (UX), where we will study how the user realizes the value additions we bring to the product.

Questions

1. How does your firm determine the price of the products?

2. Apply the pricing principles to your product. Is any pricing principle violated due to your choice of price for a specific deal? How will you rectify the situation?

3. How does your customer perceive your product offering? Does she look at it as a value add?

---

[30] Amazon's Cloudtail Is Dead – Is It Enough to Boost Indian Sellers? Inc 42, 21st June 2022, **https://inc42.com/features/cloudtail-checks-out-of-amazons-cart-will-appario-follow-suit/** accessed on 22nd September 2024

[31] **https://www.livemint.com/news/india/antitrust-case-cci-amazon-flipkart-penalty-digital-economy-fair-trade-eu-ex-ante-regulations-11726973993766.html** accessed on 22nd September 2024

4. Find the cost structure of your product and justify the pricing against it.

5. How is your product priced at various volume ranges? How can you improve on it?

6. What are the key challenges you anticipate in implementing value-based pricing in your organization? How would you address the information asymmetry between your company and your customers?"

7. Think about a time when your organization tried to quantify the value delivered to customers. What metrics were used? What difficulties did you face in measuring and communicating this value? How could the process be improved?"

Chapter 6
User Experience

Introduction

We studied the bargaining buyers and tried to address their value perceptions by moving them from the buyer mindset to the customer mindset. Next, we worked on the prices to help them realize the best value for the products and captured a part of the value for ourselves. In this chapter, we will work with the users. Eventually, the users will use the products irrespective of who foots the bill. We need to ensure the user gets the best experience and becomes the evangelist for the product. We will understand the elements of user experience, how user experience is perceived with user interfaces, the factors to consider when building a platform product, the role of documentation in better user experience, and touch upon a few tools and frameworks.

Structure

In this chapter, we will cover the following topics:

- Elements of User Experience
- User Interface
- Tools and Frameworks
- Design Thinking

Elements of User Experience

In *Chapter 4: Customers* and *Chapter 5: Pricing*, we focused on customers and the economic impact of using the products and services. We said users will influence the buyers when making purchase decisions. We also stated users can be end-users, analysts, or administrators. We will review how various users view the same product with different lenses. For this chapter, we will use some examples from varied domains. We will try to explain that with simple day-to-day terminologies.

Date	Alice	Bob	Carol	Remarks
2024-02-01	200	-100	-100	Lunch 300
2024-02-02	100		-100	Loan to Carol
2024-02-03		50	-50	Snacks 100
2024-02-04	200	-200		Loan to Bob
2024-02-05	-100	200	-100	Dinner 300
2024-02-06	-50	-100	150	Shopping 500
Total	350	-150	-200	

Table 6.1: A sample travel expense journal

As shown in *Table 6.1*, Alice, Bob, and Carol are three friends on a vacation to a nearby place. They incur some shared expenses as part of their travel. They would like to maintain a **financial journal**[1] to track these expenses. The journal only records the financial transactions that one spends. The amount one spends on herself is not in the journal. For example, on 1 February 2024, they went for lunch together. They spent `300` and split it equally among themselves. Alice paid for it; she quickly created this journal in Google Sheets and shared it with Bob and Carol. Since Alice paid for it, she only recorded `200` against her name and put in `-100` against Bob's and Carol's names. Since they only record expenses incurred on others in this journal, Alice may forget the rationale. Hence, she added a remarks column providing a short explanation. Each item on a journal entry is a **transaction**. The sum of a financial transaction is **zero**, as money cannot be created from thin air. Debited money is credited somewhere. At the end of the travel, Bob (`150`) and Carol (`200`) can pay Alice `350` to settle the accounts.

The simple table is an actual treasure trove for a product manager. Let us analyze it step-by-step. Alice, Bob, and Carol have a process to update data in the sheet referred to as the **workflow**. Let us assume Alice created the sheet and only provided viewing rights to Bob and Carol. She is the only one who can update the sheet. Now, there are **roles and rights**. Alice, being the creator of the sheet, could have maintained elevated privileges over Bob and Carol. She would have acted as an **administrator** for the travel expense sheet. Alice gave some money to Carol. There is no reason why Bob should view this transaction. A solution in this direction will bring **privacy** into the framework. We also learned domain-centric features like **double-entry bookkeeping** through this simple journal. Every transaction entered has debit and credit entries. The sum of those values is zero. There is a rudimentary emphasis on aesthetics, but we can still

---

[1] The author and two of his classmates maintained such a journal to track common expenses and used to settle at the end of the month.

see all numerals in fixed-width fonts[2]. They are right aligned. That way, someone can mentally carry out simple additions across the rows. Headers and footers are bold, demanding visual attention on them. Lastly, italics in the comments section ensure there is an emphasis to state these are different. However, readability is knowingly kept low. So, only interested people will focus on them when needed.

Workflow

Most interactive applications expect the users to follow a sequence of operations to complete a task. These groups of operations constitute a workflow. The current workflow consists of the following:

1. Create and share a spreadsheet in Google Sheets among the participants.
2. Add a column for each participant.
3. When someone spends money on another person, she must debit (+) her account and credit (-) the other person's account.
4. Since the contextual details of the transaction are not there, a remark explaining the transaction must be added.
5. After all the transactions are recorded at the end of activities, sum up all the columns. The people with negative values on their accounts will transfer money to people with positive balances.

The preceding processes are great examples of workflows. Digital transformation activities in organizations review the current manual or semi-manual workflows and try to develop software to cater to such needs. Suppose a social networking company wants to add a feature for the financial management of a group of users. They can theoretically use the similar concept we discussed but with these changes to the system:

- *As a user, I do not like my transactions shared with users who are not parties to the transaction.*[3]
- There is no restriction on the size of the user group.
- I want the app to settle the payments across the group rather than contacting every user offline for payment or collection.
- The users want the app to be available on a mobile device so that they can enter the information while traveling.

---

[2] We will have a limited coverage of fonts in this chapter. We suggest discerning readers review the Google Fonts Knowledge articles for an introductory understanding of fonts. **https://fonts.google.com/knowledge** accessed 10 October 2024

[3] The feature is described in a user story format. In a later chapter, we will discuss user stories in detail while discussing agile methodologies.

User Experience

The first constraint will make the views of every user different.

Alice's View					Bob's View				
Date	Alice	Bob	Carol	Remarks	Date	Alice	Bob	Carol	Remarks
2024-02-01	200	-100	-100	Lunch 300	2024-02-01	200	-100	-100	Lunch 300
2024-02-02	100		-100	Loan to Carol	2024-02-03		50	-50	Loan to Carol
2024-02-04	200	-200		Loan to Bob	2024-02-04	200	-200		Loan to Bob
2024-02-05	-100	200	-100	Dinner 300	2024-02-05	-100	200	-100	Dinner 300
2024-02-06	-50	-100	150	Shopping 500	2024-02-06	-50	-100	150	Shopping 500
Total	350	NA	NA		Total	NA	-150	NA	

Carol's View			
Date	Alice	Bob	Carol	Remarks
2024-02-01	200	-100	-100	Lunch 300
2024-02-02	100		-100	Loan to Carol
2024-02-03		50	-50	Loan to Bob
2024-02-05	-100	200	-100	Dinner 300
2024-02-06	-50	-100	150	Shopping 500
Total	NA	NA	-200	

Table 6.2: Alice, Bob, and Carol have different views

We know views are crucial to user experience. We consider it as an element.

Views

Views serve a purpose; the primary scope of the view must be understood. Let us be in Alice's shoes. Alice has spent some money on others, and some other people have spent money on her. She wants to know if she must make additional payments or if she should get a refund. Although Bob or Carol would have consumed the money, how much their contribution to the spending was is not the primary purpose. The details can be hidden and only shown if the breakup is needed. Now, from 5 columns, we have reduced the table width to 3. Bob and Carol move from columns to rows in the details view. We can now add Douglas, Elon, Frida, or any other number of friends to the travel group. With a minor tweaking around with views, we can meet the requirement of fitting the data in the limited screen space of a mobile device as well as adding an unlimited number of users to the views.

	Alice's View		
	Date	Alice	Remarks
-	2024-02-01	200	Lunch 300
	Bob	-100	
	Carol	-100	
+	2024-02-02	100	Loan to Carol
+	2024-02-04	200	Loan to Bob
+	2024-02-05	-100	Dinner 300
+	2024-02-06	-50	Shopping 500
	Total	350	

Table 6.3: *Alice's view of her travel account*

With minor tweaking of views, we can accommodate the data in the limited screen space of a mobile device and add an unlimited number of users to the views. When we present the view as shown, there will be discussions and emphasis on whether + and - signs are the right symbols for expanded and collapsed views or whether we should use ▶ and ▼ to represent them. Whether the click should be on the symbol position to expand or collapse or clicking anywhere else on the row is acceptable. These are relevant choices in a visual aesthetic and interaction sense. However, informational values have a hierarchy based on their importance. The following are the priorities for Alice.

- Is the travel spending settled?
- If not, is she on the debtor or creditor side, and by how much?
- When did she pay or receive benefits for a transaction?
- Who benefitted or paid for the transaction?

Now, you know what can fit in limited screen space. The rest is under a details tab; you can access it with an additional click.

Architecture

With just three people traveling together, settlement is easy. Bob and Carol pay Alice. Let us take the case of ten travelers. A (**500**), B(**250**), and C (**250**) spent a total of 1000 for D to I (-150) each and J (-100). There are various permutations and combinations possible. Let us say I and J paid to C. The rest must pay A and B. Even there also, D, E, and F can pay A; G has to pay 50 to D and the rest to B; H must pay B, and so on. The combination we discussed is just one of many possibilities; someone must track these payments so that the tasks are marked as completed. Our example considered expenses in multiples of 50, but expenses can be in fractional quantities too. There are algorithms available that can minimize the number of settlement transactions.

User Experience

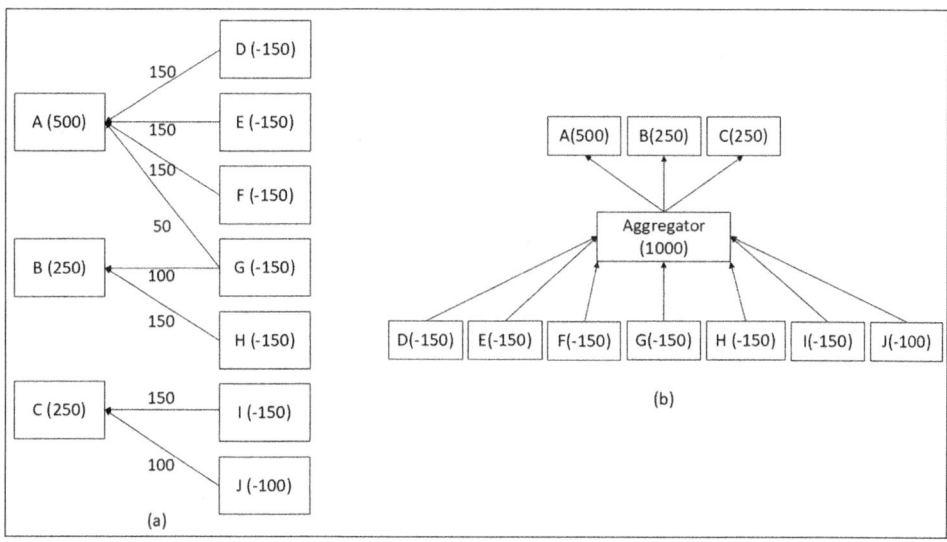

Figure 6.1: *Settlement process (a) peer-to-peer (b) hub and spoke model*

In *Figure* 6.1, we have two modes of settlement:

- We have a peer-to-peer model where the app can recommend who pays whom and how much. The users pay each other using their payment channels. One of the users acts as an **administrator** who officiates and ensures the individuals complete their part of settlements.
- We have a hub-and-spoke model. Here, every debtor pays to a central hub. The central hub pays back to the creditors when sufficient funds are collected.
  - To provide an aggregation hub for everyone, the app must be a payment aggregator, which may need a payment banking license as it collects money on behalf of other debtors and distributes it across creditors. The app vendor can register as a payment bank or partner with someone who can help them with this goal for a fee.
  - Or, the **administrator** can provide her account details in the app, everyone pays to that account, and she distributes it to the rest of the people in the group as a manual process. It is more like sharing her account details with friends and family.

Considering all these, as an app vendor, you may want to limit up to 10 people per group. You can have an **administrator** to manage the settlement process with other group activities.

Configuration

We saw the need for an administrator for workflow management. So, we need to configure it for our group. The simplest can be that whoever creates a group becomes a de facto administrator. The administrator can add additional administrators optionally. If the administrator uses a hub-spoke model for payments, she has to update the payment process in the app so that the other group members can see it. Configuration changes require views, and only administrators should have permissions for the same.

Permissions and Roles

Configuration changes require views; only administrators should have permissions for the same. Let us generalize that idea a bit. There are a few functions in the application we developed.

A1. A person should be able to view her transactions and cannot view transactions not belonging to her.

A2. A few persons in the group can add administrators (we are yet to define who is an administrator).

A3. Some persons can add notes on how to clear the dues when the travel is over.

A4. Some persons in the group can mark if the payment for the pending dues is complete.

These are examples of privileges a person or a group of persons have. This is also called permissions. Every group member has the A1 privilege. A2, A3, and A4 are available to members with the administrator role. Software can have fixed roles or it can create more dynamic role mapping.

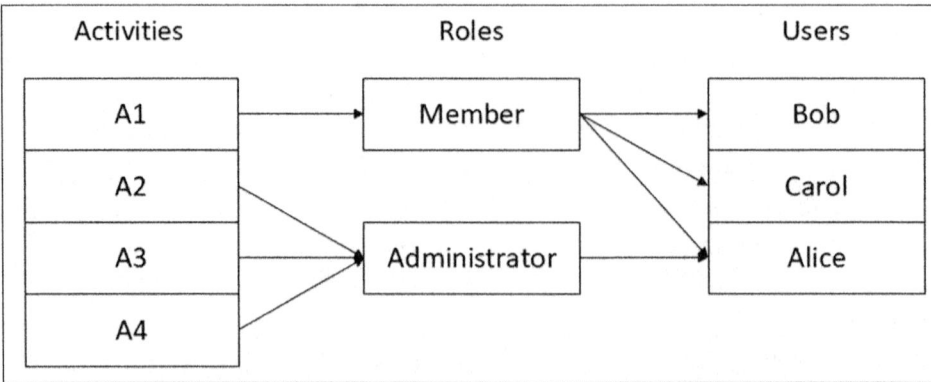

Figure 6.2: *Relationship of the activities, roles, and users*

We show the simplest form of Role Based Access Control (RBAC) in *Figure 6.2*. There are complex permissions, roles, and attributes to work on to provide the right level of privacy and security protections. Discerning readers should look at the NIST

User Persona and Profiles

User personas are business and demographic aspects of a group of users that would use a system. In our previous example, the user is an independent earning member, typically unmarried, and enjoys traveling with friends of similar age. The administrator is part of the same user population. Let us think of a school management system. Teachers and non-teaching staff are the users, including housekeeping, school peons, and so on. You have a school principal who is in her mid-forties or early fifties as the administrative head. She is a veteran in her subject but not so computer savvy. If you have to think of visual assistive technology in your application, the pages the principal uses may need focus. Similarly, the user personas of the janitor and the school peon will include their lack of formal education; they may be weak in English. So, their access pages must be made intuitive or should be translated into a local language.

However, **profiles** are more application-centric. In the school example, a class teacher manages a particular class[6] or batch of students. Students in her class will report their day-to-day needs, attendance, leave application, and so on to her. A subject teacher teaches one specific subject in the school. A mathematics teacher teaches mathematics. She is the only one who should be permitted to set up a math question paper for an examination. The application roles and permissions are associated with a user's profile. The user personas can be the guiding principles of the user interface.

In some systems, the management and administrator roles are considered overarching roles. A teacher has permission to conduct certain activities. A mathematics teacher who is a class teacher for the 5th-class students can only upload the mathematics question paper for 6th-class students. However, she cannot approve the leaves for a 6th-class student. The principal can do all these operations for all the classes. She has an overarching role in all the teachers' activities. Should she have the right to configure the email notification and server configuration settings or upgrade the system to new updates? In the user persona, we described the principal as having limited IT knowledge. Assigning such responsibility to her can lead to catastrophic consequences. Roles are not always hierarchical. An IT administrator should not access employee salary information, although they maintain the databases where such information is stored. With the advent of SaaS-based systems, IT administrators have limited access to the infrastructure platforms as they are in the vendor's control.

---

[4] Role-based Access Control, NIST Projects, **https://csrc.nist.gov/projects/role-based-access-control** accessed on 14 October 2024

[5] Attribute-based Access Control, NIST Projects, **https://csrc.nist.gov/Projects/attribute-based-access-control** on 14 October 2024

[6] Some cultures use synonyms like standard and grade.

Domains

Certain practices are prevalent in every domain. It is apparent when platforms are to integrate with a product upstream. Think of a web authentication platform, such as Login with Google, that Google provides for other consumer applications to integrate. Let us assume you want to read news on this new portal - **https://www.todaysnews.com**[7]. Today's news site wants to track who reads on their portal for better advertisement targeting and profiling. Asking the user to register is not beneficial, as users are tired of typing usernames and passwords at several websites. Remembering so many usernames and passwords is hard. They decide to integrate with Login with Google. A service that Google extends for third-party vendors to integrate. The users can log in to third-party sites using their Google username and password.

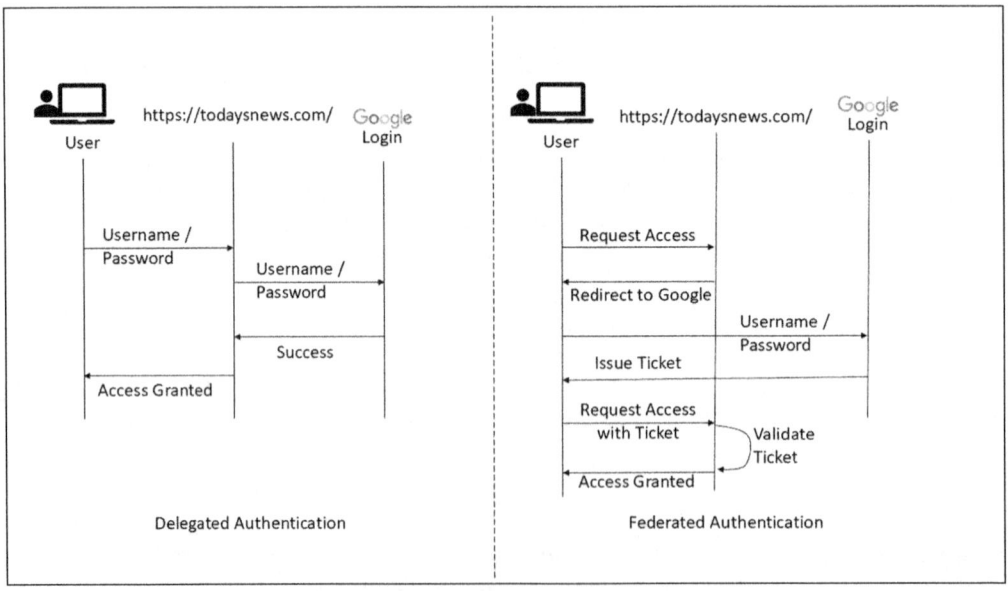

Figure 6.3: *Delegated vs federated authentication*

In the delegated authentication, you will enter the username and password on the news portal. The portal will send your username and password to Google. When Google authenticates your username and password, you will get access to the portal. Although it looks very simple to the end-user, will you be comfortable sharing your Google password with a third-party vendor? To overcome this, the authentication community came up with federated authentication[8].

- The user is redirected to Google to enter her username and password.
- Google collects and validates usernames and passwords.

---

[7] The site URL is fictitious and did not exist while writing this book.
[8] Sambit Kumar Dash, Ultimate Web Authentication Handbook, 2023, AVA Orange Publications

- Google issues a ticket for the browser to present to the news website for access.

The browser redirection changes the user experience; some people find the website switch annoying. Yet, it is a security measure that the industry has accepted. Today, payment gateways provide a similar experience to credit or debit card users. You do not have to share your card data with the online merchant. When you are redirected to the payment gateway vendor's site, you enter the card details on the payment gateway. Some experiences are like patterns; you can see the reflections in similar domains.

Culture

Culture and conditioning impact how we interact with the world. Most people in India prefer eating food with their hands. Using cutlery such as forks, knives, or spoons is uncommon in households. People who travel abroad for permanent residency sometimes enroll in finishing schools to understand Western table manners. Cutlery icons in the software may not work for Indians not exposed to Western education.

Figure 6.4: *A no-entry board with a green background is against normal conditioning*

A no-entry sign with a red background would have been apt for most people. Similarly, most Chinese people in the Western world would choose a second European-sounding[9] name. Indian names do not have a concept of First, Middle, and Last names. Indians have a family name often known as a Surname. A Given name differentiates an individual in the family. The surname does not appear at the end. Some cultures in

---
[9] Why Chinese speakers use Western names? **https://www.dw.com/en/why-some-chinese-speakers-also-use-western-names/a-18966907** accessed 15 October 2024

India use the surname first. A form that picks up Indian names can have Surname and Given name fields. While the Chinese may be comfortable with First, Middle, and Last names, Indian profile forms should have a field to display the full name rather than guessing the order. Moreover, some languages, such as Arabic and Persian, are written from right to left and ordered from top to bottom. Chinese, Vietnamese, Korean, and Japanese can be written from top to bottom and ordered from right to left. Hence, user interfaces developed for multilanguage support with these capabilities can have additional complexities. A person can experience many such examples while developing user experience for multi-cultural needs. Cultural preferences vary with education, travel, time, and willingness to adopt. The world is becoming way more cosmopolitan in its outlook than it was earlier. Business practices are understood, although adapted to suit the needs of another culture.

User Interface

The user interacts with a system through the user interface (UI). The Human-Computer Interface (HCI) is a generalization of a UI that encompasses how a person interacts with a computer. Similarly, the Graphical User Interface (GUI) is a specialized manifestation of UI on a graphical system. For example, a command-line interface can be a UI but not a GUI. The devices on which the system runs can dictate what the UI will be on such a system.

Screens and Devices

GUI depends on the size of the screens and capabilities of the underlying devices. We can classify the devices broadly into four categories.

- **Desktop and Laptop:** Typically used by professionals and academicians for work or academic pursuits. Some even use these for high-end games with enhanced graphics support. AI/ML applications can use high-end graphics systems for development and training on their GPUs. They have in-built or connected input devices, such as keyboards and mice. Some may have cameras and fingerprint sensors. Some screens may have touch panels for finger-based operations. The operating system can have an operating system, such as Microsoft Windows, Apple OS X, and Linux.
- **Tablets:** They are mid-size devices with flat screens. Generally, they have multitouch-sensitive screens for finger-touch-based navigation; an external mouse and keyboard can be connected. These are personal devices. Some professionals use them for work and academic interests. Students use them at school or home. They run Apple iOS, Google Android, or Chromebook as OS. Microsoft Surface running Microsoft Windows can fall into this category.
- **Mobile Phones:** This category has the largest number of devices. They have multitouch-sensitive screens for input. They have almost made digital cameras

redundant. Most people use these for communication, such as messaging, emails, video, phone, and so on, for work and personal use. The devices are generally not shared and can hold lots of private data for people. They have relatively less RAM or disk space than a desktop or laptop.

- **Others:** This category has the widest variety and represents anything that can connect to the Internet—the Internet of Things (IoT). It can include home automation systems, watches, CCTV cameras, televisions, refrigerators, industrial turbines, boilers, remotely managed water meters, and so on. These devices may or may not have graphical user interfaces; some may have command-line interfaces, and others may not have any user interface. Some may operate through voice or cameras as the only inputs available.

Discussing these devices as a broad category may seem futile as there are crossover use cases and devices. Describing their details is beyond the scope of our current work. Unlike laptops and desktops, all other devices can have sensors, such as GPS, compass, accelerometers, and so on. Some devices have better sensors for a particular purpose. For example, smartwatches can measure heart rate and walking steps better than a mobile phone. They can discern the activities better[10]. However, mobile phone cameras can be way better than a camera on a laptop.

Technology

Let us look at *Figure* 5.3 again. Edge devices interact with users as web applications and native applications. Native applications are more popular with mobile platforms, while desktop applications are web applications. A classic native application hosted the data on the end device. It had a database or a file locally to modify and render, think of using Microsoft Word to edit a document. The modern Microsoft Office 365 for Web is a browser-based application that stores the file on the Internet; it accesses, downloads, and renders part of the document as and when needed. Applications are becoming data-intensive, and a large part of the data is analyzed on a server in the cloud. The smallest LLM can take several megabytes of energy[11] for training. Training on edge devices is not possible. Edge devices can access the inferred results by contacting the servers through APIs. In an e-commerce application, a shopping list is on the server based on the search filters; they are continuously shown on the edge devices. The results of the search operations are downloaded to the edge devices through APIs. For example, when the user scrolls on a mobile device with the last item on the screen, a fresh API call is made to download further data from the server to update the UI. The web architecture has shifted to developing single-page applications (SPA)[12]. The edge

---

[10] Alessandra Angelucci, Stefano Canali, and Andrea Aliverti, Digital technologies for step counting: between promises of reliability and risks of reductionism, Front Digit Health. 2023 Dec 13;5:1330189. doi: 10.3389/fdgth.2023.1330189

[11] Meta AI, LLaMA: Open and Efficient Foundation Language Models, arXiv:2302.13971

[12] Chapter 1, *Supra* 7

device downloads the client rendering code and contacts the server to update the data when required. Flutter, React Native, Angular, and so on are popular frameworks for developing such applications for web and mobile applications. The application developers know that data may not be available when launching an application. The user interfaces have to be designed with this in mind. One of the ways to experience this is to connect your web browser to YouTube. After you load the web page, disconnect the network connection. A classic web application cannot render such a user interface. Those applications download page-by-page from the Internet and update the content when the page is loaded. A disconnection would mean the page cannot be downloaded and the browser cannot render the content.

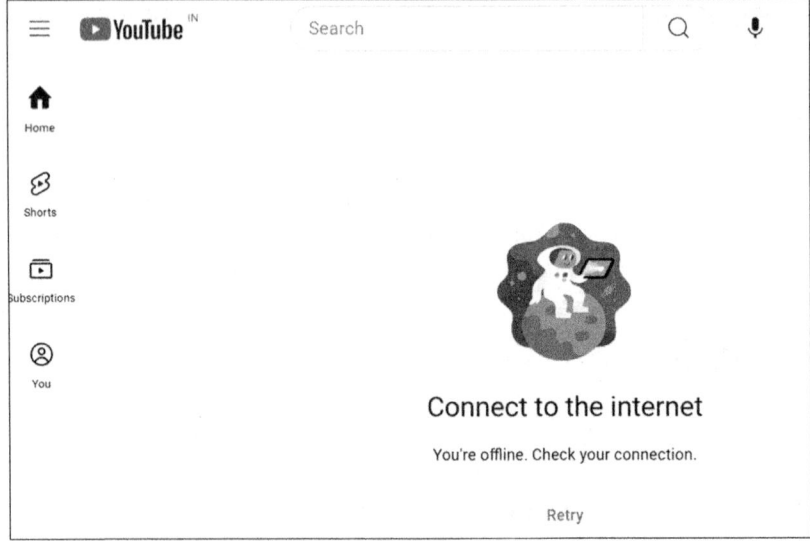

Figure 6.5: The web app captures YouTube web disconnection

In the SPAs, parts of the page are downloaded by making several REST API calls to the backend servers. The code can efficiently update only the part of the page that has received new data. For example, when you scroll up a shopping list, data is fed continuously from the API to update the screen, while the shopping cart and toolbar may remain static with no updates. While such nuances are easy with native client apps, the web apps needing server-side rendering are used to carry out many structural changes to the apps to achieve this. Many SaaS vendors provide reusable services that others can use in their applications. Some of these services are a collection of several complex services. They are essentially platforms. Amazon AWS, Microsoft Azure, Google, and so on are some of these platform vendors.

Platform and API

Platform vendors experience some of the most challenges in designing their user interfaces. Some vendors provide purely API services. These services have no user interface. The integrating application can collect the data and render its user interface. These UIs are easier to design. Other applications trigger a platform workflow from their user interface. In *Figure* 6.3 in the Federation Authentication example, when the user transitions from **https://todaysnews.com** to Google for authentication, the user should feel the transition is legitimate. If Google's user interface could show or mention Today's News on its page, that would make the user feel more confident. The payment gateway integrations face a similar design concern.

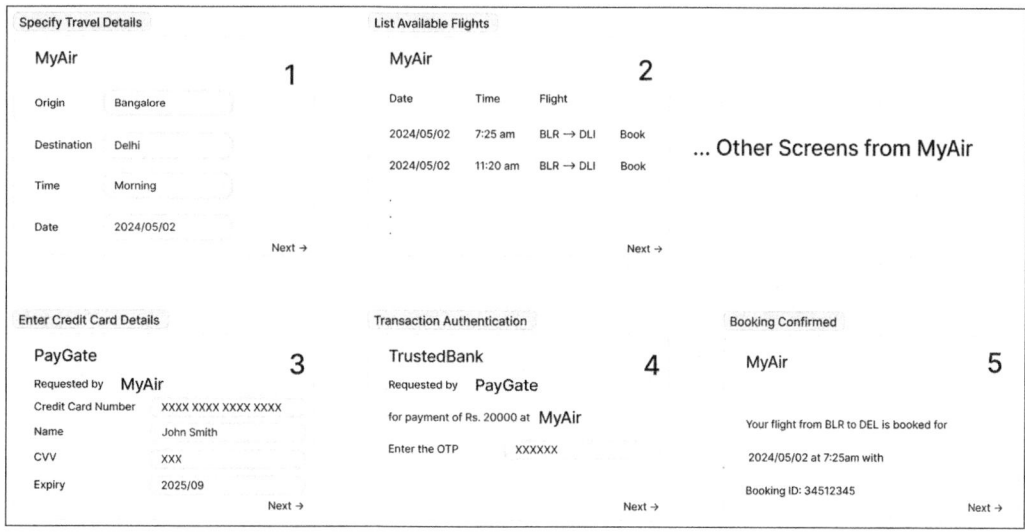

Figure 6.6: *An indicative airline booking system with payment gateway integration*

In *Figure* 6.6, An indicative airline booking system with payment gateway integration, we have some screen outlines.

1. The users enter the travel details on MyAir's website.

2. They get a list of travel options and a few other inputs (not shown) on MyAir's website. When they enter the data, they are redirected to the payment gateway at PayGate.

3. Here, PayGate has to expect the users to enter their credit card number, name, expiry month, and CVV to validate they are in physical possession of the card. When the data is validated, the user is redirected to the issuing bank (TrustedBank) portal to authenticate the transaction. PayGate also informs the user that MyAir is requesting the payment.

4. TrustedBank will show the user the amount requested by the gateway with the purpose. The user enters the OTP received through SMS and approves the transaction.

5. On completion of the transaction, MyAir shows the success or failure of the transaction.

Steps 3 and 4 are platform user interfaces. They cannot be sure of upstream or downstream user interfaces. Following a step-by-step user journey-based design may not help in these cases. It is ideal to think of these as steps that can be integrated with any form of Web UI - a redirect, an embedded iframe, and so on.

Not only is the user interface complex due to the involvement of a large number of parties in the interaction, but also the transaction has to be secured, and all successes and failures have to be tracked for failsafe operations. Here are the challenges:

1. MyAir ensures the payment is complete before issuing the tickets.

2. If a payment transaction fails, PayGate needs to report accurately to MyAir.

3. Think of a payment completion at step 4, yet the user's connection snapped. MyAir cannot issue the ticket and has to let the user know that the ticket is on hold while the payment is processed. At this point, MyAir can ask the user to complete the payment using an alternate method after some time.

4. MyAir initiated the transaction; the users will contact MyAir's support team to update the status. The exact details of payment failure are not relevant to MyAir's support team, but when they escalate the issue to PayGate, PayGate needs to verify the reasons more accurately. If TrustedBank deducted the money, they have to revert the incomplete transaction.

These are some high-level use cases we considered for the user interface. A detailed analysis of the federated authorization system needs to be worked upon. Some such scenarios are reviewed by industry experts and standardized, such as OAuth or OIDC protocols[13]. While designing the platform's user experience, one must consider its supportability, log reporting, transaction tracking, and other related issues. Some of these may be textual information.

Let us look at a multimodal user interface scenario. Suppose MyAir ties up with a digital assistant provider such as Alexa and allows airline booking through that.

1. Now, a user will state: *"Alexa, book a flight for me from Bangalore to Delhi for tomorrow morning."*

2. Alexa will provide all the options; the user chooses the flight.

3. Since payment options on voice cannot be as secured, the user is sent a link through a messaging channel.

4. The user clicks on the link and opens the browser; steps 3 and 4 kick in.

5. The user completes the task by providing the necessary credit card details.

---

[13] Chapter 5, Supra 7

A good platform design can address the needs of a multimodal user interface.

Knowledge Dissemination

Will documentation fall into the user experience? Today, most people agree that users need good documentation for a successful product. We will extend the scope of user experience further to include complete user education. While documentation is confined to using a product and its basic functionalities, user education goes much further to create an ecosystem for the user to use platforms effectively. Let us take the C language. In the 1970s, Dennis Ritchie developed a high-level programming language to program system software. The C compiler shipped with every Unix operating system. The functions and commands of the C language shipped as manual pages. However, every C programmer would refer to The C Programming Language[14] book. User education requires programmers to read a book of programming to understand and get habituated to programming concepts. In the past fifty years, understanding programming has become far more complex. There are programming languages, libraries written around them, APIs developed around them, and programmer's playgrounds for quickly writing and running simple programs. In the case of AI/ML, vendors are offering courses on the techniques. The users apply these techniques to develop complex AI applications using the tools and platforms offered. Every vendor offering a platform today provides a holistic application development experience to ensure the user understands the APIs clearly. API documentation auto-generated from code during compilation and associated playgrounds to try the APIs as you read the documentation has become the norm for most platforms. The world has not stopped at in-context documentation. In-context videos, tutorials, and workflows (What's new after every upgrade) guide users through tasks they want to accomplish with the product. Overall, user education or aids for the product are integral parts of the product user interface.

Accessibility

Over 285 million people have impaired vision, 275 million have hearing issues, and many others have mild to severe cognitive disorders[15]. Any application developed for mass acceptability should have accessibility guidelines. The US government mandated through law that ICT services offered by the US government to its citizens must cater to certain accessibility guidelines. All of these are considered Section 508[16] requirements. While the guidelines are elaborate, we state some general directions that should be practiced by user interface developers. Here are some examples:

- Use platform controls and UI components rather than introducing complex custom rendering schemes.

---

[14] Brian Kernighan and Dennis Ritchie, The C Programming Language,
[15] Accessibility Training: Introduction to Accessibility and Section 508, **https://hhs.gov**
[16] **https://www.section508.gov/**

- While using colors to highlight UI, introduce textual information that conveys the information. Thus, a screen reader can read the data.
- Text size changes in the OS should be honored by the application.
- The application should support high-contrast viewing modes.
- Screen readers cannot read complex tabular structures accurately.

Web Content Accessibility Guidelines (WCAG 2.0) are developed by W3C[17] to assist web applications to comply with accessibility needs.

Tools and Frameworks

Tools are only as good as the users who use them. We are not admirers of any specific tool or its use in any UX discussion. However, if you find any tool that improves productivity and effective communication of your experiences, it is advantageous to use them. Till about five years ago, most UX were graphical. The product managers visualized the user interactions and conveyed them to customers, engineers, and so on. Before the UX tools became popular, here are the steps most product teams followed:

1. Work with customers or pick-up interactions from the market.
2. Whiteboard the interaction with graphics artists and web developers to create static vs. dynamic mockups.
3. Explain the mockups to stakeholders for review and feedback.
4. Work with engineering to build a prototype or product depending on the complexity.

The product development and release cycles have been compressed from over a year to a few months to a fortnight. Active users can provide feedback as soon as a product is released. A popular mechanism for testing user acceptance of a new feature is **A/B testing**. In this method, a change in the user interface is shown to a random representative sample of users. User interactions with the live systems are analyzed, and user preferences are studied. The change acceptable to a statistically significant sample becomes final. With the advances in AI, **eyeball tracking** through a camera has become easy. We can study the user's focus. Technology companies have been developing physical devices to monitor eyeballs in retail stores. With eyeball tracking users on e-commerce portals, a platform can monitor users' focus on the screen and show them the items they seek in the focused location. However, the challenge remains in convincing a user to switch on the camera. It is probably ok for a fashion brand selling fashion accessories to ask users to switch on the camera; they can try fashion accessories virtually on their face. Others have to find unique ways to deal

---

[17] **https://www.w3.org/WAI/standards-guidelines/wcag/**

with these privacy requirements. They can try these trials on test users and generate statistics and AI-assisted **heatmaps** to extrapolate on real users. Link-tracking tools help track the navigation sequences the customer followed to the intended pages and targets. These can be analyzed and optimized for better UX design. GitHub Spark[18] uses AI to build web application prototypes with natural language. While AI will meet the ideation needs of the future, let us look at some of the classic tools used today.

Ideation and Expression

Good designs start with ideation. When you have to implement the idea yourself, you need no tools to express it. You could work on it and deliver the final product. However, in a collaborative world with lots of stakeholders, better visualization and expression of the design are needed. Tools only help in that aspect. The design depends on the designer's ingenuity.

Figma

Almost all the diagrams in this chapter have been developed using Microsoft Excel and Microsoft PowerPoint. It is perfectly alright to build the user experience using the tools you are most comfortable with. However, Figma[19] has been recognized as the UI designer tool of choice in the last few years. Hence, we thought of introducing it in this chapter. We created Figure 6.6 using Figma FigJam. FigJam is a collaboration, interaction design, or brainstorming tool that helps create explainable visual representations. FigJams can be collaboratively edited and commented on, making it easy for a software development team to interact in design brainstorming. Figure 6.6 has lots of limitations. For example, there are no dropdowns in the Origin and Destination fields. There is no date picker calendar or a proper time control widget. It is ok to have the brainstorming output as informal. We are yet not convinced if we will create a web page for screens 1 and 2 or implement it in a chatbot interface. In such a case, focusing too much detail on the graphical user interface may not be relevant. However, once we decide to develop a web or mobile application, Figma provides the design interface. Here, we can design the pixel-accurate GUI needed for our applications. There are various form factors, such as Android and iOS screens and Web pages for various screen sizes. There are templates for UI controls. Color schemes can be created at an organizational level. All the teams may have to use the same template in all their products. As in FigJams, collaborative editing and reviewing options are available in the design interface. Animations can be set up on the screens so that one can experience transitions from one screen to another and present a mockup for review. Developers can export Figma designs into stylesheets and use them in application development. Lastly, Figma has created an ecosystem for developers, designers, and organizations.

---

[18] GitHub Spark lets you build web apps in plain English, **https://techcrunch.com/2024/10/29/github-spark-lets-you-build-web-apps-in-plain-english/**
[19] **https://www.figma.com**

They can create libraries of their designs, templates, color schemes, tools, and so on that others can use for a fee. While PMs may not edit UX designs, they may still review them. The tools are available with freemium licenses for easy use and adoption.

Material Design

When applications are sensitive to user experiences, platforms cannot be too far away. The windowing system came into existence about three to four decades ago. With some initial hiccups, they standardized the windowing behavior with Common Desktop Environment in the early 1990s. The desktop windows are on each other with a certain pseudo-depth perception. A window created first is shown on the desktop. When another window is created, it shows above the old window, as if the old window is behind the new window. However, you cannot say how far in the depth axis the new window is from the old one. When you are rendering in two dimensions, that information is not relevant. Unlike the desktop windows, the mobile app windows overlap like stacked cards. Till you remove the top card, you cannot access the lower ones. When Google introduced the Google Glass interface, they had to design a UI for a projected screen on the human eye. There is a need to introduce actual depth into the design. That is how Material Design[20] came into existence. Every UI element has physical material in a Material Design. They not only have height and width but also have thickness or depth. So when we say Window 1 overlaps Window 2, there is a distance between them. And depending on the lighting, a shadow of Window 1 falls over Window 2. Windowing was one of the many strong assumptions of the Material Design. However, the design affects fonts, accessibility, user interaction in the 3D world, and so on. Most design tools, such as Figma, provide libraries that cater to an application compatible with Material Design, reducing the designer's efforts from these intricacies. Material design has been evolving quite rapidly; version 3 is the latest.

Delivery

In the previous section, we reviewed ways to ideate and express them to the team. Here, we put the design to development and deliver a product. As much as design tools are relevant and effective, good development and prototyping tools make application development easy and consistent.

Flutter Framework

Flutter[21] is a front-end development framework that renders high-quality graphics on client or edge devices. It is an open-source framework developed by Google. Application developers write applications in Dart Programming Language. The code is platform-agnostic. The compilers can generate binaries for the Web, iOS, Android, Linux, and

---

[20] Material Design v1 **https://m1.material.io/**
[21] **https://flutter.dev/**

Windows platforms. Declarative programming makes it easy for application developers to build applications. Hence, they can use these tools for rapid prototyping. Moreover, the framework supports single-page applications (SPA), reactive programming, and so on. While Angular, React, and React native are for web and mobile apps, Flutter covers almost all major client platforms. Flutter has widgets available for Material UI for applications to provide a consistent style across platforms. Flutter applications can support native applications of the Apple iOS Cupertino style.

Design Thinking

We looked at user experience and felt the need for better product design. However, designing a product is not only about great user experience. There is a need to go under the surface to get an in-depth understanding. Thomas Edison is quoted as the father of design thinking[22]. His innovations included the electric bulb and a periphery of other inventions that contributed to making electricity an industry. Some consider design thinking as an innovation and problem-solving method[23]. They propose six stages to the process:

1. Understanding
2. Observation
3. Synthesis
4. Ideas
5. Prototype testing
6. Implementation

While we will not elaborate on every step, early prototyping testing and receiving customer feedback are important aspects of the design thinking process. It also relies on agile teamwork, which we will review in a later chapter. The collaborative elements of design thinking should create more ideas and discussions to build a better thought-out product. For example, in a large organization, the frontline support team caters to all the products; they may not have an understanding of your specific product. If your product requires substantial initial handholding, you must insist on professional service engagements for deployment. The frontline support should be able to guide the customer to the right team so that professional services can be provided. A product manager can contact frontline support as a pseudo customer and walk through the process to ensure it is streamlined.

---

[22] Tim Brown, Design Thinking, HBR, June 2008
[23] Combelles, A.; Ebert, C.; Lucena, P.; Design Thinking, IEEE Software, Mar/Apr 2020

Conclusion

User experience can encompass many things in our day-to-day lives. A user of your application will have certain opinions, particularly on the user interfaces. While the user interface is an element of the user experience, it is not everything. The business case, audience maturity, environment, culture, and so on play a significant role. Complete design thinking helps understand the customer needs better and provides solutions that can be of value to everyone. While we discussed many topics, our coverage has only scratched the surface. We hope the readers can relate the discussed topics to their practical experiences and focus on the specific areas they want to explore as part of their practical implementations. With this chapter, we tamed the bargaining buyer. Next, we will review how to manage the bargaining suppliers.

Questions

1. Consider a few products of your choice and see on which devices they are not supported. Try to rationalize why it is fair not to support those devices.

2. A few fashion e-commerce brands went mobile only and eventually rolled back to support web-based storefronts. Analyze why such a reversal was needed.

3. Consider a screen of your application and study how the views represent various data elements. How will you rationalize the views when you move from a laptop to a mobile form factor?

4. In *Table 6.1*, you decide to capture the expenses of Alice, Bob, and Carol on themselves. How will their views change?

5. Write a chatbot interface for booking a flight from City A to B. How will you integrate payments with a credit card?

CHAPTER 7
Contracts

Introduction

We discussed the challenges of addressing bargaining buyers as an external force with pricing, customers, and user experience. Now, we move on to the force: **bargaining suppliers**. With suppliers, you have reversed your role. You are the customer and want to ensure your suppliers consistently meet your needs. Your suppliers are trying to impress you with all the processes relevant to buyers we have discussed. You want to ensure they adhere to their commitments and that their operations are consistent. You want to formalize the obligations into a contract. That is the subject matter of discussion here. You will learn the elements of a contract, the limitations, the buyer and seller relationships, conditions and warranties, and so on. We will explore the commercial aspects more than the legal aspects.

Structure

In this chapter, we will cover the following topics:

- Basis of Contract
- Implied versus Express
- Jurisdiction
- Enforcement
- Performance
- Specific Needs for the Software Industry

Basis of Contract

The economic advancement of the human race is often attributed to scientific discoveries and industrial revolutions. However, the scale of the advancements would not have been possible without the concepts of juristic persons and their internal and external interactions. In short, the human mind developed systems and processes leading to large organizations, associations of persons, and democratic governments that are artificial. These are known as **artificial juristic persons**. These persons are defined only in the legal systems and allowed to sue or be sued. They operate as one entity and interact with each other to accomplish their common goals. We define rules and regulations for them.

Natural persons to live on the earth in a dignified manner require a set of basic rights. The United Nations identified some of these and outlined part of the charter of **human rights**. Some of these are guiding principles of the **fundamental rights** of the Constitution of India. The **Supreme Court of India** is duty-bound to protect the fundamental rights of a citizen or resident. Indian governance is built on three pillars: the legislative formulates the law, the executive implements it, and the judiciary interprets the laws in the case of a conflict. The **judicial interpretation** is final. Everyone, an artificial judicial or a natural person, in the territory of India is bound by the orders of the courts. Some behaviors are considered deviant; the state considers them crimes against the state and society. They are part of a **criminal justice system**. Typical criminal laws are applied as State vs. defendant.

All laws other than criminal laws are considered **civil laws**. They come into the picture when there is a dispute and case against another person and there is no criminal intent. Some civil laws are based on a person's faith, beliefs, culture, and religion; some examples are marriage, divorce, adoption, inheritance, and succession. These are the subject matter of **personal or family laws**. It is impractical for a government to assess every interaction between parties and define laws. Hence, they give flexibility to people to establish their lawful interaction framework. For example, the Hindu Succession Act of India has defined ways to distribute the properties. However, if a person wants to deviate from it, he can create a Will under the Indian Succession Act. Contracts are a lawful framework for two parties to create mutual obligations and commitments under the Indian Contracts Act. Two parties can establish a contract on any lawful subject. Although contracts can be defined for all aspects of civil laws, we will only look at contracts relevant to commercial laws and sales and purchases of goods.

Laws are jurisdiction-based. Indian law is not applicable in the UK or USA. However, legal principles have commonalities across geographies. Most legal systems follow either civil law or common law principles. **Civil law**[1] countries such as France, Spain, Japan, and China, prefer codified law credence over anything else. **Common law**[2] countries, such as the UK, USA, and India, do not expect the law to be codified fully. For example, in India, the courts can consider all these sources of law:

- The Indian Constitution
- The legislatures are approved by the central parliament or state assembly.

---

[1] Civil law systems are different concepts from the civil law vs. criminal law distinction we discussed earlier. Civil law systems are linked to the Roman civilization. Hence, they are also known as Roman or Justinian Legal Systems.

[2] Most countries under British Common Wealth use common law principles. They have a history with British Law and some sections of their laws are similar.

- Interpretation of laws by High Courts and Supreme Court of India in previously decided cases.
- Rules and regulations developed by designated institutions, such as the Reserve Bank of India (RBI), can create rules for all banking activities.
- Judgments and orders passed by subject matter tribunals, such as Income Tax Tribunals' decisions on Income Tax-related issues.
- International treaties and agreements India is party to.
- Commonly used practices that are not codified.

While we will refer to the Indian Contract Act of 1872 in our discussion, similar legislation exists in the laws of other countries.

Definition

The basic tenets of a contract rely on the following steps:[3]

- A promisor agrees to do something or abstains from doing something and proposes it to the promisee.
- The promisee accepts the proposal and agrees to compensate the promisor with consideration.
- An agreement consists of several such agreed-upon promises.
- An agreement enforceable by law is a contract.

An agreement that is not enforceable by law is void. Sometimes, an agreement may seem lawful for a few parties (A) but unlawful for another set of parties (B). If needed, B can claim the contract is void. These are called voidable contracts. A contract could be valid when it was entered into. It is possible that as the law changed over time, the contract became void.

Parties to Contract

Any legal person over the age of majority, in sound mind, and not barred by any law, can be a party to a contract. The definition of a legal person extends to both natural and juristic persons, such as companies, associations of persons, trusts, and more. In the case of a juristic person, a natural person signs or accepts a contract. Such a person must be able to sign contracts on behalf of the organization. Otherwise, such a person has acted **ultra vires** or beyond his legal limits. Some contracts mandate the signatory be ratified by the board resolution to be authorized to make decisions related to the contract. Parties enter into contractual relationships voluntarily; the obligations are created by their choices. The civil obligations due to tort or trust laws

---
[3] Section 2, Indian Contracts Act, 1872

are non-voluntary; they are not contracts[4]. Parties must understand the agreement the same way and provide their free consent, which means, there is no:

- Coercion,
- Undue Influence,
- Fraud,
- Misrepresentation, and
- Mistake

in them consenting to the agreement[5]. All the terms are defined in the act.

In some contracts, one of the parties can take a dominant position and coerce or put undue influence on the other party to agree to their terms. The governments recognize such situations and enact legislatures to create a balancing act. For example, in the case of employment contracts, the governments realize an organization has more control over an individual. In the Industrial Disputes Act[6], the governments suggest collective bargaining by establishing an Employee's Union. Similarly, an individual consumer finds a hard bargain with a large corporation when buying goods. The Consumer Protections Act[7] provides a simpler redressal mechanism in such cases. Even a state or central government can be a party to a contract. These contracts will be assumed to be executed by the heads of the state (governor) or the Union of India (President). They can nominate a person for the contracts. However, no one will be personally liable for the contracts[8].

Some contracts are inherently **multiparty**; for example, a **contract of indemnity**[9]. A Seller (S) and Buyer (B) got into an agreement to sell and buy certain future goods. B paid an advance to S. At this point, S has not delivered any goods to B. How can S establish a trust with B? S asks a Banker (Bk) to issue a bank guarantee for the advance amount to B. Anytime B does not feel confident about S's ability to deliver the goods, she can submit the bank guarantee to Bk and recover her paid advance. This is one of the tri-party agreements as a contract of indemnity. Banks will not look at the merits of B's claims. Let's change the scenario involving an insurance company indemnifying damaged goods. B uses the services of an Insurance Company (IC) to indemnify if damaged goods are delivered to its premises. S will contact IC's staff and submit the goods to a transporter under their guidance. When the goods reach B, B finds some damaged goods on delivery. B asks IC to recover the damage. IC's inspectors verify and agree to indemnify the damages. Let us add a transporter into the equation. S is using the services of a transporter (T) to send some perishable goods to B. Due to

---
[4] Avtar Singh, Law of Contract and Specific Relief, 5th ed., 2009
[5] Section 14, Supra 3
[6] Industrial Disputes Act, 1947, Government of India
[7] Consumer Protection Act, 1986, Government of India
[8] Article 299, The Constitution of India
[9] Section 124, Supra 3

floods, T cannot use the normal route to deliver the goods to B. There will be delays due to the alternate route; the goods will lose their shelf life. Can T sell the goods in the open market and cover some losses for S? These are categorized under a **bailment** contract[10]. Many transportation contracts have bailment clauses.

In most sales situations, we deal with resellers or partners to buy most products. Only a few manufacturers have exclusive showrooms where consumers can buy their goods directly from the manufacturer. Most shops where retailers buy the goods act as agents of the manufacturers. The buyer pays the agent to purchase the goods. However, the manufacturer can offer support services in their exclusive service stations. In some cases, agents provide support services. The **agent contracts**[11] are multiparty agreements. In the case of white-leveled goods, the seller rebrands the goods in their name. The customer never gets to know about the manufacturer. The customer expects the seller to provide all after-sales support services. This is a classic case of an agent contract with an **undisclosed principal**[12].

We discussed a few special contractual agreements between parties. Some acts are carved out from the law of contracts and made part of specific laws, such as the Sale of Goods Act[13].

Sale of Goods

Even Sales of Goods is a special purpose contract with the following concepts.

- It is a contract between a buyer and a seller to transfer movable properties among them.
- The consideration is monetary only and also known as the price.
- The contract can be for specific goods that the buyer wants to acquire by paying the agreed price to the seller.
- The goods can be future goods the seller would deliver at a stipulated time.
- Payment trails can be separated from goods delivered.

A typical buying process looks like this:

- A buyer places a purchase order (PO) with the pricing and payment terms and schedules. The pricing information should include taxes.
- It also has details of the process of goods delivery.
- The conditions and warranties of the goods are also mentioned.

---

[10] Section 148, Supra 3
[11] Section 182, Supra 3
[12] Section 230, Supra 3
[13] The Sales of Goods Act, 1930

- The seller accepts the PO and agrees to supply according to the terms and conditions mentioned. A formal sales order (SO) can be used to accept the PO.
- Now, the seller can invoice the buyers to pay.
- The goods delivery notes signify the goods delivered.

The documentation can vary based on the types of goods, transport used, taxation, and internal processes involved. Before we delve further into the sales process, can software be classified as goods? While the acts are not explicit, the case laws[14] have accepted that canned software on medium (CD-ROM, USB drive, and so on) are goods. They also take away the non-tangibility part of the software and provide a test.

A 'goods' may be a tangible property or an intangible one. It would become goods provided it has the attributes thereof having regard to (a) its utility; (b) capable of being bought and sold; and (c) capable of transmitted, transferred, delivered, stored, and possessed. If a software, whether customized or non-customized, satisfies these attributes, the same would be goods.

The Software as a Service (SaaS) model is most common today. SaaS products have utility and are saleable. In point (c), we have challenges. The transfer, transmission, and delivery are unlike canned software delivery. Rather than transferring the software to a customer's control location, the customer's data is transmitted and transferred into the SaaS software. The delivery does not mean a physical delivery of software as a means of media or download; a virtual space is created in the software vendor's environment for the customer. Only the customer has access to the space. Stored and possessed signifies that storage is created for the customer's data, and the access is granted to them. Such arguments cannot be relied upon as no judicial interpretation is available so far. Ultimately, a sale agreement is a contract. Some organizations append the relevant provisions of the Sales of Goods Act and create an agreement under the Indian Contracts Act as a **Software as a Service Agreement**. We will discuss some of the compliance requirements of SaaS products later in a subsequent chapter.

The Central Goods and Services Tax Act[15] distinguishes goods from services. Schedule II considers temporary transfer or permitting the use or enjoyment of any intellectual property right as a service. Hence, SaaS products are to be licensed as services. The service account codes (SAC)[16] typically used are: Licensing services for the right to use computer software and databases (997331), Licensing services for the right to use other intellectual property products and other resources nowhere else classified (997339), or Software Downloads (998434). Similarly, custom software development and consulting are always considered services. Only software delivered on a media is classified as goods under the Harmonized System of Nomenclature (HSN) code

---

[14] Tata Consultancy Services vs. State of AP, 5th Nov. 2004, AIR 2005 SUPREME COURT 371
[15] Schedule II, The Central Goods and Services Act (2017), Union of India
[16] Annexure: Scheme of Classification of Services, CBIT and Customers, Government of India

Information Technology Software (85238020)[17]. GST Acts consider SaaS products as services.

Tenders

Any reasonable-sized purchase process involves tenders. When it comes to the government, the process is more elaborate and involved. There are requests for comment (RFC), requests for proposal (RFP), requests for quotation (RFQ), and so on. The buyers seek vendors to understand the requirements and submit their solution proposals. Buyers, through a competitive bidding process, understand the solutions available and tentative pricing. Can these be considered proposals for a contract? The bidding process is an invitation to treat, which means the buyers will select vendors based on the bidding information they submit. They will negotiate and finally submit a purchase order. The purchase order is the starting point of the contract proposal. However, a tendering process is needed to be fair. Particularly in government tenders, several criteria are set to ensure no party gets an unfair advantage. The governments publish clear guidelines[18] for the procurement process for various goods and services. A procurement process involves a decision-making committee whose decision is considered final. Such a committee should follow the **principles of natural justice** to ensure a free and fair assessment of the bidding process based on the criteria set up for selection. The principle requires the following processes:

- Every participant should be allowed to state their views.
- The decisions should not be biased.
- There should be proper reasoning associated with the decisions.

Lawful Subject Matter

A contract can be made for lawful subjects. A contract that violates any law is considered void. For example, the contract of instructing another person to commit a criminal activity for consideration is bad in law. The same applies to civil law cases as well. Here are some examples:

- Larger companies must clear the dues within specific timelines when they buy goods and services from a registered Micro, Small, or Medium Enterprise (MSME). When they fail to pay on time, they cannot claim the MSME expenses in their income tax filing. The timelines of payment obligations are determined by the law[19]. A contract cannot extend it.

---

[17] CMA Bhogavalli Mallikarjuna Gupta, All About HSN Codes in GST, TAX BULLETIN AUGUST, 2021 VOLUME - 94 - THE INSTITUTE OF COST ACCOUNTANTS OF INDIA

[18] Manual for Procurement of Consultancy services, 2024, Second Edition, Government of India Ministry of Finance Department of Expenditure

[19] Section 34B(h), The Income Tax Act, 1961, Government of India

- There are two software product developers, A and B. Both are fierce competitors in the domain. B's customer contract does not permit the customer to decompile or use evasive means to decode their product implementation. A engages an external party, C, to license B's products and analyze using reverse engineering techniques, including de-compilation, and so on, to understand the product's internal implementation. Can A and C engage in such business relationships?

- Can a company that raises public investments for its operations pay a bribe to anyone? Technically, a company has contracts with all its investors to conduct a lawful business. The investors can file suits against a company if such unlawful activities are detected. Moreover, the entities authorized to raise public money under the law are scrutinized for the lawful application of the funds collected.

A violation of law cannot be wished away or delegated by a contract. As a general guideline, if you cannot do it yourself, you cannot have an agent do it.

Implied vs. Express

Should all contracts be written and signed? The contract law does not mandate an expression. If the contract is expressed in words, it is a contract with **expression**. The contract entered into by action is called an **implied** contract[20]. Let us understand through an example. You get on a bus and ask for a ticket to a location. The conductor asks you for some money, and you pay the money. There is a valid contract where the bus has agreed to take you to a destination, and you have paid the consideration in cash. This is an implied contract; you accept it by paying the money. The ticket, online bank transfer proof, and similar items can act as artifacts or evidential value for the transaction but are not needed for the contract per se. Fellow passengers as witnesses are just pieces of evidence.

The travel example we considered is transactional and only relevant as long as you are on the bus. However, business relationships can last for several years. Several transitions may happen over the period. It can change several hands. The people who negotiated the contract can be different from those who would execute it. Hence, a written agreement will be needed. An association of persons, such as a company, is a separate legal entity from its promoters or management. In business, there is always a need to ascertain the human decision-makers involved in the agreement. If needed, the law would like to make the decision-makers personally liable if the decision was taken with malice. The concept is known as **lifting the corporate veil**. The signing of the agreement signifies the decision-maker involved in the agreement. For an artificial juristic person, a person officially approved by the **articles of association** or through

---

[20] Section 9, Supra 3

a board resolution can only sign agreements. The other parties to the agreement may ask for a resolution proving the signer's authority.

Let us talk about a business-to-consumer product like Gmail. There are almost 2.5 billion active users of the platform[21]. Each user is an independent entity in herself. When any of these users sign up for the services, Google needs to create a business association with each of these individuals. The users will share their data with Google. Google has to commit that their data will be safe in Google's hands. As a consideration, the users will allow Google to mine and profile the user data to serve them advertisements and other personalized services. Google can share these profiles with their partners and business associates. All these will be the subject matter of an End-User License Agreement, essentially a contract signed with every user of the Gmail service. Google cannot spend legal resources creating a bespoke agreement for every customer. They will form a **standard form contract** for all the users. For the customer, there is hardly any choice. If they wish to use the service, they must accept the agreement. Hence, these are also called **contracts of adhesion**. Generally, contracts of adhesion are liberally interpreted as one party proposes; the other party has almost no choice. Consent means all parties agree to the same thing in the same sense. The parties should consent freely, devoid of coercion, undue influence, fraud, misrepresentation, and mistake. In the example, Google is more powerful than the average user. Suppose litigation comes to the court related to the End-user License Agreement of Gmail. The court understands such contracts will be contracts of adhesion in nature. Of all the other things the court will analyze, the judges may assess the contract for:

- If the user read and understood the contract.
- If the user actively accepted the contract.
- If Google did not act in any manner that sabotaged the free consent of the user.

Organizations try innovative means to prove users read and accept the agreement. They send reminders through email, highlight the agreement sections that have changed from the previous iteration, force the user to scroll to the bottom of the contract before accepting, block the user from using the software unless they accept, and so on. Sometimes, the PMs struggle with the user experience due to these artificial restrictions on the application. Since the user has to click an accept button or select a checkbox, these contracts are also called **click-through** agreements. Even though the users read and accept the contract, they may not understand the finer legal details. Hence, governments bring legislation and ensure the organizations meet the required guidelines. Thus, the user is not at the receiving end of a commercial agreement. The

---

[21] Davey Winder, Gmail Privacy Alert For 2.5 Billion Users—Is Someone Reading Your Email?, Forbes, 4th Nov. 2024, **https://www.forbes.com/sites/daveywinder/2024/11/04/gmail-privacy-alert-for-25-billion-users-is-someone-reading-your-email/** accessed on 5th December 2024

European Union (EU) introduced the Digital Markets Act (DMA) and General Data Protection Regulations (GDPR) to protect and maintain the privacy of users' data. As PM, it is a good idea to review an agreement to ensure there is no violation of elements of free consent.

Let us look at another aspect of an electronic document. If the court raises a question on the user reading and accepting the EULA, the software vendor will show its internal processes, how it captures and retains the user acceptance, and so on to a technical investigator appointed by the court. High-value documents should carry an unforgeable digital signature of the signer in the electronic form. Here are some of the characteristics of an electronically signed document:[22]

- **The signature is authentic**. The signature convinces the document's recipient that the signer deliberately signed the document.
- **The signature is unforgeable**. The signature is proof that the signer, and no one else, deliberately signed the document.
- **The signature is not reusable**. The signature is part of the document; an unscrupulous person cannot move the signature to a different document.
- **The signed document is unalterable**. Once the document is signed, it cannot be altered.
- **The signature cannot be repudiated**. The signature and the document are physical things. The signer cannot later claim that he or she did not sign it.

Digitally signed documents fulfill all the expectations stated above. More importantly, they are considered the equivalent of a paper and pen signed document as per the Indian IT Act[23]. Hence, many government contracts in India can be digitally signed and submitted online. It is also true for tax filing and submission of annual reports to the Ministry of Corporate Affairs (MCA).

Jurisdiction

The courts have limits on the kinds of cases they can adjudicate, some of which are set by jurisdictions. For example, under **territorial jurisdiction**, a court can only take cases originating in the geographic area of its location. Under **original jurisdiction**, a court can take only those subject matters relevant to its function. A civil court will not adjudicate a criminal case. Courts are hierarchical. Appeals of a lower court judgment only go to the higher court under which the lower court is part. It is known as **appellate jurisdiction**. Lastly, courts have a limit on the maximum amount of relief

---

[22] Reproduced verbatim from Bruce Schneier, Applied Cryptography: Protocols, Algorithms, and Source Code in C, John Wiley & Sons (US) © 1996
[23] Section 3 and 3A, Information Technology Act, 2000, Union of India

Contracts 125

they can offer in a judgment. For example, a district consumer court can only give relief up to Rs. 5,00,000[24]. This is known as the **pecuniary jurisdiction**.

We only focus on locational jurisdiction here. The courts would like to settle the disputes in a convenient location for all parties. Generally, they look at the following:

- The preferred location of the adjudication mentioned in the contract.
- The place where the agreement was entered into.
- The place of operation for the plaintiffs or where they reside.
- The place of operation for the defendants or where they reside.
- If a location becomes prejudicial to one or more of the parties, a neutral location.

In the case of adhesion contracts, the customer has no option to choose the location; it is mentioned by the proposer. Let us understand this with a few examples. Company A in Mumbai sells gifts across India online. Their end-user license agreement contains the preferred location for dispute resolution to Mumbai, India. Here are some cases to discuss:

1. A large company B in Bangalore decided to send all its employees an annual gift. They shared the gift details and their office addresses for delivering the gifts. Company B also has an office in Mumbai. Due to some payment issues A sues B in a court in Mumbai.

2. An old man in Bangalore wants to give his son a gift as his son is visiting them. The gift is damaged and the old man requests A for a refund, but no one in A responds. So, he files a case in the consumer court in Bangalore.

3. Company A now wants an international expansion. They know California in the USA has a lot of non-resident Indians (NRIs). During the festival season, they advertised on Californian billboards and FM Radio, appealing to NRIs to send gifts to their friends and families in India. Some of the gifts were not delivered, and people sued Company A in the courts of California.

In Case 1, both the companies are reasonable in size. Company B had the legal resources to review the contract in the first place. They also have an office in Mumbai. So, the court may consider the adhesion contract is not unfair to Company B.

In Case 2, the consumer courts were introduced in India to resolve consumer grievances. The consumer cannot be forced to visit distant places to get a small relief. Bangalore consumer court may accept the case as the consumer filed the case there.

Case 3 can be complex. A has no business presence in the USA. The shipment of goods happened in India. The customers had Indian connections. Will Californian court

---

[24] Section 11(1), The Consumer Protection Act. 1986, Union of India

entertain such suits? However, A advertised in California, ensuring it has business interest in California. If A used friends or family members of the founder to liaise with the advertising agencies, those people can be considered agents of A.

Our examples only show plaints can be instituted against the jurisdictional attributes of a contract, if needed. The court's decision will depend on the facts of the case. Before trying a new territory, the legal liabilities should be understood fully.

Enforcement

Contracts are legal tools ensuring parties agree to adhere. If they are not adhered to, the aggrieved party can take the other party to court. With the significant caseloads at the court and the time it takes to dispose of a case, the process itself looks like a punishment[25] for many. Again, if there is a business relationship, there are contracts expressed or implied. We suggest you look at contracts as social agreements[26] to do something for consideration while keeping the enforceability in the courts secondary.

As PMs, we can accomplish the business objectives with little legal remediation. The most common legal remediation to a contract is a status quo ante or a state before the contract existed. When parties cannot meet the objectives, they can agree to rescind the contract. They can refund each other the considerations or compensate for the costs and part ways. Some of these can be part of the contract itself. Parties can set up contract evaluation committees with regular performance assessments, raising a red flag if there are any misses. Conditions can become irrelevant to the contract when the business environment changes. They can amend the contract to accommodate the latest changes. Dialogue among the parties on a regular cadence is good for the contract.

Let us look at the individual customers from California or Bangalore mentioned earlier. Due to some unforeseen circumstances, company A could not deliver the goods. Had they just refunded the money, they could have avoided the situation. There was no reason to force the customer to drag A to the court. Your vendors could be in the same position when they are not meeting their commitments. Understanding the contract well helps in negotiation. A good contract is about free consent or the meeting of minds. When the product documentation, contract conditions, and warranties are clear, the negotiation is easy. There are no ambiguities. If you have to review old emails or notes to justify your claims, it is clear there is little emphasis given to contract drafting. The contract is not just the legal document but all the associated scope of work, drawings,

---

[25] People get fed up with court proceedings, the process becomes punishment: CJI, 3rd Aug. 2024, **https://indianexpress.com/article/india/people-fed-up-court-proceedings-process-punishment-cji-9493237/** accessed 8th Dec. 2024

[26] Levy, K. E.C. (2017). Book-Smart, Not Street-Smart: Blockchain-Based Smart Contracts and The Social Workings of Law. Engaging Science, Technology, and Society, 3. **https://estsjournal.org/index.php/ests/article/view/107** accessed 8th Dec. 2024

design documentation, use case explanations, product documentation, and more, as one bundle.

Parties can contract with provisions for **alternative dispute resolution** (ADR). The Arbitration and Conciliation Act[27] in India provides guidelines for such dispute resolutions. Courts are not most knowledgeable in the subject matter of a contract. They can set up a committee of experts or **amicus curiae**. However, it may delay the process of law. The arbitration tribunals can have subject matter experts in the committees who can pass orders to be enforced by civil courts in India. Indian law approves ADR orders passed by internationally recognized arbitration tribunals. When a contract accepts international arbitration for resolutions, the contract should call out the law of the jurisdiction to be used; for example, this contract is under Indian law. When a contract is drafted, a legal system is kept in mind. A change in the law can make sections of the contract bad in law and may lead to a wrong judgment. Orders passed by arbitration can be enforced and challenged[28] in the civil courts in India, if needed.

In case of non-performance of a contract or a breach, it will lead to one or more parties compensating the other parties for actual material losses[29]. Only the proximate causes of the losses are looked at. For example, if there is a delay in the flight and you miss an important business meeting, it causes you a significant loss. The airline is only responsible for compensating you for the delay, not your business loss. However, if you have mentioned the purpose of using the service and they promise to honor yet fail to deliver, the losses can be attributed to the non-performance[30], a reason to document the purpose of entering into a contract with your suppliers in the agreement itself. While the contract act only provides for material losses, sometimes a contracting party may need to stop another party from proceeding further with activities that damage their business or reputation. They may attract specific or preventive relief under the Specific Relief Act[31].

Performance

The best way to discharge a contract is through performance. Every party keeps to her promises. However, there are challenges. We will look at these with some examples.

- If a contract is conditioned to an event and the event cannot be held, the contract is void. This category of cases is known as **coronation cases**. Simply put, a person booked a hotel for a specific day, thinking the King's coronation procession would be along the road. The event got canceled. The person can request a refund for the hotel booking advances as the contract is void.

---
[27] Arbitration and Conciliation Act, 1996, Union of India
[28] Section 34, Ibid
[29] Section 73-75, Supra 3
[30] Hadley vs Baxendale, 1854
[31] The Specific Relief Act, 1963, Union of India

- A particular singer was to conduct a show. She was sick on the evening of the event. The performance of the contract could not be completed. In contrast, a building contractor is constructing a building, and the mason working earlier has fallen sick; the contractor arranges an alternate mason to complete the task. It is not a non-performance, as the specificity of the performer is not in the contract. In the case of the singer, the **specific performer** was the subject of the contract, but not in the case of the mason. Sometimes, service contracts are carried out with a certain person in mind. In such cases, non-availability can lead to non-performance.
- A contract where **time** is important must explicitly provide the expectations. If no timeline is specified, then the court can decide a reasonable time.

A non-performance due to the fault of a party can be considered a breach. A penalty, if specified, can be imposed on a breach of the contract. If the causes of non-performance are beyond the control of the performer, then the contract is considered void. This principle is called a **force majeure** in the legal literature. In case of a force majeure, the penalty is not imposed, but each party should return any benefits or advances they are given for the performance. Contract law does not accept **unjust enrichment**. The consideration for a contract is lawful only on the performance of the subject matter.

The common law contracts are far more stringent than the contracts of a civil law country. Any deviation from the contract is considered a breach that makes the contract voidable under the hands of the affected party. However, civil law countries consider the contracts a long-term association and not to be breached by a few violations. They provide for curative actions. Here are some examples:

- If the buyer receives defective goods, the seller can work again and send fixed goods if the buyer agrees.
- If there is no payment on the scheduled date, the seller can give additional time. However, the buyer may have to compensate in terms of interest.
- If the goods do not meet the quality decided by the contract, the buyer may pay less money for the lower quality of the goods after negotiating with the seller.

Some of these provisions are part of the United Nations Convention on Contracts for the International Sale of Goods (CISG). While India is not a party to the convention, the effects of the conventions are felt in international contracts.

Specific Needs for the Software Industry

We discussed a few salient features of contracts. Here, we focus on some commonly seen contractual elements in software technology companies. Softwares are built in layered stack format. There are lower-level foundation technologies over which vendors build applications. The foundation technologies reach a large audience base;

they have less value added for the end customer. The specialization increases as you go up the stack. We will roughly classify the contracts into three parts, protecting:

- Licensee's rights
- Licensors' rights
- Service Provider Rights

Licensee's Rights

Sometimes, foundational technologies are commodities and are supported by open-source initiatives. Yet, obtaining technical support for some open-source software requires contracts with vendors who optimize open-source products for enterprises. Today, almost all enterprises use one or more components developed through community open-source initiatives where they support enterprises with some form of enterprise license. Those using enterprise licenses for open-source software would like to get proper **product support**. While community support for open source is another possibility, most community licenses are without warranties and best efforts only.

If you are employing a vendor who provides you with a product component, you wonder, why cannot they develop or acquire the other parts of your domain and become your competition? When you have not shared your customer data or know-how and just used the software as a platform, there is no real reason to be worried about a competitive fallout. Netflix uses Amazon Web Services (AWS) for its content distribution. Amazon Prime Video is one of its biggest competitors. Netflix is the market leader, while Amazon Prime Video, with all of Amazon's muscle, is a distant competitor. Large companies operate business units such as independent companies, and it is not unlikely for one business unit to have a customer who competes with another business unit. You would always like to protect against **vertical integrations** by your software vendors.

Can you write a clause in the contract stating the vendors cannot compete in the same domain? Generally, a contract that asks someone not to do something without due consideration is hard to justify in the courts. However, if you have shared your customer information with your vendor and the vendor uses that information to reach your customers or market information to price their products and services, it is tantamount to acting in bad faith. Whenever you engage in any business transaction with anyone, if you believe there is a possible exchange of confidential information, you must ensure a **Non-Disclosure Agreement (NDA)** is signed for such interactions. NDAs can provide protection when a licensor acts in bad faith. NDAs generally state there has been an exchange of information between the two parties. They will only use the information for mutual benefits and interests. They will not share the information with any third party nor use it to the detriment of participating entities. The data exchanged is confidential and shall be wiped out as soon as the engagement ends.

Sometimes, the contracts demand **exclusivity** from the vendor's business. The vendor will not supply its goods or services to your competitor. This exclusivity means you expect the vendor to only develop products and services for you. These clauses are not always enforceable. First of all, the definition of a competitor can be very generic. Some organizations are so spread out in their business that tracking what parts of the company will qualify as competition is questionable. Can a supplier for Microsoft not supply products or services to Google? Again, one has to see how much experience or learning of Microsoft is used by the vendor to provide services to Google. Both are technological behemoths serving many different verticals. Secondly, are the services by the vendor so unique that it can take away a significant business advantage of Microsoft over Google? This problem should be addressed through business acquisitions rather than legal contracts. The customer should think of **vertically integrating** with the vendor by buying out the business unit from them.

If you use a third-party platform, you are interested in ensuring it can support your application and its **Service Level Agreements (SLA)** with its customers. For your customer's SLA, you would like to establish an **Operations Level Agreement (OLA)** with your vendors. If you have an SLA of 99.9% uptime with your customer, you would like the platform provider to support the same. What if the platform only provides a 99% uptime? The probability of failure for each system is 0.01. Reliability experts will suggest running two parallel systems. With two parallel systems, the failure probability will be: $0.01 \times 0.01 = 10^{-4}$. The effective reliability of the system will be: $1 - 10^{-4} = 0.9999$ or 99.99 percent. Is your OLA including such an arrangement with your vendor?

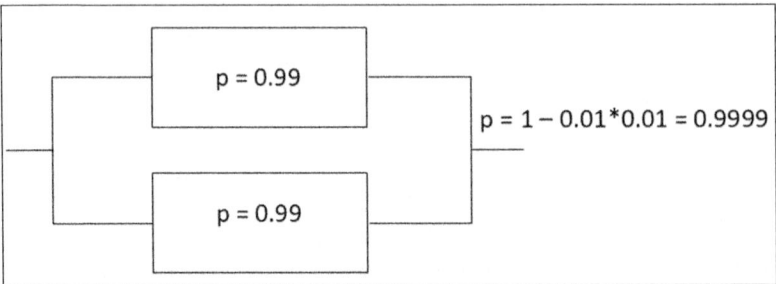

Figure 7.1: *The reliability of the system increases with two parallel systems*

Both the supplier and buyer want their interests to be protected. Sometimes, contracts are drafted in ways that show more of the positional status of the buyers and suppliers than protection of the actual business interest. Think of a Fortune 500 giant buying an IT solution from a startup in the early stages of its existence. The software component is of significant value to the buyer. The deal is equally important for the survival of the startup. However, the price decided barely gives enough profits to the startup. At this point, the buyer wants an indemnity clause worth millions of dollars. Millions of dollars is not a big amount for a Fortune 500 company. When such an indemnity gets triggered, the startup will declare bankruptcy; it is a lose-lose situation for both the

Fortune 500 company and the startup. In such circumstances, it is ideal to consider three aspects to ensure the business interest of the buyer.

- **Hold the buyer harmless** for any malfunction or false claims of the vendor's software.
- **Indemnity insurance** for potential losses in case of an unforeseen exigency.
- **Source code escrow** that can ensure the buyer has a right to the source code in case of the failure of the startup business.

Who would pay for such insurance expenses? Of course, the buyer. So, hard bargaining to squeeze margins from the sellers may not work in the best interest in these cases. Some vendors understand these needs and incorporate the insurance element in the product itself. In the digital certificate world, people apply this concept innovatively. CA/Browser Forum decided to release a guideline for certificate issuance in 2007, where not just the domain name but the actual physical verification of the company's attributes shall be validated before issuing a digital certificate for a company. The browsers will highlight the company's details so that users can confidently access their websites without worrying about phishing. The Enterprise Validation (EV) certificates have an indemnity clause that protects the buyer from general fraudulent attacks with a 2 million USD. The amount can be up to 5 million USD, where negligence can be attributed to the Certificate Authority (CA). The CA needs to buy insurance from a company of repute and is exonerated from such a duty only when they have revenues above 500 million USD[32]. The validation aspects of EV certificates are no longer given much credence; browsers have stopped highlighting EV certificates in the UI[33]. Yet, the insurance aspect is still relevant. CAs still charge a premium of 5 to 10 times the price of a domain validation certificate, which is baked into the certificate price.

We have discussed exigencies so far; what about normal operations? In case of failure to discharge the obligations, how does the licensee know her rights? When software is licensed, the licensee should know the intended behavior; when the performance does not meet the expected behavior, some legal remediation is needed. How will the legal parties understand the intended behavior or what was agreed to in the first place? The **documentation** comes in handy here. The documentation should be clear enough to state the intended behavior, the general understanding of the industry about such products, and if deviations from the general industrial practice are in the application. Let us assume a device manufacturer licenses a general-purpose Windows 11 OS and embeds in the device, assuming some real-time OS (RTOS) capabilities. When they

---

[32] CA Browsers Forum, Guidelines for the Issuance and Management of Extended Validation Certificates, Version 2.0.1, 6th May 2024

[33] Catalin Cimpanu, Extended Validation (EV) Certificates Abused to Create Insanely Believable Phishing Sites, **https://www.bleepingcomputer.com/news/security/extended-validation-ev-certificates-abused-to-create-insanely-believable-phishing-sites/#:~:text=EV%20certificates%20abused%20for%20phishing,company%20named%20%22Verified%20Identity.%22** accessed 15th Nov. 2024

are about to release the product, they realize the system does not meet their needs. They are looking for a possible solution here. If the documentation of Windows 11 OS has those capabilities listed and they are not met, the licensee is covered. If RTOSes provide a specific feature, then the licensee would not get any protection as Windows 11 is not an RTOS.

Some vendors give product documentation lower priority than the software component or binary. A PM has reasons to be concerned. A product without proper documentation cannot be properly represented in the courts, as the courts cannot ascertain the intended behavior and the deviation from that—the basis of legal contention. One may argue that documentation can be buggy, product behaviors can change over releases, and most businesses do not sue for product feature malfunctions, so why invest so much in documentation? It is crucial to understand if the feature in the discussion is a condition or warranty to the contract. Conditions to a contract are non-negotiable and must be adhered to as much as possible. For warranties, we have time to cure. If a product feature is likely to become a condition for a contract, the license agreement should highlight it from the product documentation.

SaaS-based products are data intensive. The licensees, while using the licensor's product, share data. The data can reside on the licensor's servers for data analytics and future use. The licensors may have to share the data further downstream with their vendors. They may need the data for extended periods. Some of these are also defined by the audience the products are targeting. For example, if the licensee is ultimately interested in providing a solution for the European markets, General Data Protection Regulations (GDPR) will be applicable. If the licensor does not provide GDPR compliance, the licensee has to make alternate arrangements with the licensor. It is always a good idea to mention the purpose of these special arrangements in the contract so that the licensors know the ultimate goals for such additional conditions. While conditions and warranties can be explicitly called out, a good explanation in the contract makes judicial interpretation easier. Judicial people, lawyers, or advocates may not be most knowledgeable in the subject matter and need product managers to explain the functional challenges to them while drafting the contract, defense, or instituting a legal suit.

Licensor's Rights

As much as licensees are interested in protecting their rights in a software contract, the licensors would like to protect their interests and rights. Licensors are concerned that the licensee may develop or acquire competencies in their business and start a competing operation. Licensor's product features, the software binaries, APIs, and SDKs are exposed to the Licensees. So, the exposure of the licensor's intellectual properties (IPs) is significantly higher than that of the licensee in the software industry. Here are some things they would like to add to their contracts.

Contracts

- They typically add a **non-compete clause** stating the licensee shall not use the license to indulge in an activity detrimental to the licensor's business.
- They could also keep a **cool-off period** in the contract—the licensee cannot enter a competitive business within, say, three years of cessation of their contract.

Legal non-compete clauses are hard to enforce. Generally, the law is pro-competition as it is good for the consumers.

At the same time, the law protects the intellectual property. We will discuss the role of IP in greater detail in a later chapter. In such situations, the licensees typically can set up a subsidiary, hire industry experts, give them no access to the licensor's software, and ask them to build parallel software in a cleanroom environment. Some subsidiaries are so meticulously maintained that the team cannot communicate with anyone outside their project teams. The idea is to develop the software in isolation and not be influenced by the licensor's IP. However, the licensor should mention the **patents, trademarks, copyrights**, or other IPs used in the product. Explicitly mentioning can act as a warning for the licensee if they decide to develop similar technologies. They cannot easily deny the awareness in case of an infringement.

Just like licensees, the licensors would also like to **limit their liabilities** to a minimum. Open-source licenses mention anyone can use the software as-is without any warranties. Paid software vendors will normally keep the maximum liabilities up to the license fees. When such limits are exceeded, insurance clauses can be added to the contracts to limit the liabilities. If the licensors provide their software as a binary, they may add protection clauses against **reverse engineering**.

In the SaaS world, the licensee provides their data to the licensors. The licensors provide guidelines and follow industry-standard methods that can deter data breaches. Every licensee would like to conduct a vulnerability assessment and penetration test (VAPT) against the licensed software to ensure the absence of critical vulnerabilities. Let us assume licensee A attempts a vulnerability assessment against the licensor's product, and the licensed product is vulnerable. Licensee A may access the data of licensee B. A licensor must maintain due care against such adventures of their licensees. Here are some things they can include in a contract.

- **No VAPT tests** are permitted against a production system.
- Test environments can be provided to the licensee for a limited time.
- The discovered vulnerabilities, the payloads, and data collected as part of the test would be shared with the licensor.
- The licensor can run malware detection tools on the production systems, and any violation can blacklist the IP addresses of the originators.

VAPT tools are similar to those used by hackers to perpetrate cybercrimes. Hence, SaaS vendors should take these kinds of contractual safety measures. The licensees carrying out VAPT tests must follow ethical hacking practices and notify before trying any tests.

A relative newcomer in any field would like to **associate partners** to advertise their services for better market visibility. However, such associations should not be misleading. For example, Licensee A hosts its SaaS-based accounting software on Microsoft Azure and offers its customers buying through Microsoft Azure Marketplace. Suppose Licensee A claims their application is ISO-27001 certified and is a Microsoft-certified accounting package. Both these claims are misleading. While Microsoft Data Center is ISO-27001 certified, any application hosted is not automatically approved by reference. Secondly, mere approval to sell services through Azure Market Place does not make the product a Microsoft-certified accounting package. The contract must protect against such claims. However, Microsoft runs Azure Partnership Programs. These programs are meant for co-branding and marketing partner solutions with Microsoft. These programs are outside the purview of the hosting license of Microsoft Azure.

Service Provider Rights

Software organizations run with the help of knowledge workers. Organizations cannot be knowledgeable in every discipline; they acquire knowledge in specific core competencies. They hire full-time employees or train their employees in these areas. However, sometimes they need commonly available skills for a quick turnaround of a project or specialized skills to guide them in the initial setup of the systems and processes of the organization. In both cases, they need service providers to augment their intermittent needs. Some of these service providers are large IT companies, such as TCS, Infosys, IBM, Cognizant, and so on, providing expertise in multiple vertical and horizontal domains. Some are independent consultants focused on a specific area of operations. Generally, the contracts are governed by a **Master Services Agreement** (**MSA**) that provides a general guideline for a service provider engagement, payment schedules, and so on. There are extension agreements for specific projects. All the nuances of an MSA are not our focus. We will highlight only a few common ones that the contracting parties should know.

The **type of contract** plays a significant role in service provider engagement. The engagement can be of two types:

- **Contract of work:** The service providers only offer human resources. The client manages the work content, allocation, schedules, readiness assessment, and so on. The service providers are providing staff augmentation to the project. However, the client has all the requisite knowledge and experience.
- **Contract for work:** The client only describes a high-level requirement and expects the service providers to carry out the planning, content, design, and

so on for the project delivery. The client may not have the requisite skills for the activity and has to trust the service provider.

A strong dissatisfaction creeps in when clarity is not established between both types of engagements. When a contract of work is misunderstood as a contract for work, the service provider is seen as incompetent. When it is the other way around, the client starts micromanaging an expert in the domain. Both are lose-lose situations for the parties. Yet, most service engagements can fall into these traps. A contract of work engagement can attract labor laws for the client, as the law may view the worker as an extension of the client organization. Compliance with prevalent labor laws has to be worked out. Geography and location of labor can determine the holidays and other employee benefits. Not all of these will fall under the purview of a product manager. The human resources department may intervene to apply the applicable policies. Micromanaging a contract for work engagement will lead to distrust and disrespect for the experts in the domain. It can lead to substandard work, limited engagement from service providers, and bad execution. The clarity in the type of contract will ensure a win-win relationship for both parties.

In the IT industry, highly skilled talent is always in short supply. A client can solicit the service provider's employees for direct employment, as it may work out cheaper for the client. SPs understand this well. The contracts have clauses for **non-solicitation of employment**. Some service providers offer to **build, operate, and transfer (BOT)** service models. They hire for the clients, provide the necessary management services, and eventually transfer a functional setup to the client. In these setups, they explicitly call out management and engineering leaders who will not be transferred to the client. These ensure the service provider maintains the necessary capability for a subsequent engagement.

The client wants to protect its intellectual property and would not want the service providers to learn and use them for the competition. They sometimes impose unrealistic expectations that the SP cannot engage with a competitive organization for several years. Some jurisdictions can find these unconstitutional as improperly drafted contracts can be challenged as taking away an SP's right to earn a living. While sharing information, it is protected well by non-disclosure agreements (NDA); a blanket ban on offering services to anyone else in the domain is untenable. However, the SP must do away with all sensitive documents or information as part of the engagement once the engagement is terminated.

Every organization developing technology-oriented products wants to protect its intellectual property. One of the ways to dilute the IP is by not formally applying for patents, trademarks, copyrights, or so on. Since SPs are engaged in developing technological activities, they can get newer ideas, and the client would like to exploit those IPs in their products and services. The IP laws are designed to reward the actual creators or inventors so that they can apply their minds. The law also wants an ecosystem that will encourage the creators. Here, the clients provide the necessary infrastructure or monetary support as part of the ecosystem. Hence, they would like to be assigned the IPs and exploit them for economic benefits. The human beings involved in the IP should be recognized as the inventors or authors, as the case may be. If the members of SP's team are not recognized as inventors or authors, it violates the author's **moral rights**. We will discuss this concept in further detail in the chapter on intellectual properties. A contract cannot violate any law, nor can it override the provisions of any law. While the contracts can demand IP assignment to the client, they cannot deny the right of SP's member to be recognized as a creator.

Other elements in the MSA may include the payment schedule, the price list of the resources, and engagement models, like time and material vs. work content, the time validity of the contract, termination conditions, quality assessment conditions for completion, and so on. We touched upon only a few aspects of the MSA. The detailed MSA can run up to tens or hundreds of pages depending on the complexity of the projects. It is always advisable to have formal drafting and review of MSAs through legal experts.

Conclusion

We reviewed the legal framework on which the contracts are based. We focused on commercial contracts and the sale of goods or services agreements. We looked at some ways parties would like to enforce the implementation of the contracts and ways to measure the performance. Lastly, we looked at some of the salient features of contracts used in the IT industry. We discussed the outlines and principles of contracts and avoided detailed legal treatment of the issues involved. While we used the contracts to manage the bargaining suppliers, new entrants would always want to take away your market share and industry leadership positions. One way to counter them is by developing intellectual property and creating entry barriers. We will discuss those in the next chapter.

Questions

1. Review the master service agreements you have with various vendors and learn how intellectual property is treated.

2. Are RFPs and RFQs contracts?

3. What are the conditions and warranties in contracts?

4. Review a contract with your vendor and find one-sided terms. Discuss with the legal team to rectify those.

5. Can you contract a third-party organization to reverse-engineer your competitor's software?

Chapter 8
Intellectual Properties

Introduction

So far, we have tamed the competition by executing a compelling product vision. We transitioned the buyers to customers, provided them with a product at a mutually beneficial price, and ensured the users got a holistic product experience. We review the contracts with our suppliers periodically and ensure our relationship is active and expectations are set right. Our business is all set to fly. Now, we are getting noticed. New entrants are evaluating the markets for the next opportunity; our success attracts their attention. The newcomers have not come to the limelight, so we may not even know who they are. We have to protect our territory, as a ruler would protect his castles with moats. Intellectual Properties (IPs) are the modern-day moats. They add value to our customers and create goodwill for us in their minds. We do not want that association taken away by newcomers easily. We will learn about various IPs and how they protect our business interests.

Structure

In this chapter, we will cover the following topics:

- Basis of Intellectual Property
- Types of IPRs
    - Copyright
    - Trademarks
    - Patents
    - Design
    - Others
- Process of IPR Application
- Respecting Other's IPR

- Open Source
- Innovation and IPR
- Incentivizing Innovation

Basis of Intellectual Property

Dealing with buyers and suppliers is direct. They reach you, and you reach them. There is continuous relationship building; you know the success is mutual. With competitors, there is an adversarial relationship. You will show down their products when you meet in a bidding process; they will do the same for your products. You develop battle cards against each other's products, a show of strength and upmanship. How do you deal with a new entrant? Do you want to deal with a new entrant head-on? In the early days of Freshdesk (now called FreshWorks), then incumbent helpdesk solution Zendesk entered into a Twitter war, calling Freshdesk a rip-off.[1] Freshdesk had the perfect opportunity to invite all Twitter users to try their 30-day trial offer. Freshdesk considered it as their first visible campaign in the market. In short, Zendesk made customers see Freshdesk as a real competition. A few years later, ServiceNow and BMC competed in a similar market. ServiceNow was the newer player and used to show that BMC was not innovative enough. BMC sued ServiceNow for infringement of 11 patents[2]. Although they settled the matter, it was clear BMC handled the case differently than how Zendesk could. They could do so because they had formalized the IPs and used IPs against a threat from a newer competitor.

Before we delve into IPs in detail, let us understand some principles from economics. Resources are scarce. That is why the economic principles of demand and supply work for them. In an open market, a resource should go to the claimant, who can give maximum economic value to society. That will be the most efficient use of the resource. The same prompts municipal corporations to auction seashores for mechanized fishing contracts or open spaces, stadiums, and so on for event management companies or the national government to auction mobile spectrum to telecom companies. Such transferrable resources with a basket of rights are called properties. A property transfer gives away some of the rights to the transferee.

Let us understand it with some examples. With the rapid urbanization of India, cities such as Bangalore keep expanding on all sides. The city limits reach other rural human settlements, such as villages. The villagers use the surrounding areas of their countryside as agricultural lands. Builders and land developers in Bangalore would reach the villagers, buy their property, and approach the local administration to

---
[1]C.S. Swaminathan, Charles Assisi, Freshdesk vs Zendesk: Everybody loves a good fight, 18th May 2015, **https://www.livemint.com/Companies/pd77zXkfC1fzdFwZ7xBNQJ/Everybody-loves-a-good-fight.html** accessed 13th Dec 2024

[2]BMC Announces Resolution of Patent Infringement Disputes Against ServiceNow **https://www.bmc.com/newsroom/releases/bmc-announces-resolution-patent-infringement-disputes-against.html** accessed 13th Dec. 2024

Intellectual Properties

convert the land from farming to residential. The process is called mutation. Land is sovereign property. Land ownership does not mean an owner can join the neighboring territory or country. Registered land ownership with the government gives the owner limited rights for a specific purpose, such as residence, forest, factory, fishing, farming, and so on. In short, land ownership does not give away sovereign rights to the land. Moreover, ownership of immovable property like land is artificial and limited and does not permit the owners to do whatever they like.

Before the Industrial Revolution and Renaissance, there were only artisans and performers. They were individuals or groups who would develop a piece of art or sculpture or perform a play under the patronage of a rich or famous person, like a royal. Most such art would be in the private collection of a royal family. However, some would paint a mural in a church or chapel that came to public visibility. The artists worked for some rich people and got their earnings. The rich people retained the piece of art. The famous artists Michelangelo and Leonardo Davinci, playwright William Shakespeare, and composer Guillaume Dufay belong to this era. While their work had a mass appeal, they had to deliver it personally, and there could only be one instance of their masterpiece.[3] With Gutenberg's printing press, books could be printed into multiple copies and distributed, but the process was still slow to adopt. The printing press owners were not good authors, and the authors did not have the means to set up a printing press.

Some visionary artists, such as Raja Ravi Varma in India, had the lithographic printing press to disseminate their artwork.[4] The first copyright act came in 1709 when a printing press got a monopoly to print and distribute books for 14 years.[5] Authors or creators conceive a work. They give publishers or distributors the right to reproduce and disseminate to the masses and collect revenue. Governments legislated the formal procedures under Intellectual Properties (IPs). There are several IP types other than writing and authorship, which we will discuss in this chapter.

Just like the concept of software products we discussed in *Chapter 1, The Practice of Product Management*, there are other forms of products representing human ingenuity. Books, artwork, cinematography, industrial products, and so on, can all be manufactured by anyone who can set up a large factory. The creators have to be incentivized both with money and recognition. The government allowed the creators to own properties that are outcomes of their creativity. They can now transfer the property or license certain aspects of its use to a publisher or distributor to make

---

[3] ...Shakespeare's plays had never previously appeared in print, including As You Like It, Julius Caesar, Macbeth, The Tempest, and many more... What is a First Folio? **https://www.folger.edu/explore/shakespeare-in-print/first-folio/** accessed 13th Dec 2024

[4] Kalpana Sundar, Raja Ravi Varma: Controversy of India's most iconic artist, 18th July 2022, **https://www.bbc.com/culture/article/20220715-raja-ravi-varma-indias-most-influential-artist** accessed 13th Dec. 2024

[5] The Statute of Anne: The First Copyright Statute **https://www.historyofinformation.com/detail.php?id=2955** accessed 13th Dec. 2024

releasable chunks to sell to a large audience. For example, the author writes this book as a creator, and there is the publisher and distributor. We have signed an authorship contract that gives the author remuneration for his work and his name as the author as recognition; the publisher has the right to publish, sell, and distribute. This book is an intellectual property with many rights. Without money and recognition, the author may not have authored the book. The publisher has employed editors, reviewers, and artists to improve the publication, selling, and distribution. They are collectively part of the publisher; they are not authors of the work. Sometimes, in autobiographical works, you find an additional person who significantly assists or storyboards the core author's ideas. In those cases, the assisting person is also considered an author.

There was a change in education. The artisans learned their skills from family apprenticeships. That changed to formal vocational education and training with universities. They not only taught but also researched and developed new knowledge. The new knowledge piggybacks on the old knowledge. So, the researchers should have access to the latest and greatest in the field and not be affected by monopolies given to business exploitations. Every country provides a certain freedom to the research community to use its intellectual property.

The business outlook is changing significantly. Two or three decades ago, the entrepreneurs developed businesses. They introduced unique capabilities into the market, convinced early adopters, generated revenues, and bootstrapped a business. They may get some initial investors or seek public funding to scale up the venture. Today, the founding members are quickly approaching the investors for funds. Developing the markets takes time. The investors want to see the founders utilizing the funds judiciously. The IPs act as possible milestones for progress even before the product goes to market. Moreover, governments are incentivizing startups to file patents. For example, one of the ways for a startup in India to avail of government benefits is by proving the innovation potential of the startup.[6] A company's valuation can increase with the quality of intellectual properties it carries.

When new technologies or business practices come into practice, they are unregulated. As their popularity increases, laws are needed to regulate them and create a level playing field for everyone. Intellectual properties reward human ingenuity by assigning some monopoly rights while mass-produced alternatives can still be in the market. For example, industrial products like cars are produced in massive batches in factories. However, companies such as Rolls Royce still produce bespoke vehicles for the connoisseur. These are handmade by artisans.[7] They are expensive and have a unique market of their own. Japan does not manufacture Katanas for the armed forces. However, experts keeping the old manufacturing techniques still produce for martial arts enthusiasts. The markets have shrunk, but they need protection from mechanized

---

[6] **https://www.startupindia.gov.in/content/sih/en/startupgov/startup_recognition_page.html** accessed 15th December 2024

[7] **https://www.rolls-roycemotorcars.com/en_GB/bespoke** accessed 15th December 2024

alternatives. Some IP laws, such as Geographics Indicators, are directed to protect classic human art and crafts. With the advent of Artificial Intelligence (AI) and Machine Learning (ML), machines can carry out cognitive fields such as idea generation and human expression. Will we need laws to protect some of the human mental activities? As the industry embraces AI-ML, we may see changes in IP laws. With this note, let us review the various IP types and their relevance to the software industry. With rapid digitalization across all domains, software is becoming relevant to many classic businesses.

Types of IPRs

Here are some of the intellectual property granted by law: Copyright, Trademarks, Patents, Designs, Trade Secrets, Geographical Indicators, Plant Varieties, Semiconductor IC Layouts, and so on. With the software products, we mostly interact with the first four kinds. However, in e-commerce, exposure to other IP types can be helpful.

Copyright

The Copyright Act[8] applies to literary, musical, dramatic, sound recordings, artistic, cinematograph, computer programs, and so on, where expression is the primary factor of the work. As per the act, computer programs[9] encompass binaries, source code, databases, and so on. The computer programs are literary works. Hence, the following rights apply to the copyright holder:[10]

- reproduce the work
- issue copies of the work
- perform or communicate to the public
- translation of the work
- adaptation of the work

The copyright owner can sell or rent a copy of the program. This basket of rights is known as copyright for a computer program. Rights for other forms of copyrightable material are different and stated in the act.

Copyrights are assigned automatically. The authors create the work and become the copyright owners[11]. However, they can assign the copyright to another person or entity wholly or partially. In most employment contracts, if the employees have worked on something as part of the employment, they assign the associated rights to

---
[8] The Copyright Act, 1957, Union of India
[9] Section 2(ffc), Ibid
[10] Section 14, Ibid.
[11] Section 17, Ibid.

the employer. Computer source codes are ever-changing and contributed by many developers. The source control acts as a good way to track time. A copyright notice, such as Copyright @ Akme Corporation[12] 2010-2020, All Rights Reserved, should be added to the metadata of the published work. In a computer program, it can be a comment in the source header; in a binary, it can be in the resource string of the files, and so on. One can also register the copyright periodically, for example, the released versions of the computer software or documentation. Copyright is for sixty years from the date of publication.[13]

Assignment for copyright can be with some specifics as mentioned in the act[14].

- It must be in writing.
- The document should mention the remuneration and considerations for the assignor.
- There is a term for which the assignment should be valid. It is for five years if there is no mention of a term.
- The assignment is also valid for a specific territory. No mention of territory shall make it valid for the whole of India.
- If the assignee does not act on the assignment for one year, the assignor will get back the rights.

The Delhi High Court observed some of these in their judgment on Pine Labs vs. Gemalto.[15] The mere mention of an assignment in a Master Services Agreement (MSA) is not enough for a copyright assignment. All the details needed for such an assignment have to be provided.

Licensees can license some rights from copyright owners. They do not get to own the copyright; they cannot further license the product. The licenses are written agreements. However, some of the licenses can be adhesion contracts as the copyright owners reach out to users. EULA for Microsoft Windows may reach over a billion users. Licensees cannot sue for infringement. However, licensees with exclusive rights can be a party with the copyright owner to sue an infringer.

An infringement is a violation of copyright by anyone. In case of a copyright infringement, the owner can file a suit in a court of law. Discussing all possible infringement is beyond the scope of this book. We will highlight only a few examples relevant to software products here.

---

[12] A fictitious company; use your company name. The years are the first publication year to the last publication year. Since the software is updated almost every year, companies use a range.
[13] Section 22-29, Supra 8
[14] Section 19, Supra 8
[15] Pine Labs Pvt. Ltd. vs. Gemalto Terminals India Pvt. Ltd., 2011 (48) PTC 248 (Del.)

- Copyright law approves some usage of copyright as fair use.[16] Fair use is free from copyright violations. For a computer program, creating copies or backups for the protection of the software is fair use if the final usage is for the intended use of the software. There are several others, including caching information for better search.[17]

- Suppose a disgruntled employee working for Microsoft took the MS Windows source code and released it in the public domain. Now that the source is in the public domain, can anyone use it to develop derivative work? Copyright law is supposed to protect in such cases. The software is still copyright protected. An unauthorized access is still an infringement.[18,19] It is important to understand the licensing of any code from the public domain. The code could be copyrighted and published by a person with malicious intent. The same argument also applies to unauthorized use of binaries of copyrighted software.

- Computer programs installed on a machine have the license keys. The programs use some electronic protection mechanisms to keep the license information safe. However, hackers can use software tampering measures to overcome the license restrictions. These tampering measures are illegal under the Information Technologies Act.[20] Abetment of such activities by providing tools is also prohibited.[21]

- Generally, a literal copy of a literary work protected by copyright is an infringement. Software programs do not work in isolation. They need to interact with the underlying operating system runtime. With web services, other client applications will send data confirming Application Programming Interfaces (APIs) and use the result to render a web page. APIs act as communication interfaces across various software layers. Google used roughly 11000 lines of Java API to develop its version of Dalvik Virtual Machine for Android. Thus, the VM can interoperate with Java Programs for easier application development. Oracle considered this a literal copy of the source code and demanded compensation for USD 8.8 billion. After several years of judicial activities, the US Supreme Court held Google's use of the software for the APIs was within the purview of fair use under interoperability.[22] Interestingly, the Indian law

---

[16] Section 52, Supra 8
[17] Caching is generally considered safe as with the Google Library Project.
[18] Statement from Microsoft Regarding Illegal Posting of Windows 2000 Source Code, 12th February. 2004, **https://news.microsoft.com/2004/02/12/statement from-microsoft-regarding-illegal-posting-of-windows-2000-source-code/** accessed 17th Dec. 2024
[19] Section 58, Supra 8
[20] Section 65A, Information Technology Act, 2000, Union of India
[21] Section 65B, Ibid.
[22] Google LLC v. Oracle America, Inc., Docket No: 18-956, The Supreme Court of USA

also considers independently developed software for interoperability within fair use.[23]

- Even non-literal copying can be considered an infringement of software. USA courts have employed four tests (given as follows)[24] to identify non-literal infringement. Expressions are copyrighted, not ideas. The purpose of any software (what the software achieves) is an idea and cannot be copyrighted. Simply developing a competing software product is not a copyright infringement. However, expression elements in software are not limited to the source codes and machine executables. Hence, other tests are suggested to identify similar expressions.

    o **Structure, Sequence, and Organization (SSO)**[25]: Courts have accepted the program structures as an expression, hence copyrightable. In Whelan and Jaslow, the courts applied this test to identify substantial similarity between a program written in EDL language for mainframes and another written in BASIC for IBM Personal Computers.

    o **The Paperback Approach**[26]: It has three steps:

    - Find the generalized concepts to specialized concepts, thus distinguishing ideas from expressions.
    - Find the essential elements and non-essential elements in the expressions.
    - Find the overlap between two software implementations for their similarity of essential and non-essential elements. A significant overlap of non-essential elements can be a moot point in determining infringement.

    o **Abstraction, Filtration, and Comparison Test**[27]: A three-step process with the following characteristics:

    - **Abstraction**: Evaluate the code structure for modules, routines, subroutines, and so on, organizing the elements in the order of increasing generalizations.
    - **Filtration**: Filtering out expressions that cannot be copyrightable. They can be already in the public domain, well-known practices in the domain, or the like.

---

[23] Section 52(ab), Supra 8
[24] Apsi Adithyakumar, Copyrightability of Computer Software in India, Indian Journal of Integrated Research in Law, Volume II Issue II | ISSN: 2583-0538, Mar-Apr, 2022
[25] Whelan Assocs., Inc. v. Jaslow Dental Laboratory, Inc., 797 F.2d 1222; 1240 (3d Cir. 1986); 479 U.S. 1031 (1987)
[26] Lotus Development Corp. v. Paperback Software International, 740 F.Supp.37 (1990)
[27] Computer Associates International, Inc. v. Altai, Inc., 982 F.2d 693; 119 A.L.R. Fed. 741; 61 USLW 2434, 37 Fed. R. Evid. Serv. 348

- **Comparison**: The remaining cores of the programs have the golden nuggets. Infringement is arrived at by comparing those.
  - **Extrinsic and Intrinsic Test**[28]: The courts use a two-step test to compare user interfaces of two copyrighted software.
    - Extrinsic Test: Determines the copyrightable elements in the systems.
    - Intrinsic Test: Once the copyrighted elements are known, an analytical dissection is carried out as part of the intrinsic test.

PMs do not need to apply these tests in any legal case. They should be aware of the existence of these tests. When copyright lawyers apply the tests, the PMs can suggest and help them with the features. It is ok to get some inspirational ideas from the competition but not to be obsessed with their expressions to the extent that your implementation looks very similar. Lastly, developers should not look at copyrighted source code or designs when developing a product. With such a possibility, cleanroom development practices can be followed. The engineers work in complete isolation and do not discuss their projects with anyone outside the team. They do not take any technical input from anyone else. They may not have access to the internet. Even if they have, it is only for a few restricted sites. The team has a project manager, who is the only conduit to the external world. All her communications are strictly archived and monitored for any external influence. In the end, the software the engineering team builds cannot be considered influenced by any outside code.

While we scratched the surface of copyright laws, we understood discerning readers would like a deeper understanding. We suggest they review the handbook[29] published by the Government of India.

Trademarks

Copyrights protect the expressions in the software. What about the software's titles and brand identities? In businesses, branding provides the association of origin. It is critical to even software products. Trademarks provide the legal framework for the association of origin recognized by a jurisdiction. Due to their prevalence in the software industry, we look at only the following trademark types.[30]

- Wordmark: words, names, textual representations

---

[28] Brown Bag Software, a California Corporation, Formerly Telemarketing Resources, Inc. v. Symantec Corp., a California Corporation John L. Friend, an Individual and Dba Softworks Development, 960 F.2d 1465 (9th Cir. 1992)

[29] A Hand Book of Copyright Law, DPIIT, Ministry of Commerce, Govt. of India, **https://copyright.gov.in/documents/handbook.html** accessed 17th Dec. 2024

[30] Non-conventional trademarks have been registered for sound, such as MGM's roaring lion, and color, such as Cadbury purple, and so on.

- Device mark: logos, visual marks, icons, and so on.
- Domain Names

Some companies' legal departments provide a detailed list of trademarks registered.[31]

Trademarks need to be distinctive. Generally, an Abercrombie test[32] is used to identify distinctiveness under three guiding principles:

- **Inherently distinctive**: Arbitrary, Fanciful, and Suggestive Marks
- **Non-inherently distinctive**: Descriptive, Geographic, and Personal names
- **Marks with no distinctiveness**: Generic Marks

Here are some examples of Arbitrary, Fanciful, and Suggestive Marks:

- **KODAK**: Photographic Supplies
- **Apple**: Computers, Apple as goods is a generic name, yet, for computers, it is an arbitrary mark.
- **Camel**: Cigarettes, again a generic name for an animal but distinctive for a cigarette brand.
- **Shell**: Gasoline

Here are some descriptive marks.

- **Homemakers**: For family housekeeping
- **Joy**: For perfume
- **Trim**: Fingernail clipper

Trademarks are registered for the first two categories, namely, inherently distinctive and non-inherently distinctive marks. No trademark is issued for generic marks.

When trademark examiners review an application for registration, they compare the similarity with other known marks and trademarks. The comparison can be visual, phonetic, or structural. A person with ordinary intelligence and imperfect recollection should see distinctiveness with these comparisons. Although examiners try to be as objective as possible, there are limitations to human observations. Sometimes, the marks have no distinctiveness, have associations with religious symbols, are disrespectful to a community, are immoral, or have similarities with other national symbols. The examiners refuse such applications under absolute grounds of refusal.[33] In some cases, the marks have similarities with an earlier registered trademark.

---

[31] Adobe Trademark List for General Distribution as of August 9, 2024, **https://www.adobe.com/content/dam/cc/en/legal/licenses-terms/pdf/adobe_trademark_database_external.pdf** accessed 18th Dec. 2024

[32] Abercrombie and Fitch Co v. Hunting World Inc., 537 F.2d 4; 189 U.S.P.Q. 759

[33] Section 9, The Trademarks Act, 1999, Union of India

Trademarks are registered for a class. However, there are many descriptions of goods and services under it. For example, the most general goods and services description under **class 42**[34] is *scientific and technological services and research and design relating thereto; industrial analysis and research services; design and development of computer hardware and software.* A phonetically similar trademark for rubber technology research can overlap with a trademark to be used for cloud computing, creating a relative ground for refusal.[35] One can narrow the scope to cloud computing and get over such objections. A territorial limit can be another way to resolve relative grounds of refusal; for example, the trademark is only applicable to the state of Karnataka[36].

Like copyrights, trademarks can also be assigned automatically on consistent use. However, registration helps in two ways:

- Once you register a trademark, a new entrant cannot register for a substantially similar trademark. For Zendesk and Freshdesk, trademark registration may not have helped as part of a name (desk) cannot give protection as shown in the Indian case Amritdhara Pharmacy v. Satyadeo Gupta.[37]
- If the new entrant does not register the trademark and starts their business with a similar name, you can sue them for infringement. A lawsuit for infringement is straightforward. It has to be established that unauthorized persons use substantially similar marks not assigned to them; their business gains due to such acts need not be justified. Protection is available in the Trademarks Act[38].

When a trademark is not registered, the remedy is common law and the law of tort, known as passing off. In simple terms, an unknown brand tries to pass off its goods and services with similar names from another brand. The following conditions are needed to ascertain passing off:

- A person misrepresents an ultimate consumer of goods and services through trade.
- It injures the business of another trader.
- There is an actual loss of business or goodwill due to this.

The challenge in such cases is to establish actual losses. Passing off can occur across trademark classes and may not be captured as part of a trademark registration. For example, Hybo Hindustan advertised men's underwear with a similar arrangement to

---

[34] The classification is standardized internationally by the World Intellectual Property Organization (WIPO), **https://nclpub.wipo.int/enfr/?class_number=42** accessed 18th December 2024

[35] Section 11, Supra 33

[36] A draft of Manual of Trade Marks Practice & Procedure, 15.3.5, Ministry of Commerce and Industries, Govt. of India.

[37] 1963 AIR 449

[38] Section 134, Supra 33

the Mercedes-Benz logo for its product, VIP Benz.[39] Daimler-Benz claimed that Hybo Hindustan tarnished the Mercedes-Benz brand.

A company should register as soon as it conceives the trademark. Once it uses a mark in one market without registering and expands its business to another, and a similar mark is seen in the new market, it can derail launch plans in the new market. The brand goodwill is lost if the company has to launch with another trademark. Moreover, trademark registrations can take several months.

Lastly, domain names are significant for software companies, as almost all transactions happen over websites. In the early days, some people registered common domain names and reached companies and asked them for a fee for the domain. For example, a Google employee discovered Google's domain (google.com) had expired and registered it in his name, and Google canceled the registration but rewarded him for being vigilant.[40]

A Uniform Domain Registration Policy (UDRP)[41] is under the Internet Corporation for Assigned Names and Numbers (ICANN). As per this policy, a complainant with a business interest in a domain name can request ICANN with the relevant proof and convincing evidence that the site is in bad faith to their business interest. However, if the defendants could prove that they are running a valid business or on fair use from the website, ICANN would not transfer the site. The USA has the Anticybersquatting Consumer Protection Act (ACPA), 1999.[42] This law codifies pass-off defenses for domains. So, the provisions go further than bad-faith defense. There are several reported cases of cybersquatting in India. The domain has been granted to the trademark owners in the pronounced judgments. Here are some for reference:

- **Yahoo Inc v Akash Arora**[43]: The court granted an injunction against usage of the domain yahooindia.com
- **Rediff Communications v Cyberbooth**[44]: Cyberbooth was prohibited from using the "*Radiff*" domain name.
- **Titan Industries v. Prashant Kooapati**[45]: The defendants were prohibited from using the Tanishq name on their website.
- **Satyam Infoway v Sifynet Solutions**[46]: The court held that the defendant's domain "*siffynet*" was against the plaintiff's interest, leading to a pass-of.

---

[39] Daimler Benz v. Hybo Hindustan AIR 1994 Del 239
[40] **https://www.businessinsider.com/this-guy-bought-googlecom-from-google-for-one-minute-2015-9** accessed 18th Dec. 2024
[41] **https://www.icann.org/resources/pages/policy-2024-02-21-en**
[42] Anticybersquatting Consumer Protection Act (ACPA), 15 U.S.C. § 1125(d)
[43] 1999 (2) AD (Del) 229
[44] AIR 2000, Bombay 27
[45] Delhi High Court Suit No. 179 of 1998
[46] AIR 2004, SC 3540

As soon as a business interest is seen in a new domain, it should be procured to avoid unnecessary legal concerns later. Domains must be renewed at regular intervals, ensuring non-expiry. Most domain registrars provide multi-year and advanced registration these days.

Patents

We protected the expression elements in the software code and user interface through copyrights and our branding, names, and domains as registered trademarks. But what about the ideas? Interesting ideas come to employees, but not everything gets to a product. What if the employee quits and joins a competitor? When an idea is in someone's mind, similar ideas are also in other people's minds. They will work on these ideas and can be new entrants in the field. Converting these tacit ideas into explicit knowledge and getting exclusivity on them for a few years is a good way to create a barrier against new entrants. That is where patents come into the picture.

At the beginning of this chapter, we discussed ServiceNow vs. BMC wrangling over a patent dispute. BMC sued ServiceNow for infringement of eleven patents, claiming every aspect of ServiceNow product had infringed BMC patents; ServiceNow had no patents.[47] Eventually, they settled the dispute,[48] but all these put significant pressure on ServiceNow's product development strategy. Today, ServiceNow has over 2000 patents, with another 600 under review. ServiceNow had been lucky to have overcome the adversities and fought back with full force. They call it out as a potential threat in their annual report.[49]

A government grants an inventor and her assignee exclusive rights to use the idea for a limited period[50] when the following conditions are met.

- The subject matter is patentable.
- The idea is capable of an industrial application.
- It is novel.
- It is non-obvious and has an inventive step.
- The disclosure is complete in the specification of the application.

Patentable Subject Matter

Domains are not covered by patent laws. The patentable subject matter is a considerable concern for the software industry, as computer software, mathematical

---

[47] Joseph Tsidulko, BMC Sues ServiceNow, Claims Widespread Patent Infringement, September 23, 2014, **https://www.crn.com/news/cloud/300074139/bmc-sues-servicenow-claims-widespread-patent-infringement** accessed 24th Dec 2024
[48] Supra 2
[49] ServiceNow, Annual Report, 2023
[50] Section 53, The Patents Act, 1970, Union of India

formulae, business methods, and algorithms are not patentable.[51] Moreover, scientific discoveries[52] are not patentable either. However, there have been several disputes between software companies on patents.

Industrial Application

Judicial interpretations have suggested machine or transformation tests to determine software patentability. An overly simplified explanation: Software embodied inside a computing machine or a process capable of transforming material from one state to another inherently has an industrial utility;[53] Hence, it is patentable. However, it has been held in certain cases, such as Bilkis v Kappos, that it is not the only test to justify a software patent. All software patent claims state the methods followed by a system defined with a computer that can execute them. In short, if you have a software program or algorithm that provides some business benefits when implemented on a general-purpose computer, you can apply for a patent to protect your idea.

We will discuss patent US 7,310,769 B1,[54] where the author has been the inventor. The author was developing a plugin for AutoCAD to convert the views from AutoCAD drawings to PDF. The plugin printed the views in PDF format. However, AutoCAD used some custom font technologies and would print the output as line art, not text characterized by fonts. A human being can read such line art as text. However, there was no textual encoding information. Hence, such text information could not be selected or used for copy-paste operations to another application or read by a screen reader. The industrial application for such a technology is easily established.

Novelty

The author's plugin was part of the AutoCAD application. The author could query the text information from AutoCAD using the APIs in his plugin. He estimated the location of the text in the printed views. He had access to Adobe's libraries for PDF manipulation. So, his program could post-process the generated PDF and insert the text-encoding information.

Optical Character Recognition (OCR) was a research area for Adobe for a substantial

---

[51] Section 3(k), Ibid.
[52] Section 3(d), Ibid.
[53] Andrei Iancu & Peter Gratzinger, Machines and Transformations: The Past, Present, and Future Patentability of Software, Northwestern Journal of Technology and Intellectual Property, Volume 8, Number 2 (Spring 2010)
[54] Sambit Kumar Dash, Text Encoding Using Dummy Fonts, Assignee: Adobe Systems Inc, Filed: March 12, 2003. US 7,310,769 B1, USPTO. The patent term has expired as of April 2024. It is in the public domain. The discussion does not detriment the assignee's interests. Adobe Systems India Pvt. Ltd. had employed the author during the patent application filing.

period. Nicholson and King[55] devised a hybrid image model when overlaying text-encoding information over an image document using a PDF-like file format. However, their requirements were slightly different from the author's.

- They were interested in digitizing an image-to-text.
- They wanted an actual font that matched the visual look of the image. They could replace the image with a reconstructed document with computed fonts.
- Embedding an actual font increased the document by a few hundred kilobytes to a few megabytes.

The author was not interested in the shapes of the glyphs in the font. However, fonts are the only way to embed encoding into a PDF file. Hence, he proposed a dummy font where all encodings were mapped to one glyph, a rectangular box. The invisible outline box could be placed on any character location when rendered in the PDF document. This approach was novel to the **prior art**[56], where identification and selection of the glyph was a non-trivial step.

Non-Obvious and Inventive Step

The suggested changes to using a font with only one glyph could significantly reduce the size of the files. Moreover, the technique was not obvious to a person skilled in the art. The author conceived the idea almost eight years after the prior art. One can argue that such a technology is not easy to conceive with just having the skill in art. Patent attorneys or examiners take the closest prior art, examine the objective technical problem, and argue if the solution is obvious. In our example:

- The closest prior art was the Nicholson and King proposal.
- The problem was file size reduction—this was not something the prior art could have achieved.
- Introducing a universal font to hold the text encoding was an inventive step per the examiners.

Complete Disclosure

Complete disclosure in the context of patents becomes debatable. The government wants the inventor to disclose all steps so that the idea can be exploited for commercial use. If a licensee or assignee of a patent cannot gain commercial advantage, then the disclosure is of little use. However, the licensees believe the disclosures are for the

---

[55] Nicholson and King; Method and apparatus for producing a hybrid data structure for displaying a raster image, US 5,625,711 A, USPTO, Filed: 31st Aug 1994, The patent term has expired as of Aug. 2014.
[56] ibid

complete product development. If you read the patent by the author,[57] the specification describes the hybrid document in detail. However, it does not discuss embedding the special font in the PDF document. A person skilled in the art of PDF would know this by reading the PDF specification and associated documentation. The complete disclosure is about the invention and achieving the desired result of the invention.

Patents can involve legal nuances and tests to decide on patentability. We discussed only a few simple ones with some personal examples. We will now look at some other aspects of patenting.

Preliminary Application and Continuation

The governments give priority to the patent disclosed the earliest. Hence, inventors sometimes disclose the patent description before the final claims. Such a patent application is called a preliminary application. The claims can be furnished within one year of the application. Similarly, when a patent is under review and the assignees want to broaden the scope of the claims, they can apply for a continuation application. Searching dummy font-encoded text[58] is a continuation of the patent application for text encoding using dummy font.[59] Continuation applications have a similar expiry as the original application.

Infringement

A patent is granted to the earliest invention disclosed to the patent office. Suppose A and B were working on a similar idea independently. A came up with the idea first, but she did not patent the idea. B filed for the patent. Later, A came up with a product exploiting the idea. It comes to knowledge of B. B can sue A for patent infringement. If A can successfully prove that she had the knowledge and priority before B's idea, the court can revoke the grant of B's patent. Without a published disclosure, it is always hard to convince the courts. The defense for patent infringement will challenge patentability in most cases. Some typical defenses are:

- There are prior arts that are similar to the patent.
- The patent is superfluous and does not have any inventive steps.
- The disclosure is incomplete.

The other aspect that the defense tries is fair use.

- The usage was only for research, experiments, and education.
- The patented information can be used for the development of new products as long as the product hits the market after the expiry of the patent.

---

[57] Supra 54
[58] Sambit Kumar Dash, Searching dummy font encoded text, US7765477B1, USPTO, expired 12th March 2023.
[59] Supra 54

- The use is for the government.
- The plaintiff has misused the patent or provided misleading information to the patent office.

The party infringing a patent may not be aware of the existence of a specific patent. If two companies are working in similar areas, there is a likely chance that they have patents with overlapping domains. In such a case, they negotiate and agree not to sue each other for infringement for patents related to a specific domain. Novell and Microsoft agreed that Microsoft would not sue Novell's SuSE Linux customers for any Microsoft patent violations and vice versa.[60]

Design

Industrial activities produce various objects with shapes, configurations, patterns, and ornaments. These can be distinguished purely by visual means.[61] These add aesthetic value to a product and should be protected. Similarly, an integrated circuit layout on a printed circuit board can be a form of design to be protected.[62] In the software domain, fonts are unique as fonts can be thought out as code and hence can be copyrighted. Some glyphs are used as trademark symbols from fonts. Similarly, fonts also stand out independently as a pattern for industrial design.[63] Colloquially, many call these designs design patents. However, industrial designs are not patents. Industrial designs have a term of 10 years that can be extended by another five years.[64]

Others

Trademarks, Copyrights, Patents, and Designs are the most important IPs we deal with in software. However, we are exposed to other forms with the digitalization of enterprises and e-commerce as the goods sold are not software—for example, Geographic Indicators.[65] At the beginning of the chapter, we discussed artisans and their art to be protected from over-mechanization. GIs are a way to achieve that. Pochampally silk patterns are GI assigned to the artisans from the region using their traditional process. A duplicate manufactured elsewhere cannot claim to be

---

[60] Microsoft and Novell Announce Broad Collaboration on Windows and Linux Interoperability and Support, 2nd Nov 2006, **https://news.microsoft.com/2006/11/02/microsoft-and-novell-announce-broad-collaboration-on-windows-and-linux-interoperability-and-support/** accessed 26th Dec 2024

[61] The Designs Act, 2000, Union of India

[62] The Semiconductor Integrated Circuits Layout-Design Act, 2000, Union of India

[63] Savan Dhameliya, Protection of Font and Typefaces under the Indian Copyright Law, 17th Nov 2024, **https://iprmentlaw.com/2024/11/17/protection-of-font-and-typefaces-under-the-indian-copyright-law/** accessed 26th Dec. 2024

[64] Section 11, Supra 61

[65] The Geographical Indications of Goods (Registration and Protection) Act, 1999, Union of India

Pochampally silk. Similarly, farmers can develop crops and animals of hybrid qualities using traditional breeding techniques.[66] They have to be protected as well.

Should you patent every idea? What would have happened if Coca-Cola had patented its formula? The patent would have expired; every known soft drink manufacturer would be producing their Coke. Coke would have lost its brand identity. For an idea to be patented, the discoverability upon infringement should be easily identifiable. Secondly, the process should be unique enough that another person trying to infringe will find it hard to imitate with an alternate method. If these characteristics are not there, patenting may not help. However, the technology can be kept as a trade secret. When your approach is for the current market condition, for short-term economic gain, it is ideal to keep the approach a secret. Patents are rights over 20 years. If your technology does not have such a long horizon, patenting does not help. Enforceability of trade secret infringement can be difficult. Some countries, such as India, do not have any statutory provisions specific to trade secrets. Moreover, in a trade secret, the content is unknown. When sharing trade secrets with someone, a written record must be maintained with a proper Non-Disclosure Agreement (NDA). The owner should maintain a formal record of the secret. For example, she can write the secret and register the post to herself in a sealed envelope or store it in a secured vault, and so on.

Process of IPR Application

The government grants monopolistic rights through IPs and there are well-defined processes from application to final disposal of the case. Hence, a legal advisor such as an IP lawyer is a good intermediary to assist in this process. Indian IP laws do not mandate an intermediary to apply for any IPs. However, the experience and knowledge of an IP expert help quickly dispose of the case. Most of the IP-related applications can be submitted online these days. The process is as follows:

1. The applicant submits an IP application with all the required details in a well-structured form.

2. The IP examiner reviews the application for correctness; if there are discrepancies, she returns the form requesting additional information.

3. With the satisfactory submission and the relevant fees, the examiners review the form. They study prior art or similarity of trademarks by employing various search mechanisms. They reject the application when they find substantial overlap of ideas, expressions, designs, and so on.

4. The applicant can appeal to the appellate authority, providing additional information or modifying the application. Only modifications can be permitted to specific sections and areas and should not be for the complete specifications.

---

[66] Biological Diversity Act, 2002, Union of India

5. The appellate authority can publish the application for public comments when convinced by the applicants' information, or she can reject the application for further review.

6. Most IPs are published for some time for public comment and review. A party aggrieved by the grant of the IP rights will raise objections, stating how the possible application affects their rights over the IP or a prior art makes the application unsustainable.

7. The examiners review all the objections and finally confer the rights on the applicant.

After a successful grant, the IP owner can use or license her rights. While we describe a simplified version of the IP registration workflow, the exact duration of the examination and waiting time can be months or even years in the case of patents. Hence, as soon as an IP is identified, it should be registered.

While our explanation of the IP registration process mimics the Indian system, almost all World Intellectual Property Organization (WIPO) members follow a similar process; the nations have similar IP laws. India has been a WIPO member since 1975. With liberalization, India amended many IP acts in line with international recommendations. IPs have to be registered in each country for recognition. They do not get automatic recognition in another country. However, if country A recognizes the IPs of country B, B will reciprocate in recognizing A's IPs. India is a signatory of the Patent Cooperation Treaty (PCT). If needed, an Indian citizen can file a PCT patent application, which will be honored by all 157 member countries.

Respecting Other's IPRs

No one develops software in isolation. Sometimes, you use code, libraries, and APIs from other vendors to work with your software. One should know the license restrictions and recognize the IPs as per the license. For example, white-labeled software used in your code should not expose the vendor information to an external customer. However, some vendors like their brands advertised even though they are internal to the system. Intel asked all the OEMs to display their logo externally on laptops and desktops as part of their Intel inside[67] campaign.

We will look at the cases where you have used a service provider with a contract for work or a contract of work arrangement. As per the service agreement, IPs developed during this engagement will be assigned to your entity. However, authors and inventors have special rights with their authorships and inventions. These rights are statutory; a contract cannot take them away. These are known as moral rights. As per

---
[67] Ingredient Branding, End User Marketing and "Intel Inside", **https://www.intel.com/content/www/us/en/history/virtual-vault/articles/end-user-marketing-intel-inside.html** accessed 27th Dec. 2024

the copyright act, an author has a right to claim authorship for his bona fide work and damages for misattribution of work not contributed by him.[68] A source control system is a good way to retain the developer's moral rights. In patents, the human inventors get the first right to the invention. They assign the rights in favor of the company they are working for. All the inventors must be recognized, irrespective of the assignee. In contractual employment, sometimes it is assumed the contractual employee cannot be an inventor. The inventor and assignee relationship is not an employee and employer relationship. The inventor can contact the patent adjudicating authority (controller in India) and submit a request for the inclusion of his name in the patent application.[69] All office actions of a patent are public information. Inventor conflict does not reflect well against a company's reputation; such disputes unnecessarily drain resources.

There are situations where you are competing with a platform provider. You have used their services in the past but now want to own that platform yourself. You are integrating downstream. It is natural for them to accuse you of infringing their IPs. The right way to develop software is a cleanroom. Your application developers work independently without any influence of any of the software you licensed earlier. In Google v Oracle[70], the rest of the Dalvik VM was not considered an infringement as Google developed the code in Cleanroom. The only contention was the 37 APIs they used from the JVM and the associated 11,500 lines of the code.

Open Source

Open Source started as a movement from the Free Software Foundation by Richard Stallman in 1984 with the GNU project. The GNU project talks about free as in freedom and not economically free. It has four levels of freedom:[71]

- The freedom to run the program as you wish for any purpose (freedom 0).
- The freedom to study how the program works and change it so it does your computing as you wish (freedom 1). Access to the source code is a precondition for this.
- The freedom to redistribute copies so you can help others (freedom 2).
- The freedom to distribute copies of your modified versions to others (freedom 3). By doing this, you can give the whole community a chance to benefit from your changes. Access to the source code is a precondition for this.

Some of these freedoms are not available to commercial software. After years of initial wrangling with commercial software, open-source powers almost all major software platforms. Every software organization today uses or contributes to some form of

---
[68] Section 57, Supra 8
[69] Section 24, Supra 50
[70] Supra 22
[71] Taken verbatim from **https://www.gnu.org** accessed 27th December 2024

open source. Open-source licenses are copyrighted codes assigned to a community, yet the license allows others to develop derivative work with certain restrictions. For example, some licenses require the derivatives to share source code. Some more permissible licenses, such as MIT and Apache, may expect attribution of the software in the derivative. We will not discuss the open-source licenses in detail here but review them in the context of compliance. However, most open-source licenses mandate their usage be acknowledged.

Innovation and IPR

IPs are a way to quantify human endeavor and ingenuity. While most people focus too much on patents to convince their innovativeness to businesses, much of their ingenuity can be in building brands, business methods in selling, customer service, and so on, that cannot be patented. If you have a catchy logo that adds to your brand identity, it is a trademark that will add value to you. Good packaging can be an industrial design. Your company name and associativity to the customer's mind are all great IPs. Customer or people's goodwill, though adds value to an organization, it is not discussed as an IP. Tata as a brand is attributed to trust and durability in India. It is just a reflection of the goodwill of Indian people, not any recognized IPR. For a company, the innovation can be directed toward improving the overall value of its products and services. Picking up IPs on the way is just an added advantage.

Incentivizing Innovation

The best way to incentivize innovation is by ensuring people excel in their work. We recommend the following as a means to foster innovation.

- Making the product vision clear to all employees.
- Enabling them to define and operate a working environment and content that aligns with the vision.
- Improve collaboration across departments for the free exchange of ideas.
- Open and frank communication across hierarchical boundaries.

Often, companies focus significantly on patents to drive their innovation. Here are some notable ones:

- Cash and gifts for filing new ideas.
- Reviews of ideas and coaching to employees to generate better ideas.
- Providing additional time to employees to pursue the patent application process.
- Cash awards and recognitions when the patent is filed and granted.
- Special mention of patent holders in various forums in the company.

Figure 8.1: *The author's employer gave this citation to commemorate the patent grant*

Companies should review patent portfolios and incorporate them into the relevant products. Very few companies achieve this. The realization of patented ideas in the product is a good way to ensure the products are always at the forefront of technology. PMs can significantly contribute in this direction.

Conclusion

We started with an understanding of the basis of IPs. We delved into copyrights, trademarks, patents, and industrial designs as IPs and their impact on the software industry and products. We looked at how they are helping us in creating a barrier against the new entrants taking over our markets. We discussed the legal implications of the IPs and how to protect them. We learned how to register IPs. We reviewed some lesser-used IPs in the software industry, such as Geographic Indicators, Biodiversity, and trade secrets. Lastly, we looked at a few practices that organizations employ to foster innovation.

With the advent of AI, will IP laws remain the same? We leave the readers to review these articles[72,73] to form their opinions on this topic. We believe the legal community is divided and is waiting for courts to provide a clear direction with cases.

In the next chapter, we will look at how to defend against substitutes and how compliance creates a deterrence in that direction.

Questions

1. You are about to start a new business; should you have a logo? Is it a good time to register your logo as a trademark?
2. Think of a technology problem you worked on. Assess if you can patent the idea.
3. You need a website for your business. But someone has already registered the domain. How will you get access to your website?
4. Are patents the only means to justify innovation?
5. Outline the activities your organization is undertaking to foster innovation.

---

[72] Harshal Chhabra and Arihant Sethia, The Impact of Artificial Intelligence on Intellectual Property Rights: A Case for Reform in Indian Patent Law by "Innovative Oversight" Approach, 24th Nov 2024, IJLT, https://www.ijlt.in/post/the-impact-of-artificial-intelligence-on-intellectual-property-rights-a-case-for-reform-in-indian-p

[73] YAGAY and SUN, Intellectual Property (IP) in India in the Era of Artificial Intelligence [IPRs Laws], 10th March 2025, https://www.taxmanagementindia.com/visitor/detail_article.asp?ArticleID=13756

CHAPTER 9
Compliance

Introduction

Like new entrants enter the market to compete, substitutes try to completely overthrow the existing approach to addressing the customer problem with newer approaches and innovative devices. The substitutes often enter the market completely unannounced, catching the incumbents' products and solutions unaware. No one can ever guess they can be a prominent force in the market. The transition can be so sudden that one day, the businesses realize the rug has been pulled under their feet. The incumbent needs protection against such a tsunami of change from substitutes. When used astutely, business compliance can provide good protection from the threats of such rapid changes. In this chapter, we review why compliance is important for businesses. While most see the role of compliance in risk mitigation, they protect from disruptions of substitutes as they are not prepared to meet the compliance requirements.

Structure

In this chapter, we will cover the following topics:

- The Need
- Penal Provisions of Non-Compliance
- Gating Criteria and Business Loss
- Cost of Compliance
- Messaging
- Compliance in SaaS Business

The Need

Compliance is an afterthought. First, a new domain of businesses establishes itself. When businesses become popular and a need for regulations is realized, the laws and rules are formulated. The businesses are asked to comply with them. That is pretty much the genesis of a compliance process. Hence, most people think of compliance as an overhead. However, authority and society consider these as reasonable restrictions imposed to restrict the rights of the business and impose certain obligations on the business. We will understand this concept with some examples. The Constitution of India gives the right to livelihood under the broader interpretation of the right to life under Article 21. Any person can start any legally valid business. Suppose the person wants to separate her business liabilities from her personal liabilities. This is an additional right. She can register for a Limited Liabilities Partnership (LLP). The LLP requires certain restrictions and some disclosures of her firm's financials to the government as part of the LLP compliance process. Suppose she decides to have other people invest in her business who are not working for her business on a day-to-day basis. Moreover, the business liability should be kept separate from the investors' liabilities. For this additional right to be honored, she can register her business as a private limited company. The disclosures for private limited companies are higher than LLPs as part of the company's compliance process. If she wants to raise funds from the general public on a stock exchange, she has to float a public limited company. The disclosures are far more stringent. They require independent board members, auditors, and company secretary-like officials to audit the finances, company board activities, and so on. Every form of organization we discussed gives certain additional rights. Authorities impose some reasonable restrictions through compliance requirements on the owners and promoters.

The Dutch East Indian Company, established in 1602, is considered the first company to have traded stocks on exchanges. Yet, with so many advancements in financial disclosures and accounting practices in four centuries, we see significant changes in the laws to bring transparency in disclosures and accounting practices worldwide every couple of years. Compliance requirements are fluid and keep changing over time. Organizations have to review and comply with the newer rules and regulations introduced. The ideal accounting practice in Indian laws is double-entry bookkeeping on accruals. When the Indian government introduced the goods and services tax (GST), it did so around the standard accounting practices. Since micro, small, and medium enterprises (MSME) were not maintaining formal account books, the government incentivized them by providing a channel to obtain free accounting packages,[1] thus creating a level playing field across the organizations.

We discussed the Certificate Authority (CA) business earlier and revisited due to the strong presence of compliance. The CAs issue digital certificates that can be used to sign and verify documents, authenticate users, and establish trusted electronic communications. The certificates are of very little value unless there is a large technology ecosystem to accept and use them. Industrial bodies have developed standards and Request for Comments (RFC) that the CAs adhere to when creating the certificates. The CAs have to be trusted by the web browsers. They would like to evaluate the processes used by the CAs and certify them as trusted CA partners. They may develop a well-defined process for inclusion into the ecosystem. Browsers

---

[1] We discussed this in *Chapter 4: Customers*.

and CAs have developed a forum[2] where they interact and let each other know of their technological advancements. They comply with the membership guidelines to maintain their membership in the forum[3] and to be part of the approved CA list. The listed CAs issue **server certificates** (SSL certificates) that encrypt the communication channel while accessing the servers through web browsers. Some of the international CAs in the market are Let's Encrypt, GlobalSign, Sectigo, GoDaddy, DigiCert, and so on, as per their market share.[4]

One can digitally sign an electronic document using a digital certificate. The same signing technology principles are used to authenticate a user. These certificates are called **user certificates**. As per the Indian IT Act, certificates issued by CAs approved by the Controller of Certifying Authorities (CCA) are valid for legal non-repudiation. You can only use those to sign contracts, file taxes, submit government contracts, and so on. CCA has only approved 23 CAs[5] —some of these are government entities and issue certificates for consumption by government departments. The CCA mandates that CAs should keep all Personal Identifiable Information (PII) in India. It can be a significant task for global certificate vendors to operate specific data centers in India. Very few global SSL vendors provide CCA-approved user certificates in India. Some of them had collaborated with Indian vendors to offer such services earlier. Running a data center in India has not been a commercially viable option for them.

The technology around certificate management has become commoditized. There are several open-source certificate management platforms on the market, such as OpenCA and EJBCA. There is no need to depend on the traditional global players for the technology. Moreover, the user certificate vendors have slowly expanded into identity vetting (e-KYC) or document signing markets that use biometric user recognition services. eKYC and online document signing are used in the financial markets with anywhere banking. With increasing compliance requirements, the regional vendors are getting a substantial boost in the market.

A CA works on absolute trust, and CAs issue root certificates trusted by all the relying parties. What if the CA is compromised? To ensure the CAs are taking due care, the CAs disclose their certificate policies and actions taken to comply with them in a Certification Practice Statement (CPS). The authorities, such as the CA/B forum or CCA,[6] ensure the CPS is maintained. What can be a substitute technology for CA business? Distributed trust with blockchains does not require a CA. A distributed ledger can record any data and timestamp it. Anyone having access to the ledger can validate the data. So, blockchains do not require a certificate authority. The Indian IT Act defines two entities - digital signatures and electronic signatures. What we have so far discussed falls into digital signatures. However, electronic signatures have a wider

---

[2] CA/Browser Forum, **https://cabforum.org**
[3] **https://cabforum.org/about/information/potential-members/**
[4] **https://w3techs.com/technologies/overview/ssl_certificate** accessed 7th February 2025
[5] **https://cca.gov.in/licensed_ca.html** accessed 7th February 2025
[6] Section 30 (cb) Indian IT Act 2000

interpretation. Today, Adhaar-based KYC and trusted third-party assisted subscriber certificates are the only recognized techniques approved in Schedule II under electronic signatures.[7] While blockchains have the required technological capabilities, the existing compliance requirements can protect the user certificate vendors for some time. Even if the law adopts newer technologies, large-scale adoption of that technology can take a few years. Incumbent vendors have found some protection from substitute technologies.

Compliance requirements are not always imposed by external authorities alone. Some large organizations develop policies that all the business units adhere to for better operational efficiency. An e-commerce vendor may introduce a free replacement of damaged goods for low-priced products. As the products are low priced, they do not want to involve the support executive's time in resolving the issues. Organizations may impose a policy of approval from a BU head for purchases of a certain value or more. While the intent is for better organizational efficiency, sometimes implementations are in letters rather than in spirit, defeating the purpose.

Penal Provisions of Non-Compliance

When a statutory policy affects a business, non-compliance can have serious consequences. Companies can go out of business, and the law can make the founders and managers liable for civil and criminal actions.[8] Penal provisions are severe when they affect commoners or involve public money. Sahara India was involved in several financial improprieties and was asked to refund all the money collected from the public under private placement. The founder was kept in jail for a long time. A substantial part of the money with interest was recovered.[9] The company's assets were attached or divested to repay the debt. Overall, it affected the company's reputation and business. Reading through the case, one can understand that such large companies often depend on legal interpretation and are professionally prepared to take these risks.

In *Chapter 5: Pricing*, we discussed how e-commerce players have used discounted pricing to retain dominant positions in the market. Instances of predatory pricing have been observed where the products are priced way below the variable cost of production. While some cases are still pending in the courts, general guidelines for such businesses can be the following:

- Lower pricing should also mean the players maintain a low-cost structure so that they are not inconvenienced by charges of predatory pricing.

---

[7] Schedule II, Indian IT Act 2000

[8] Sumeet Kachawa and Tara Sahni. Business Crime Laws and Regulations India 2025, ICLG, **https://iclg.com/practice-areas/business-crime-laws-and-regulations/india** accessed 10th February 2025

[9] **https://www.businesstoday.in/latest/corporate/story/subrata-roys-sahara-scam-where-is-rs-25000-crore-submitted-to-sebi-and-how-to-claim-refund-405829-2023-11-15** accessed 7th February 2025

- Be prepared for a legal battle and keep it part of the risk mitigation for compliance. Most large companies maintain in-house legal counsel and engage litigation lawyers to review major business decisions and assess legal ramifications.

Lastly, they can acquire aspirational customers with a relatively inexpensive luxury experience, for example, cheaper alternatives to expensive perfumes, self-service dining options, self-installable furniture, or privately labeled goods. They attract a new market without affecting the existing market yet create lingering doubt and pressure in the core market. The customers in the core market do not wish to shift to cheap alternatives, but they demand better value and experience from their suppliers.

When Reliance Jio entered the mobile market, they were prepared for the Competition Commission of India (CCI) investigations. When Amazon or Flipkart are in the e-commerce business on a large scale, they are prepared to defend anti-trust provisions in India. For a startup, these statutory compliance cases can become a nightmare.

Gaurav Dahake, a graduate of IIT Kharagpur, developed the Tatkal for Sure browser extension and sold it for Rs. 30. A person can install the Chrome extension and go to the IRCTC website. The extension could autofill the customer information in seconds, thus making the booking of tickets very fast for passengers under the emergency train ticket quota (tatkal). IRCTC, the primary booking portal of the railways, considered this a violation of the Railways Act and booked a case against him. The provisions under the section even had criminal remediation with a jail term. The case took several years, and the business could not take off. Eventually, the Karnataka High Court acquitted him of all the charges.[10] However, it affected the portal significantly. Their web page says they have shut down the business.[11] Today, IRCTC is not the only website that books railway tickets.[12] Companies take data from the Centre for Railways Information Systems (CRIS) and have developed parallel booking systems collaborating with IRCTC. When regulations are at the core of the business, the risk should be assessed and mitigated for the product to be successful.

Complying with all the legal frameworks in business is hard. The lack of understanding of laws cannot be an excuse for not adhering to them. While we just discussed compliance related to business, there are several legal requirements for running an office, employment, corporate structure, capital structuring, procurement, material movement, and more. Not all of them fall into a product management domain.

---

[10] **https://timesofindia.indiatimes.com/india/hc-quashes-case-against-iit-grad-who-sped-up-tatkal-bookings-through-software/articleshow/113141024.cms** accessed 8th February 2025

[11] Sorry and thank you for your immense support! We are no longer in operations ever since the pandemic hit in 2020. **https://tatkalforsure.com/** accessed 8th February 2025.

[12] Companies like MakeMyTrip, Ixigo, RedBus.in, etc., allow railway booking through their websites. They advertise themselves as IRCTC-approved websites.

With significant inroads into SaaS and AI, data is becoming the core of many businesses. The user's data is collected and uploaded to the servers. The data has to be secured confidentially. Similarly, many businesses on the internet do not own the content. They provide a platform between content creators and subscribers. In such cases, they act as an intermediary for the business. Today, a business needs to maintain legal compliance with the following laws of its operational jurisdiction:

- Data Protection and Privacy Laws
- Any legal provisions imposed on intermediaries.

The European Union has the most progressive laws in these directions. They apply not only to companies operating out of the EU but also to companies external to the EU with business interests in the region. The first one is the General Data Protection Regulations (GDPR).[13] The act ensures ethical collection and use of the data. The companies must collect the minimum data from the users:

- Stating the details of the data collection and the purposes of their use.
- Giving the option to opt out of the service and deletion of the data when the user does not use the services any longer.
- Sharing, if needed, the information with a law enforcement agency only when requested lawfully.
- Retaining the data securely for use and legal audit and compliance.

EU law is considered a pioneer in the field. Other nations and states in the USA have developed their regulations.[14] While every law has its provisions specific to its jurisdiction, there is a general alignment with the principles developed in GDPR. India also passed her Digital Personal Data Protection Act, 2023, and will soon notify it along with the Digital Personal Data Protection Rules, 2025.[15]

The Indian IT Act 2000 has a wide definition of intermediary encompassing internet service providers (ISP), telecom service providers, network service providers, web-hosting service providers, search engines, online payment sites, online auction sites, online marketplaces, cyber cafes, and so on.[16] It is understood that these kinds of organizations do not own the content and are not directly responsible for the content. However, they should abide by government orders to provide information when any objectionable content is transmitted through them and remove it when asked.[17] The Indian government has released detailed rules for the intermediaries to take due

---

[13] GDPR, Legal Text, **https://gdpr-info.eu/** accessed 8th February 2025
[14] Data Privacy Laws: What You Need to Know in 2025, Osano, **https://www.osano.com/articles/data-privacy-laws** accessed 8th February 2025.
[15] MeitY releases Draft Digital Personal Data Protection Rules, 2025 for public consultation; Feedback/comments sought from public by 18th February, 2025, **https://pib.gov.in/PressReleasePage.aspx?PRID=2090048** accessed on 10th February 2025.
[16] Section 2(1) w, Information Technology Act, 2000
[17] Section 79, Ibid

diligence to ensure the content does not violate legal provisions.[18] In case of failure to maintain due diligence, the protection they get as intermediaries shall not be available.

Some intermediaries have reached a size where they can enforce their dominant positions. We have seen it in the past when AT&T got monopolistic control over the USA telecom market and was split into several smaller entities called Baby Bells after the court order. Today, Alphabet, Amazon, Apple, ByteDance, Meta, and Microsoft are in such a dominant position. They have control of substantial user data; they touch upon every individual who accesses the internet today. However, the services they offer are of immense value. The EU wants to keep the competitive elements active in the markets while these large companies can operate without stifling competition. Digital Markets Act[19] is a set of regulations for such gatekeeper companies to operate on a level playing ground with smaller companies. The gatekeepers offer twenty-two services identified as core platform services (CPS). These six companies provide several of these CPSs. They can force competition out and push the users to their CPSs. For example, Meta has social networking (Facebook and Instagram) and messaging (WhatsApp). They can force users of Facebook and Instagram to move to WhatsApp. The act gives guidelines for do's and don'ts for these gatekeepers. Here are a few examples.

Do's

- Allow third parties to interact with their platforms.
- Allow business users to access data generated in the CPSs.
- Provide advertisers tools to verify their advertisement metrics independently.
- Allow business users to negotiate and contract outside of Gatekeeper's platform.

Don'ts

- Gatekeepers should not rank their services higher over their competition in search results or e-commerce merchandise lists.
- Prevent consumers from linking up to businesses outside their platforms.
- Preventing users from uninstallation and installation of software of their choice.
- Tracking users without obtaining their consent.

While DMA affects the gatekeeper companies, the EU Artificial Intelligence Act[20] has a wider implication for every company that provides a service with AI. The law classifies AI into four classes.

- Prohibited unacceptable risky activities.

---

[18] The Information Technology (Intermediary Guidelines and Digital Media Ethics Code) Rules, 2021
[19] EU Digital Markets Act 2022, **https://digital-markets-act.ec.europa.eu/index_en**
[20] EU Artificial Intelligence Act, 2024, **https://artificialintelligenceact.eu/**

- Regulated high-risk activities.
- Lighter transparency obligations for medium-risk activities.
- Unregulated low-risk activities.

The law focuses on the first three classes and demands proper disclosures from the providers of such systems. It has been in force since August 2024, and the EU expects complete compliance in the next three years.

Gating Criteria and Business Loss

In areas where statutes are crucial, non-compliance can lead to legal actions and can have criminal repercussions. What if compliance is for a standard or a condition of the contract bidding process? The business may not qualify to participate. These can have economic or long-term image implications. On the other hand, a company that successfully qualifies would like to create barriers for others by narrowing the provisions of the compliance requirements. Let us look at the CA business again. When it comes to a CA as a user identity issuer, local government regulations are of paramount importance. The server identity or the Secure Socket Layer (SSL) protection is governed by the CA/Browser forum. During booming e-commerce and internet in the early 2000s, Verisign was one of the major players in the CA market. Verisign had two businesses. They are the owners of .com, .net, and .org top-level domains. They owned 44% of all issued server certificates.[21] Technically, they provided the DNS infrastructure of the domains and issued certificates to protect them. They were a prominent player in the CAB forum. It is natural for players such as Verisign to introduce more stringent regulations for Extended Validation certificates through the CAB forum. The EV certificates had more stringent validation, insurance clauses, and so on, and were several times more expensive. At some point, Verisign owned over 70 percent of the market share of EV certificates.[22] We discussed the EV certificates and their subsequent failure in *Chapter 7, Contracts*. With cloud computing, the number of certificates needed for SSL communications skyrocketed. Symantec acquired the Verisign certificate business.[23]

Not just Symantec, but others in the CAB forum now understand there is a direct market opportunity for CAs to gain from the explosion in the internet servers due to cloud computing. Typical browser vendors such as Google or Microsoft could not enter the CA market as that would be a conflict of interest. A browser vendor

---

[21] **https://investor.verisign.com/news-releases/news-release-details/verisign-leads-ssl-market-444-percent-unit-share-latest-netcraft** accessed 13th February 2025
[22] ibid.
[23] **https://www.verisign.com/en_US/verisign-repository/symantec/index.xhtml?loc=en_US** accessed 13th February 2025

certifying legitimate servers to connect to would have been antithetical to the open internet. Moreover, these were the same companies that later dominated the cloud computing market. Some companies came together and created a consortium called "*Let's Encrypt*" and issued SSL server certificates for free through them.[24] Moreover, CAs were not immune to vulnerabilities and were not always compliant with the norms set forth by the CAB forum. The Symantec CA vulnerability 2017 made Mozilla and Google Chrome remove the CA roots as trustworthy.[25] Symantec ended up selling the SSL CA business to DigiCert. Today, *Let's Encrypt* has over 60% market share of SSL certificates, while DigiCert commands only 3.4%.[26] Most server certificates used in cloud servers are free Let's Encrypt certificates. A trigger of events of compromised CA and non-compliance with the CAB forum requirements ended Symantec's CA business.

Cost of Compliance

Non-compliance is a business risk. Either it can lead to legal ramifications or force one to close the business due to serious losses. Similarly, compliances for company, labor, export-import, taxation, and so on are non-negotiable, though they do not fall into the responsibility of a PM. For the other forms of compliance, you need to assess if you want to:

- Avoid the Risk
- Reduce or Mitigate the Risk
- Transfer the Risk
- Accept the Risk

Let us think of a cloud service provider. The customer data is in the cloud, with the potential risk of data breaches. You know, the EU has strict laws on data privacy. You know you cannot meet them in your product today. The best option for you will be not to venture into that market. You **avoided** that risk along with losing the business. Sometimes, it may not be practical to avoid.

In the cloud, there is every possibility the hackers are trying to steal data from your servers. It cannot be removed, but you can **reduce** it by better access control and implementing industry-standard best practices, like an ISO-27001 or conducting Vulnerability Assessment and Penetration Testing (VAPT).

---

[24] **https://letsencrypt.org/sponsors/** accessed 14th February 2024
[25] Timeline of Certificate Authority Failures, **https://sslmate.com/resources/certificate_authority_failures** accessed 14th February 2025
[26] **https://w3techs.com/technologies/history_overview/ssl_certificate/ms/y** accessed 14th February 2025.

Compliance

You use third-party or open-source software. The software is outside of your control. Suppose there are patent violations by the open-source vendors.[27] You do not want to take such a burden and decide to **transfer** such risks to your customers. You document the end-user license agreement that way.

You have outsourced a part of your product to a Ukrainian entity, and there is a war going on between Russia and Ukraine.[28] They cannot work as effectively as they would in the time of peace. You have not found an alternate team elsewhere. You have **accepted** the risk and project delays due to that. Moreover, you may be considered a hostile company in Russia if you have a potential market there.

Let us assess the cost to incur in meeting the compliance needs. Here are the typical steps involved.

- Assessing the risk and employing the right expert for the compliance assessment.
- Developing the plan to meet the technical and management needs for compliance.
- Roll out the plans to the affected team and get the management buy-in.
- Finding the right external auditor to audit the progress and plan based on their availability.
- With all the activities in place, you can assess the cost of first-time compliance. However, that is not enough. You will periodically evaluate, amend the policies, and be compliant over several years. You will need to assess them and include them as a recurring cost of compliance.
- You implement the controls in all departments and review them with the internal auditor or expert.
- Once they are satisfied, you invite the external auditor to certify.

As you can see, the work involves quite a few departments and can take several months to years to be compliant with some standards. Before pursuing any compliance project, you should evaluate the costs judiciously.

Some standards are discretionary in nature of capability assessment; some examples are ISO-9001, CMM Level 5, ITIL, and so on. As you climb up the levels, you start projecting a better process capability of your services. However, the value has to be understood by your customers and service consumers. Initially, the standards are adopted by a few competitors; it is a differentiating proposition to some prospects.

---

[27] Microsoft and Novell decided not to sue each other or their customers on patent disputes. It made SuSE Linux a better interoperable Linux in the Windows ecosystem. **https://news.microsoft.com/2006/11/02/microsoft-and-novell-announce-broad-collaboration-on-windows-and-linux-interoperability-and-support/** accessed 14th February 2025.

[28] Nigel Walker, Conflict in Ukraine: A timeline (current conflict, 2022-present), 16th September 2024, House of Commons Library, UK Parliament.

Over time, as many organizations acquire such capabilities or independently expand their business and develop their markets, reliance on standards-based capabilities may lose the differentiating edge. For example, the Information Technology Information Library (ITIL) has defined a list of best practices for the IT Service Management (ITSM) industry. Pink Elephant is an organization that certifies the process capability of the ITSM tools. In the list, some organizations have achieved compliance with all process metrics vs. some that have barely scratched the surface with one or two processes.[29] Some of these companies have been in business for several decades and have established their image in their customers' minds. Business success, profits, or revenues do not always correlate to the number of processes they are certified. Somewhere the compliance costs have to justify the revenues gained.

Messaging

Compliance can be useful when the customer can connect to it and is ready to offer a better price. Sometimes, the customers do not see the value of compliance. A technically savvy and aware customer can directly connect. The buyer may be a businessperson. While influencers can see the value, a lot is lost in translation. PMs should look at effective communication. Here is an example:

> *Our products are compliant with the EU GDPR standards.*
>
> vs.
>
> *We collect your phone numbers, names, and addresses to operate the product. We share the data with our third-party service providers to send you alert messages about service operations. When a customer leaves the platform, we delete the data within six months. Our practices are compliant with the EU GDPR. We obtained certification in 2024.*

While the first statement is good enough for a business operating in the EU region, the second one is elaborate and applicable even to the non-EU regions. It is easy and creates an impression of an organization that takes personal privacy seriously.

It is easy to overstate the compliance level of a product. In the PinkVerify certification we discussed earlier, we saw companies certified from two to twenty-one processes. It is easy for someone to state compliance with PinkVerify for ITIL without clearly stating the number of processes or providing the specific processes. Things like these will be considered misstatements of facts. These are not unusual in the industry in general. For SaaS applications, security compliance is a serious concern. ISO-27001 and Service Organization Control (SOC) 2 are relevant standards. However, many products that run their applications from a public cloud infrastructure, such as AWS, Azure, or GCP, would use statements such as *"running from a compliant platform."*

---

[29] **https://www.pinkelephant.com/en-US/pinkverify/pinkverify-certification** accessed on 15th Feb 2025.

The core platform compliance does not cover the SaaS product. Buyers should be cautious of these facts. In the code for self-regulation of advertising content in India,[30] misrepresentation and false claims of facts are strongly discouraged.

Non-compliant claims are not akin to compliance information only. You see them in competitive information sharing as well. However, absolute exaggerated claims that are beyond practicality into being funny are generally acceptable. Some campaigns, such as *Thanda Matlab Coca-Cola*,[31] Best Adhesive for All Kinds of Furniture,[32] Nothing Official About It,[33] and so on, are merely funny in their market and appreciated and enjoyed by the target audience.

Compliance in SaaS Business

Compliance varies based on the domains of operations. We only discuss a few areas affecting almost every organization delivering a SaaS product.

Operations

All SaaS products store customer data in servers and locations outside the customer's control unless the customer has special conditions worked out in their agreement, like deployment on a private cloud or customer-specific account of a public cloud. That would give jitters to a customer for sure. Is her data in safe hands? Are there any processes or principles followed to keep her data safe? If the customer is a government, they can create standard guidelines or gating criteria for all SaaS vendors to honor. When one department approves, other departments can use the approval without evaluating again. The US FedRAMP is one such government-approved cybersecurity risk management program for cloud software providers. The Australian Government has a similar program called IRAP. We have mentioned ISO-27001 and SOC-2 earlier. When you certify your product for a cybersecurity audit, the following basic questions are answered:

- **Data Residency:** Clarity of the geographical region where the customer data is stored. Some countries mandate that their customer data cannot leave their geographic boundary.
- **Physical Security of Infrastructure:** The security measures taken for the

---

[30] The ASCI code, The Advertising Standards Council of India, **https://www.ascionline.in/the-asci-code/** accessed 16th February 2025.
[31] Thanda Matlab Coca-Cola, **https://www.youtube.com/watch?v=B-19panyC7I** accessed 16th February 2025.
[32] Old Fevicol Ads – Funny Ads, Pidilite Fevicol, **https://youtube.com/playlist?list=PL1F3HbfShZToQ_IIJiE5VNJbtZNhJVk1E&si=j7F_Zejbqc4OIbli** accessed 16th February 2025
[33] Pepsi – Nothing Official About It, **https://www.youtube.com/watch?v=zfFE426tq6o** accessed 16th February 2025.

data center. People should have physical access to the infrastructure, identity badges given to them, the tracking mechanism for the same, and so on.

- **Identity and Access Control:** People who can access the data center and from where. Some organizations may mandate that the customer infrastructure can only be accessed from the office premises through node-locked machines. Some demand that access be given to residents or citizens of a particular country only.
- **Business Presence in the Country:** Some compliance measures require the business to have an entity in a country. Some organizations resort to partnerships to fulfill these needs.
- **Operations Team:** The engineers working on the product should not have direct access to customer data. A specific operations team should access the customer environments.
- **Failover and Disaster Recovery Setup:** Ensuring the infrastructure is available and tested to ensure the failover works.
- **Review and Audit:** Schedule for review and audit of the complete working system periodically on all control parameters.

Here are a few things that the SaaS vendors should keep in mind.

- The operations processes are for the complete stack. If they use a certified public cloud infrastructure, they can benefit from its physical and core platform compliance by reference.
- The artifacts generated in the compliance process can divulge a lot about the security infrastructure. They should be shared judiciously, only as needed.
- The controls can overlap across standards. Hence, it is a good idea to employ an expert who can identify the similarities and ensure the compliance cost is kept low.

Open Source

In *Chapter 1, The Practice of Product Management*, we looked at the history of software products. The software was considered a value addition to hardware. Unix developed around the late 60s and early 70s in the AT&T Bell labs and was shared with academicians at UC Berkeley. The Berkeley Software Distribution (BSD) was available to everyone with the source code for free. It can be considered the first open-source software. Later, Richard Stallman formalized the process of developing an open-source alternative Unix-like operating system called GNU. GNU was released under the GNU Public License (GPL). GPL mandates the licensors to release the source code if they distribute the software. Any derivatives of the software also have to be distributed under GPL. Industries did not like these provisions and were skeptical about using the software with a GPL license. GNU Linux, which has a GPL license, was not getting acceptance as people were concerned that linking with Linux libraries would amount to derivative work. It led to Library GPL (LGPL); mere linking with the library would not amount to derivative work.

In the meantime, people in the industry and community understood that for open source to flourish, the industry must use and contribute to it. When the Netscape and Microsoft battle culminated in Internet Explorer shipping on all Windows desktops, Netscape disclosed its code under the Mozilla Public License (MPL). The intent was to make Mozilla sources easier for all the non-Windows commercial platforms. MPL was considered a pioneering idea in developing an industry-friendly open-source license. Apache projects were released under the Apache License, which did not expect disclosure of sources for derivatives. Similarly, the MIT licenses do not expect the licensees to disclose their sources.

Some open-source licensors wanted the best of both worlds. They wanted the research and non-commercial users to use open-source compatible licenses while commercial users pay under a commercial license. The network tool NMAP[34] is a great example. It has a dual license (GPL v2-like) and a commercial embedding license. Moreover, parsing the NMAP output with a text parser is derivative work. Today, most open-source communities run a commercial arm for customer support. While the application is free, support is offered for a fee. For example, Julia is an open source language. The founding developers of Julia language work for JuliaHub, providing enterprise platforms, consulting, and support services. RedHat is the primary contributor to Fedora Linux.

SaaS vendors do not distribute software, so technically, they can be immune from all the distribution-oriented licenses and restrictions of their derivative work. Technically, you can modify GPL software, use it in your cloud infrastructure, and do not have to expose your source code as you are not technically distributing the software. Affero GPL[35] plugged that loophole. It considered network usage as distribution; thus, those users should have access to source code.

Here are some general guidelines for a SaaS product company.

- For every software release version, maintain an accurate record of all third-party licenses with the version numbers.
- Understand the license changes from previous releases and new software licenses and their versions.
- Understand the open-source licenses and attribute them in your documentation if required.
- Changes to any open-source software should be maintained in source control. If the license mandates, it will be easier to disclose the source code.

---
[34] NMAP Public Source License, **https://nmap.org/npsl/** accessed 24th February 2025.
[35] GNU Affero General Public License, https://www.gnu.org/licenses/agpl-3.0.en.html accessed 24th February 2025.

- Avoid using software whose license restrictions are unknown. A source file may be part of a larger package with unfriendly license terms affecting your product.
- Periodically, audit your open-source license usage.

Licensing

SaaS businesses have a relatively complex contractual relationship with customers and users. In the simplest form, you have a website that has a large number of B2C users who are also paying for the services. The end-user license agreement and sales agreement with warranties and conditions are part of the same document. There is also a data privacy policy mentioned in the same document.

Let us introduce a business-to-employee (B2E) business, such as an HR system or an ERP. Here, the users are employees of your customers. The fact that the employees have access to the portal. The customer has an identity management system that gives access to its employees. The customer's access management system is gating the users; they do not come to your portal directly. When you have a sales agreement with the enterprise, the employees are part of it. There is no specific end-user agreement needed. But it is not entirely true. URLs on the internet are open; what if a stray person, out of curiosity, accesses your portal, and you start tracking him with cookies? Even their data has to be protected. You have to have some form of data protection agreement with them.

We extend the above idea further to mobile applications. Mobile applications are available at a platform (Android or iOS) app store. The user is responsible for installing it on their phones. Consumers can download enterprise applications without understanding, but they can use them. They may fill in some registration information. Through the application installation process, the application can collect device fingerprints and send them to the vendor's servers. The vendors are responsible for that data and have a legal relationship with such consumers. Hence, the end-user license agreement should think through these possible use cases.

The product could be a SaaS marketplace connecting buyers and sellers. The buyer and seller relationships are different from the vendor-marketplace-customer relationships. The product should capture these effectively in the relevant agreements. As a SaaS product vendor, you should work on effective license compliance. You should engage the right legal team to review them.

Conclusion

Compliance is a double-edged sword. While most businesses feel it is a necessary evil, it also opens new markets. If you have a compliant product with a great customer base, it is unlikely that the customers will search for a non-compliant substitute. The compliance requirements are stringent, and it takes time to incorporate all the controls. Hence, it is a barrier to protect against the substitutes taking over your business. However, compliance requirements may emanate from statutory laws, ecosystems, open-source, internal operational management, and so on. Some become mandatory, and non-compliance can lead to legal civil or criminal actions. Some are mere business losses or losses of reputation for the product or the company. Adherence to strong compliance processes becomes necessary for risk management. Product managers should assess them as part of business viability. We have looked at all the five external forces that affect the business and understood business functions to tame the forces. In the next chapter, we organize all the functions effectively using the agile process model.

Questions

1. Find the standards and laws you should comply with for your business operations while developing your products.

2. Do you have to comply with all the standards at the same time? How will you plan the compliance requirements in your product roadmap?

3. Study the other organizations in your domain and find the areas where you perform better than the competition in meeting compliance needs.

4. How do you message the adherence to standards to your customers or prospects? Can better compliance lead to better business value?

5. How do you ensure adherence to third-party licenses in your products?

Chapter 10
Agile Process

Introduction

We have discussed how external forces affect our products and developed functions that can minimize disruptions caused by those forces. All these functions require coordinated efforts from many members of the organization. We need a process model that can make this coordination possible. Organizations have been using agile process models for over a decade. We will review the rationale behind the models and how to apply them effectively for our framework. Agile processes are simple, yet they need steady practice and an effort from the organization to use them in the spirit and not the letters. Our focus here is to help you understand the rationale behind the principles and apply those in your specific context.

Structure

In this chapter, we will cover the following topics:

- The Need
- Components of Agile Process
    - Requirements
    - Estimation
    - Process Model
    - Iterations
    - Retrospective
- Roles in a Scrum Model
    - Scrum Teams
    - Scrum Master
    - Product Owner
    - Communication Across Teams

- Tools for Product Release
  - Burndown
  - Readiness Assessment
  - Minimal Viable Product
  - Go to Market
- Working in the Mixed Models

The Need

While product organizations build products continuously, they like to keep each release to a meaningful chunk. They invest **resources** for a specific **period** to achieve a certain objective or **scope** with **quality**. It is traditionally called the project management triad. We will discuss a few well-known project management principles from this triad, as shown in the following figure.

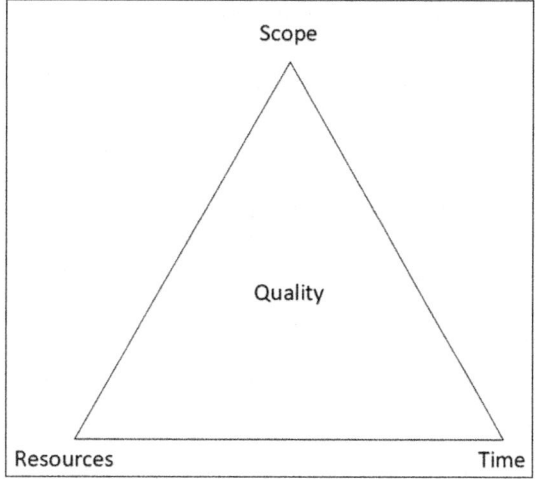

Figure 10.1: *Project Management Triad*

Quality at any cost is often unachievable. Where the industry average of 10-12 defects per 1000 lines of code required USD 50 per line of code, NASA spent USD 1000 for each line of code to achieve 0.1 defects per 1000 lines of code.[1] While NASA can afford such resources to achieve quality levels in mission-critical applications, being obsessive about quality can be unreasonable for a regular software development project. Depending on the market you focus on, you have certain quality expectations, and every product organization should try to meet the right level of quality.

Before SaaS products became popular, traditional product development was heavy on

---

[1] Dennis Jenkins, Advanced Vehicle Automation and Computers Aboard the Shuttle, NASA history pages, **https://www.nasa.gov/history/sts1/pages/computer.html** accessed 5th January 2025

content or scope. The customer would buy a version of a product for perpetuity and pay an upgrade or license fee to move to the new version. Unless they got a feature-heavy version over the previous version, there was no incentive to migrate. Complex operating systems and software platform products would take several years to develop. For example, Microsoft Windows Vista (2001-2006)[2], Adobe InDesign 1.0 (1996-1999)[3], Apple Mac OS X 10.0 (1997-2001)[4], and so on. One of the threats companies faced was their previous versions - a lingering doubt with the customer in migrating to the new version. When products took several years to develop, the market moved fast, and the launched products had a mismatch of market expectations with available features and quality levels. Microsoft Windows Vista and Mac OS X 10.0 had reputations for being poor-quality operating systems, lacking features, and the expected performance on low-end devices. Sometimes, products could not win the race when one version did not do well enough in the market, and customers did not buy. Companies were scared to rearchitect their flagship products as they could go out of business after one such release. Luckily, Microsoft and Apple held their positions in these difficult situations. Apple was going through its lowest point (1997-2001) when Mac OS X launched and took some drastic steps with Mac OS X to achieve a quick turnaround. Apple released OS versions every year and hardware upgrades every three years after that.

Then, many software followed waterfall, iterative, or variations of those as their software development lifecycle (SDLC) process models. The marketing and product management teams came with marketing and product requirement documents (MRD and PRD) over several months. Engineering and product interlock happened when the engineering teams agreed to the defined scope. The architects and designers defined the high-level designs, followed by low-level designs. Finally, the developers would build the product, and testers would test and find issues that the developers would fix. After several months, the marketing and product team can comment on the alpha or the internal preview version of the product. It would have taken several months from when product teams identified the requirements to a working prototype. Sometimes, even years! During the alpha testing, when everyone had a reality check of the implementation, they realized they would miss the timelines; the implemented features were not meeting the requirements, or the requirements were over a year old, and customers would have moved on, yet they could not change the scope that easily. They would slip the release or augment the engineering teams with people from other projects. Adding new people to the team created confusion, required training, and could affect quality, thus delaying the project.[5] They would now work on several internal milestones called beta releases to ensure the product achieved the goals. After every milestone, flaws were found and release could slip further. Non-functional artifacts

---
[2] **https://microsoft.fandom.com/wiki/Windows_Vista** accessed 6th January 2025
[3] The last version of PageMaker was released in 1996.
[4] **https://web.archive.org/web/19990116231607/https://product.info.apple.com/pr/press.releases/1997/q2/970107.pr.rel.macos.html;** https://www.apple.com/newsroom/2001/01/09Apples-Mac-OS-X-to-Ship-on-March-24/
[5] Several examples can be seen in: Fred Brooks, The Mythical Man-Month, 1975

such as MRDs, PRDs, High-level Design documents, and Low-level Design documents were prepared. These deliverables made everyone feel accomplished. However, the production code would be less than perfect; it did not meet the customer's needs when the product was released.

Seventeen pioneers promoting alternate SDLCs for software development came together to suggest a common theme across all their approaches. They called it the Agile Manifesto.[6]

We are uncovering better ways of developing software by doing it and helping others do it. Through this work we have come to value:

- **Individuals and interactions** *over processes and tools*
- **Working software** *over comprehensive documentation*
- **Customer collaboration** *over contract negotiation*
- **Responding** *to change over following a plan*

That is, while there is value in the items on the right, we value the items on the left more.

They proposed twelve principles. Here they are:[7]

1. Our highest priority is to satisfy the customer through early and continuous delivery of valuable software.
2. Welcome changing requirements, even late in development. Agile processes harness change for the customer's competitive advantage.
3. Deliver working software frequently, from a couple of weeks to a couple of months, with a preference for a shorter timescale.
4. Business people and developers must work together daily throughout the project.
5. Build projects around motivated individuals. Give them the environment and support they need, and trust them to get the job done.
6. The most efficient and effective method of conveying information to and within a development team is face-to-face conversation.
7. Working software is the primary measure of progress.
8. Agile processes promote sustainable development. The sponsors, developers, and users should be able to maintain a constant pace indefinitely.

---

[6] The Agile Manifesto, **https://agilemanifesto.org/** accessed 6th January 2025. Stated verbatim.
[7] Principles behind the Agile Manifesto, **https://agilemanifesto.org/principles.html** accessed 6th January 2025. Stated verbatim.

9. Continuous attention to technical excellence and good design enhances agility.

10. Simplicity—the art of maximizing the amount of work not done—is essential.

11. The best architectures, requirements, and designs emerge from self-organizing teams.

12. At regular intervals, the team reflects on how to become more effective, then tunes and adjusts its behavior accordingly.

A process model used for a long period becomes ritualistic and preachy. People start following it by the letter rather than the spirit. The team must question and validate the processes against the principles of agile methodology. The parts of the process that do not align with agile principles should be removed or modified.

The agile process model and regular software releases worked perfectly for software vendors. Customers could get their features and bug fixes on a regular cadence. Imagine an IT administrator deploying software for all the enterprise servers, desktops, or client software every three to six months. If you were developing client and server software in that period, most customers would not like to upgrade as frequently as you would like to release the product. While you could convince customers to upgrade the enterprise server in six to nine months, they insisted either the servers work with the old clients or upgrade clients a year or so later. These were the plights of the enterprise application vendors and their customers.

Consumer internet companies such as Google, Microsoft (MSN), Yahoo, Amazon, and so on were not bound by any Service Level Agreement (SLA) of enterprise customers. They were innovation-driven and wanted releases every two-three weeks. They all maintained several websites, which the consumers had to approach for the services on their web browsers. Technically, the software development, testing, and deployment were within their control. Interestingly, most of their services were free and ran multi-year beta programs.[8] The customer was not more tolerant about engineering surprises or bugs. These next-generation internet companies saw value in the agile processes. However, the deployment was a challenge for them. They were worldwide services; many of them were to be always on. The scales were massive and had to be dynamically changed. Continuous integration and deployment (CI/CD) architectures addressed these concerns effectively. The next-generation mobile platforms (iOS and Android) became closed ecosystems for application deployment. Application management is not the customer's problem anymore. Then, software vendors provided SaaS-based services for enterprise applications through a universal client such as a web browser. Microsoft, SAP, Adobe, and so on, the traditional business-to-enterprise vendors, started a significant transition in this direction. With SaaS, the

---

[8] After Five Years, Gmail Finally Sheds the 'Beta', **https://www.nytimes.com/2009/07/08/technology/companies/08google.html** accessed 6th January 2025

deployment dependency on customers went away. Today, the scale of computation for AI has favored SaaS for analytics. The client devices act as edge devices for inferences. So, software vendor organizations would prefer a quick cycle of releases so that they can update the models quickly.

SaaS-based applications are a reality today. Virtualization, workload management, cloud and mobile migration, and AI-based inferences are all realities we have to accept. We will build and deploy software fast at an unprecedented scale with ever-growing requirements. Agile process models have worked best for such needs. Technologies and processes always evolve together, meeting each other's needs. We will look at a few agile methodologies used for software development.

Components of Agile Process

Most software development activities involve similar activities, regardless of the kind of software. You must elicit requirements, plan, design, develop, test, integrate, and deploy. These activities do not change based on the SDLC process model used. The classic SDLC used almost a decade ago had very similar activities. We do not show deployment as customers deployed them on their premises after buying. A few classic SDLC process models are shown in the following figure.

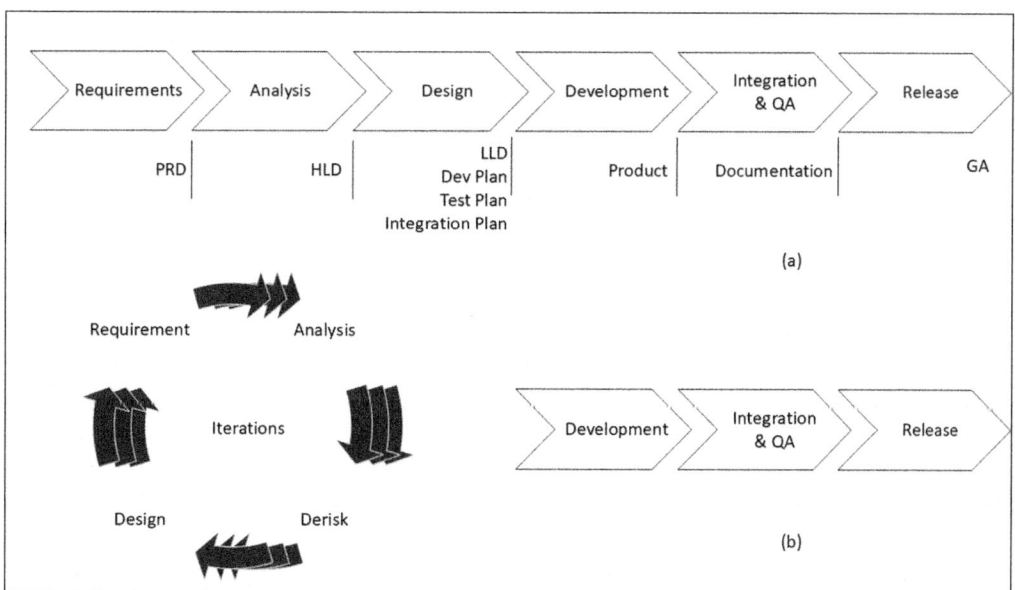

Figure 10.2: SDLC processes (a) Waterfall (b) Iterative

However, in the classic SDLC models, the final product reached the customer after the release. The overall time taken could be several months or even years from requirements elicitation to final release. The progress was ascertained from the intermediate documents and artifacts delivered. There was no working implementation.

People would develop some working prototypes or screen walkthroughs for customer feedback, but those may not make it to the final product. That was a serious issue from an overall release and intermediate risk mitigation perspective. Can we get a release in less time if we use agile methodology? The answer is yes and no. We will be doing more releases where each release has a lot less number of features. If we look at the overall time taken to release all the features, the agile methodology may take longer but at a much better predictability. It can get clearer with a schematic.

In *Figure 10.3*, we have a backlog of seven items. We release two items per release and develop these over four iterations.

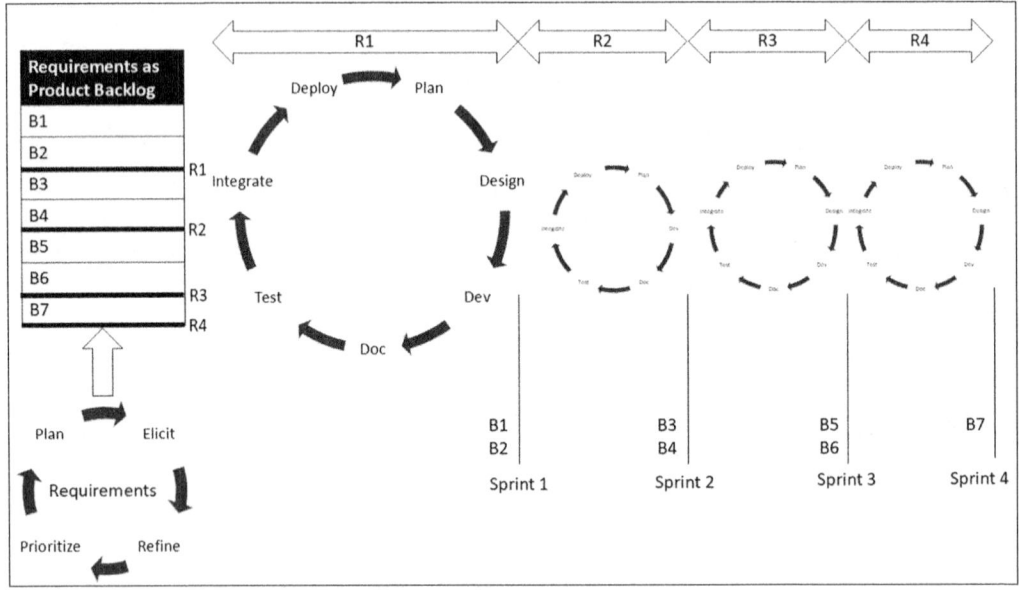

Figure 10.3: *Agile process model*

Every release has overheads. Once the release is ready, you will need integration and release readiness testing. In the waterfall model, we would have put all the backlogs in one release, and that would have less overheads. The teams adopting agile models for development get these doubts. With early product releases, you are getting customer feedback and acceptance of the product in the market. Moreover, short releases are easier to plan and execute. In long-duration projects with improper planning, the work fills up all the available time and demands more time. We will discuss this further in the section on agile planning and estimations.

Requirements

PMs collect the requirements continuously in the agile process models. Requirements

Agile Process

can come internally from the organization or externally from customer and customer engagements. Here are the typical sources:

- Customers and prospects
- Competition and their products
- Analysts
- Pre-sales and sales team
- Support and customer success team
- The engineering team and architects
- Management

Their ideas and expressions can vary, and so can the communication channels. Some organizations have product request portals where anyone can add their product requests. Such portals should allow for free-flow communication and not impose too many barriers in the submission format.

PMs prefer the final requirements be in a user story format. In the negotiation section of *Chapter 4, Customer*, we discussed focusing on the problem while eliciting requirements. The user story format is a way to achieve it. Suppose you work for a mobile wallet platform such as Paytm, Google Pay, and so on. In the last strategy meeting, the management wanted the PM to plan to make the wallet a super app.[9] As a starter, they wanted to look at the travel industry. Can a PM add a story like this?

> *As a PM, I want to make PayUSafe*[10] *a super app.*

A PM is not the application user. Secondly, the super app is way too vague. The PM decides to narrow the scope of the super app to travel, investments, and so on. Now, he writes,

> *As a wallet user, I would like to book my travels through PayUSafe.*

The wallet user is a defined user-persona but travel booking has a wide scope. Is it airlines, buses, trains, cruises, local sightseeing, and so on.? These large-scope stories are called epics. It is a good idea to start a user story as an epic. Epics set forth a focused direction for the team to suggest innovative solutions.

As a product manager, you have attended the organization's strategy initiatives tasked with making your application a super app for travel. In your BU leadership meeting, you propose the directions. The team members voice their concerns. The concern that the requirement is vague is the most common; hence, you should improve upon it and use the group to arrive at an objective set of requirements. Such meetings are to

---

[9] Super apps are mobile apps or internet portals where you can meet all your daily needs. The user should be glued to the app and not leave outside of it for all her daily needs.
[10] Fictitious name

brainstorm and align with the strategic direction. Brainstorming[11] is to be time-boxed with three distinct steps.

1. Idea generation (15 mins): Everyone suggests her idea to the group to be listed
2. Elaboration (30 mins): People explain their ideas to others to highlight their point of view.
3. Selection (15 mins): Everyone votes. The ideas voted higher in rank get priority.

The team suggested a few things; we highlight the top two of them here:

1. Airlines booking to start with.
2. Look at the possibility of partnering with travel portals.

The epic is broken into two further ones:

1. As a wallet user, I would like to book flight tickets.
2. *As a wallet user, when I initiate an air ticket booking, PayUSafe will book tickets through TravelMate.*[12]

The preceding Item 2 talks about a partnership between PayUSafe and TravelMate. It raises some questions about the user interface of the integration. Here are some hypothetical possibilities.

- PayUSafe can launch TravelMate; the user will book the tickets in TravelMate, but payment can only be with PayUSafe as the payment gateway. TravelMate can offer beyond air travel; the user can access that.
- PayUSafe can implement all the user interfaces in its control and use TravelMate as an API in the backend.
- PayUSafe can develop a user interface SDK. TravelMate can use the SDK to provide their workflows. PayUSafe can release embedded TravelMate as a library as part of its final release.

Each of these will require different components. They can influence the user interface significantly. Moreover, there is work to develop a partnership with TravelMate. TravelMate should agree to support integration with not just development but also with customer support. What will happen if a traveler needs in-person assistance to change something? Should they come to PayUSafe or TravelMate? What seemed like a very high-level epic slowly got into lower-level epics with reasonable clarity and sometimes with alternative proposals.

---

[11] Brainstorming is one of many idea-generation techniques. You can use whatever works best in your organization. Here are a few articles to guide you in the process: **https://hbr.org/2022/04/get-better-at-brainstorming-our-favorite-reads** accessed 13th Jan 2025
[12] Fictitious

When do you stop? You can stop when your development teams agree they know what to do. Let us take a simpler epic.

As a wallet user, I would book flights through PayUSafe.

It essentially means the user needs a flight search option that looks like this:

As a wallet user, I can provide:

- *a source airport*
- *a destination airport*
- *a date and time of my travel*
- *initiate a search,*

I will get various flight options available to me.

We have not clarified the user interface yet. We have the option of a web portal, a mobile app, a chat interface, and even a personal AI assistant, all with their unique interaction workflows. That is where the PMs can work with the UX teams to elaborate and design user journeys, interaction designs, and so on. Suppose we decide to make it a form-based workflow of either a web or mobile application. We have a reasonable story for engineering to work on.

As a wallet user, **in the search form**, *I can provide:*

- *a source airport*
- *a destination airport*
- *A date and time of my travel*
- *initiate a search,*

I will get various flight options available to me.

We have mentioned a search form, but not if the source airport will be a drop-down. Should the date and time selector be some specific type of control, or should you click the buttons for search or use the platform search button? It is best to leave these to UX and engineering teams to mull over and suggest what is doable within the technology constraints. When the UX is overdesigned, the engineer spends time achieving it rather than implementing acceptable trade-offs. A user story should have the flexibility for teams to make that decision effective. What if you have a relatively novice engineering team or release the requirements for a contract for a work project? You have to define trackable requirements. The user stories can be precise in such cases.

Let us bring this user story to a sprint for engineering to work on. On the first day of the sprint, the team would do a detailed estimate and task breakdown. Let us assume we have worked out the interaction design and the UX mockups. Now, we have to decide the acceptance criteria. Acceptance criteria can be test cases or test assertions. Here are a few simple ones:

T1. *There is a text box to enter the source airport.*

T2. *When I enter three characters for the source airport, I will get suggestions for the possible airports.*

T3. *T1 for destination airport...*

T4. *T2 for destination airport...*

T5. *The destination airport suggestions should not contain the source airport.*

T6. *When I send the same source and destination airport, the API should handle it as an error condition.*

While T1 to T5 are application-level test cases, T6 is a condition asserted in the code. There may be an automated test case to handle it.

This part of the user story is still unclear.

I will get various flight options available to me.

The output listing is still ambiguous. Here, we can create another user story. The story can be completed in the same or next sprint, depending on the availability of the team. For the input form, the acceptance criteria for now can be:

T7. *I will get a list of search results based on my input criteria. The list would be used to test whether the search algorithm[13] is working fine visually. However, the rendering of the same would be later modified in user story B25.*

What we discussed is called backlog **refinement** or **grooming**. The PMs interact with various stakeholders and improve upon the stories. It starts as a business direction, to epics, user stories, acceptance criteria, and so on. Starting as a relatively open-ended epic gives scope for expansion, while the final user story in a sprint has to be thorough and with a measurable outcome.

You place the user stories in a prioritized list (backlog) to be picked by the agile teams. How do you prioritize the backlogs in the first place? The Kano model shown in the following figure is one step in that direction.

---

[13] The details of testing the search algorithm are not mentioned.

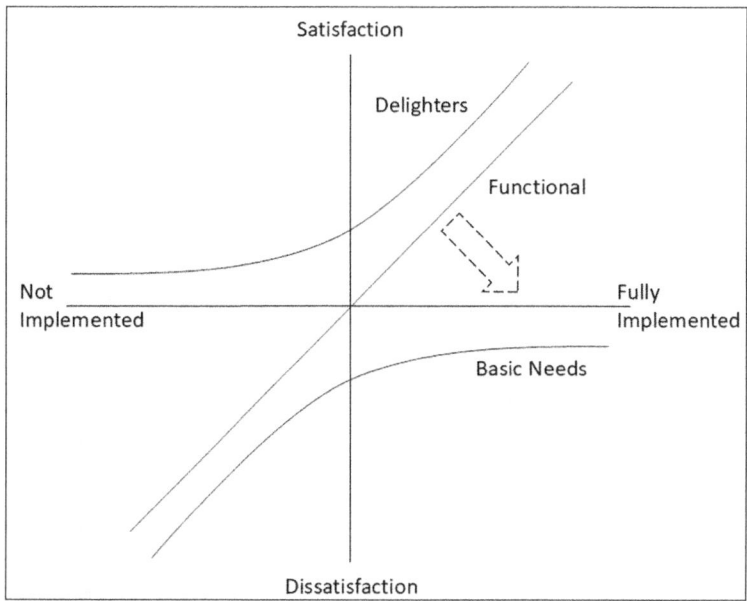

Figure 10.4: *Kano model*[14]

One of the ideas can be to find the customer preference for a feature. For example, the selection of UI components. If the standard platform control works for most cases, increasing complexity by introducing a custom control may not make much sense. However, what the customers considered **delighters** earlier may soon become **basic**. Applications with night mode were a novelty a few years back, but today, many applications have it. Applications that use navigation prefer to have night mode. It is important to develop a feature till customers see the value but not when they find the features esoteric. Customers prefer a product to be bug-free. However, if you decide to test till no bugs can be found, the cost of quality can go up. Customers may not see immediate value unless the bugs affect their day-to-day workflows; otherwise, bug-free software is a basic necessity. The use of AI and LLMs in software started as delighters, but today, it is entering the mainstream in certain domains, and people look at them as **functional** needs. While the Kano model is a great way to classify features, other attributes are crucial in backlog prioritization. For example:

- Number of customers requesting the same features.
- Revenue associated with the feature: one large customer can hijack the release to implement features they request.
- New technological features introduced by the competitors.
- Proximity of feature to other improvements in the release, thus reducing development cost: a developer working on the UI for the flight search interface can fix a bug in the results page.

---

[14] Kano Model, **https://www.scrum.org/resources/kano-model** accessed 12th Jan 2025

Once we prioritize backlogs and rank, we develop and release them. Then how do we decide how many backlog items to commit to in a release?

Estimation

As a PM, you have a reasonable backlog; you want to develop it through several engineering teams you have. You want them to give you a release every three months. In classic SDLCs, such as waterfall and iterative models, you had a group of architects and senior engineers who would review the features, break them down into detailed work breakdown structures, and put in timelines to complete those tasks by an average engineer. The planning cycles used to be long and often inaccurate as there were many unknowns. The engineers have differing capabilities to the extent of productivity multipliers of 10; the best developer may be 10 times more productive than the average for a well-defined problem.

There are two different estimations in agile processes - **relative sizing** and **absolute task sizing**. The first relative sizing is called **t-shirt sizing**. These are typically carried out by experts or architects for high-level epics. Just like t-shirt sizes of Small (S), Medium (M), Large (L), eXtra Large(XL), and eXtra eXtra Large (XXL), they rank the epics in each bucket. But these are high-level epics. You know, in the last release, you could only accommodate one XXL and one S feature for the release. So, you would only focus on two such epics to be worked on by the teams.

From our example:

> As a wallet user, I would book flights through PayUSafe.

It probably would be an XXL-sized epic to review for breakdown. Let us assume we have discussed the approach with TravelMate with experts and have started to outline a strategy. We reach a reasonable-sized story in the air travel search form. These are the kinds of stories where the agile teams review and estimate the story based on their understanding. Neither the expert nor the PM should influence the estimate. They can be there in the estimation meetings to give additional information as facilitators. Let us look at the story:

> As a wallet user, in the search form, I can provide
> - a source airport
> - a destination airport
> - A date and time of my travel
> - initiate a search,
>
> I will get various flight options available to me.

People would immediately ask if they could use some standard controls. The UX person in the team can outline a sketchy design on the whiteboard for the engineers to understand. Then, the engineers can look at the design and are convinced of the work to be done. They will have concerns about where to store the data or which APIs are available from TravelMate. The experts can answer or keep these questions to clarify from TravelMate but ask the engineers to estimate, assuming the availability of an API. The engineers ask what various flight options mean. The PM can state the output format is not fully decided and is a separate user story, and this story is focused on the input form only. In short, the engineers will size the story in **story point** format. Story points are simply numbers the teams assign to every story based on the time to complete them and their understanding of complexity. The valid numbers are 1, 2, 3, 5, 8, 13, 20, 40, 100, and ?. The first few numbers (till 13) are part of the Fibonacci series. Each Fibonacci number is the sum of the previous two numbers. Hence, each Fibonacci number is roughly twice its precedent. A story estimated at 8 is approximately twice a story of 5 points; it may take twice as long to implement. Here are the guidelines for the estimation process:

- Every team member needs to be part of the estimation process.
- They have their own decision. They should not show their estimates to others while estimating. Everyone shows their estimates at the same time. Hence, this is called **planning poker**.
- They can discuss their views and opinions, but the final estimate is individual.
- Consensus has to be arrived at in the story point estimation meeting. If the group is divided into two values adjacent to each other, take the larger number. However, if there are a number further apart, the discussions and explanations can build a consensus.

The first story is probably the hardest to estimate. But, once the team has a few stories estimated, they can estimate relative to each other. For example, if the team has estimated the input form, the results page estimate can be easier. It could be as simple as asking, now that you have estimated the input form, if the results page is the same size, half the size, twice in size, or some other size.

Some of you may be wondering why story points work. Here are a few reasons:

- Human beings cannot accurately estimate the time to be taken when all the tasks are unknown in the activity, but they are good at estimating the size of something relative to another task.[15]
- An activity where consensus is established becomes a team responsibility; teams make individuals commit to their decisions.[16] This behavior is seen in

---

[15] Humans can't estimate tasks, Agile, By Allan Kelly, March 17, 2011, **https://www.allankelly.net/archives/741/humans-can-estimate-tasks/** accessed 12th Jan 2025

[16] **https://hr.berkeley.edu/hr-network/central-guide-managing-hr/managing-hr/interaction/team-building/steps** accessed 12th Jan 2025

other fields such as microfinance—the loans given to groups of people are more committed, and they pay back.[17]
- It also utilizes a well-known estimation technique known as wideband Delphi.[18] Here, experts share their knowledge and rationale for estimates. The other experts understand the viewpoint, form their opinions, and reach a consensus—similar to the planning poker exercise.

There is also an **ideal time** estimate[19] used for estimating stories. However, when all the tasks associated with the stories are not known, they do not provide good results. It may work for small stories and bug fixes. We encourage everyone to use story point estimates for your products.

Process Model

Agile process models are a set of process models that align with the manifesto and follow the principles. All the signatories of the manifesto are pioneers of at least one such process model, for example, Kent Beck (eXtreme Programming), Ken Schwaber (Scrum), Jeff Sutherland (Scrum), and so on. Today, Scrum, Kanban, and Scaled Agile Framework (SAFe) are the most used frameworks. Any other process model or their variations, if they meet the core agile principles and the manifesto, are good frameworks to follow.

Scrum

Scrum is a team-based software development process and is very popular in enterprises. The engineering team is divided into groups of five to seven with complementary skills. The teams are complete in their work activities and responsible for the delivery of all the backlogs they pick up. There are no hierarchies in knowledge, experience levels, or reporting structures. Depending on the needs of the hour, they take up various roles and responsibilities to accomplish a task. The term comes from the scrum formation to either start or move the Rugby game forward after an interruption. We will review this process model and roles in detail later.

Kanban

Kanban is a visual depiction of tasks and their state in a queue or swim lanes. They help understand the overall progress of the project or tasks. For example, many software

---

[17] Efa Wahyu Prastyaningtyas, Sri Umi Mintarti Widjaja, Hari Wahyono, Endang Sri Andayani, Jack Febrian Rusdi, Methods for studying group loans, join responsibility, and women's empowerment, MethodsX, Volume 9, 2022, 101749, ISSN 2215-0161, **https://doi.org/10.1016/j.mex.2022.101749**.
[18] Project Management Institute (2021). A guide to the project management body of knowledge (PMBOK guide). Project Management Institute (7th ed.). Newtown Square, PA. ISBN 978-1-62825-664-2
[19] The time taken to complete a story when you have absolutely no distractions.

projects involve experts in specific areas. In a story of adding an End User License Agreement (EULA), you need legal input from various product teams. However, you may only have one legal person in the organization for all these activities. In such cases, Kanban boards are a good way to understand how a specific resource is utilized; you may have to reassign the task if needed. Most agile management tools provide Kanban dashboards with swim lanes to know what task is in progress, what is to be done, and what is completed. You can filter the data based on sprints and specific team members. You can move a task from one lane to another to reflect the correct status. A typical Kanban board is shown in the following figure.

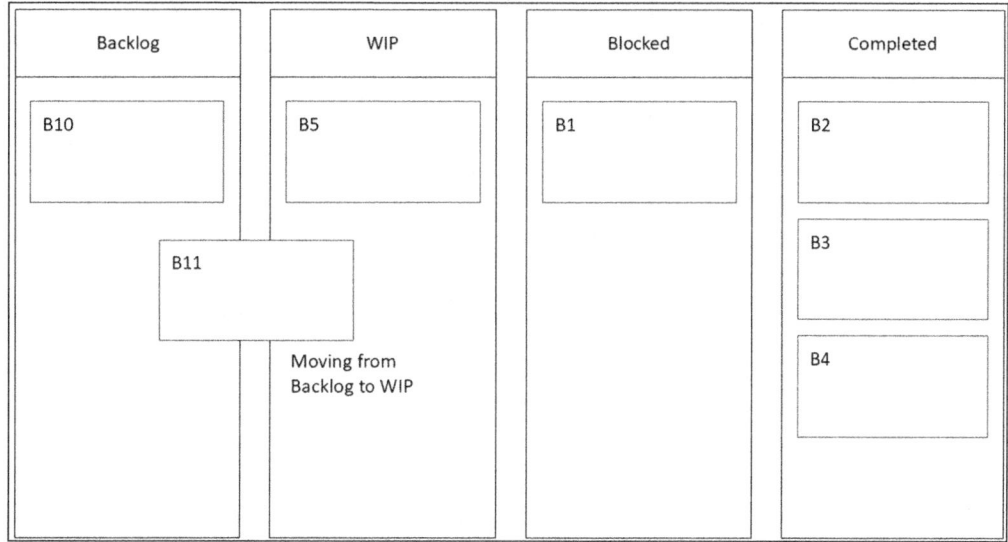

Figure 10.5: *A typical Kanban dashboard*

SAFe

The original agile models were software engineering-centric. Large organizations that want to bring the agile framework into large interrelated projects can look at SAFe as a methodology. While Scrum and Kanban processes are for an agile team's activities of planning, development, testing, deployment, and so on. SAFe also gets into agile backlog management, innovation management, product architecture, and so on. A complete discussion on SAFe will be beyond the scope of this book. However, people interested should explore the web resources.[20] Interestingly, SAFe also recommends SAFe Scrum and SAFe Kanban to manage means for agile team activities. The SAFe versions of the processes are not entirely different from the Scrum and Kanban process models we discussed here.

---

[20] **https://scaledagileframework.com/**

Iterations

All activities of the agile team happen in multiple short iterations, each lasting two-three weeks. These are called sprints. Humans can accurately plan activities when they are of short duration. Ideally, we would like to have releases every sprint. However, that may not always be practical. It could be a collaborative effort across the teams, system integration may take time, or customers may not prefer frequent releases when the product UX is affected. Typically, a release spanning three months will have 4-6 sprints, depending on the length of the sprints. The backlogs are refined and ordered. The time and resource dimensions are fixed here. You can only decide on the scope. The POs specify a minimal set of user stories for the product release. They also provide some bonus features the team can work on if there is time in the sprint. This additional feature list is called a **feature buffer**.

Agile process models believe in a steady work environment and do not expect any last-minute cramming to release the product. The team will plan their sprint at hourly level tasks and adhere to completion in the sprint. Before they start the planning activity, they should estimate the time available in the sprint.

- Remove the holidays from the available schedule.
- Each team member would specify their non-availability due to leaves, training, other non-sprint activities, and so on. Those will be removed from the planned hours.
- Multiply the remaining hours by a factor between 0.6 and 0.75.[21] The remaining hours are considered the total hours available for the sprint.

On the first day of the sprint, the team would pick up the top few backlog items and plan for them. The planning is far more detailed here. The team would break down the story into multiple tasks. These tasks can be technical. For example, in the input form for the air travel story, the data should be persisted. There is a need to design a table schema to do so. The table schema design and implementation is a task under the air travel story. The team should identify all such tasks needed for the story. The tasks are segregated and assigned to all the team members. Team members can estimate their tasks in actual hours. What if the hourly estimates exceed the total available hours? Then, the team cannot complete the story in the sprint. The story is split into two: one with a zero story point and the other with the estimated story points. The story with zero story points[22] is taken in the current sprint. The team should complete all the tasks in the story and ensure the acceptance criteria are met for the story completion.

---

[21] Focus factor – the percentage of time the team is working on sprint activities. In a day of eight hours, people can effectively work for five to six hours.

[22] Such stories are also known as spikes. In scrum, teams can take up spikes to improve understanding or estimate better. Some initial sprints of a release can be filled with spikes. Some call these sprints sprint 0.

The team gets the story points as a reward. **Sprint planning** is an involved process and can take a whole day.

Once the planning is over, the process does not permit any change to the scope. The team should only focus on executing the tasks. There is a standup[23] meeting of the team where each person tells the other team members before the start of the workday.

- The task she has done the previous day.
- What she plans to do on that day.
- If there is any bottleneck

A standup should have no additional discussions. However, if there are any bottlenecks to be discussed among specific people, they stay back after the standup. It is typically called a **parking lot** discussion. These meetings are not status meetings; they must be used for coordination among the team members. Each team member should update their task progress with hours worked and the additional time needed to finish the task at the end of the day.

Sprints are classic **Plan-Do-Check-Act** (PDCA) models in management literature. We have already reviewed the **Plan** and **Do** process. The **Check** part is captured at the sprint demo. The team sets up the environment for the **demo**. It is ideal if the teams can show out of one deployment to convince the work has been integrated properly. There can be challenges. However, non-availability of time should not be one of them. Integrating everyone's work for the demo is a task for story completion. The demos are carried out on the last day of the sprint. A customer representative or the PO should be there to provide feedback on the demo. Demo is not the place to test the user story or check acceptance criteria. The team should do their due diligence on both before showing the demo to announce the completion of work to the best of their abilities. Every demo leads to some new ideas or bugs. They have to be verified against the acceptance criteria; if found to be additional enhancements, new user stories should be created and pushed to the backlogs for a subsequent sprint. Additionally, every team member can conduct intermittent demos to solicit feedback from the team and PO as parking lot activities after the daily standups. However, those are optional.

Retrospective

However well-developed the processes are, when there are teams of people, they have conflicts. One of the ways to express these is by involving the team to act and improve the process. Due to unplanned travel, the PO could not attend standups, and the team made some decisions that led to an improper story implementation.

---

[23] Standups have to be limited to 15 minutes. Each team member should get two minutes to explain their activities. If the people are meeting face to face, they should be standing and discussing, as when people sit and discuss, the urgency is lost. One can be flexible on the standing part in remote video conferences, but a time limit should be imposed.

The team could state it in the retrospection meeting. The idea of the retrospection meeting is to state:

1. What worked well?
2. What did not work well?
3. How can we improve upon them?

The improvements are captured and passed on to the next sprint planning meeting to act.

Roles in a Scrum Model

What we discussed about the agile processes is relevant for Scrum. However, we have used the term team in the previous sections very loosely. We will elaborate on them here.

Scrum Teams

A group of five to seven people work as equals in a scrum team. There are no hierarchies in the scrum team. One of the team members acts as a scrum master. However, she is just another team member. Has her scrum delivery tasks. It is best when a team has no functional delineation, and everyone can take up any tasks if needed. Organizations face challenges with backend, AI, iOS, Android, Java, Python developers, testers, specific CI/CD developers, and so on. A team ready to take up each other's tasks as a full-stack development team is ideal. Moreover, developers who like to learn one skill and excel can look at another secondary skill to learn from team members. In some cases, manual testing is a must. For the other cases, the automated unit testing framework should be developed. The tests can be conducted before deployment to qualify for a release. Today, only a few organizations are purely dependent on manual testing. A scrum team takes and owns all the decisions for their activities.

Scrum Master

The team selects a Scrum Master (SM) among the team members or someone whom the team can trust through her experience and abilities. She is part of the team. She contributes to the sprint activities deliverables as well. An engineering manager can be an SM as long as she is not applying her supervisory influence on the team. The SM essentially removes the roadblocks from the scrum activities. They ensure the team is represented correctly in other forums and establish communications needed with non-scrum entities. However, the final decisions of a scrum team are taken through consensus. The SM can facilitate the process without acting as an arbitrator. SM can again help resolve conflicts within the team as a facilitator of communication and mutual respect among the team members. While no specific experience level is needed for an SM, SMs are generally good communicators.

Product Owner

A Product Owner (PO) is part of the scrum team but is not involved in the day-to-day sprint activities. She represents the customer and is present in planning, standup, demo, and retrospective meetings. However, she cannot influence the team's decisions. In a planning meeting, she can clarify the story and enable the team to understand it. She cannot influence the story points or detailed planning of the tasks. In standups, she addressed the team's concerns with the user stories. She cannot direct the team to solve a task in a specific manner. A PO's expertise in technology is not needed in the role. In the retrospective, she is like another team member who can voice her opinion on what worked and what did not. During the demo, the PO decides whether to accept the user story as done. For the decision to be fair to everyone, the PO must set the acceptance criteria properly. Improper acceptance criteria can frustrate the scrum. The team works hard, producing an output, and looks up to the PO to judge it fairly. In this role, fairness in action, expression, and communication is expected of a good PO.

Communication Across Teams

What, we discussed in this chapter, are toy problems where one scrum team is working with its constituent members. However, in large software projects, you have hundreds of engineers, each team working on their area of competence. For large teams, SAFe will be the advisable agile framework to follow. We will discuss simple enterprise scrum methodologies that can be used for seven to ten teams easily. A scrum team makes the team operate in their silo and be oblivious to the project objectives. As team sizes increase, there has to be more communication across the teams. In the enterprise adoption of the scrum, the SMs of the scrum teams meet on a weekly or bi-weekly cadence to discuss their team status, dependencies, and bottlenecks. These are called **scrum-of-scrums**. All the POs should be present in these meetings to ensure the proper alignment of dependencies. The senior management stakeholders may join these meetings as observers. A slow-moving scrum team can delay the project. In such cases, the stories from one team can be transferred to another team. Can story point estimates of one team be trusted by another? Ideally, there will be differences. However, over time, the teams develop a common understanding of sizing. Or, you may ask the new team to re-estimate the story again. Again, this movement is only possible if the skills are aligned across teams. Many large enterprises that have feature-based teams can have challenges there. Moreover, transferring a team member from one team to another is not advisable.

Tools for Product Release

The elaborate PDCA requirement of agile processes requires good tools. Luckily, there are hundreds of great products in the market addressing such needs. Here are a few well-known ones: Atlassian Jira, VersionOne, Jama, GitLabs, GitHub Projects, **and so on**.

Most such products work with integrated CI/CD solutions. People using Atlassian Jira may have BitBucket as a source repository or Confluence for team communications, **and so on**. We suggest evaluating your complete process requirements and choosing the tools that address all your organizational needs. We do not recommend any tool of a specific organization in this book. They all have certain advantages and disadvantages over the others. What we will be discussing here are measures suggested in the processes for better management.

Burndown

Burndown is the only trackable tool suggested in the Scrum methodology. A scrum team is on a mission to complete the tasks. While inside the sprint, they are not interested in analyzing anything beyond it. In every standup, they should bring up the sprint burndown chart and evaluate what tasks are affecting the pending hours to complete their stories.

In *Figure 10.6*, we have a sample sprint burndown chart. If you remember, the team members entered how much time they spent on the task and how much is further needed to complete it.

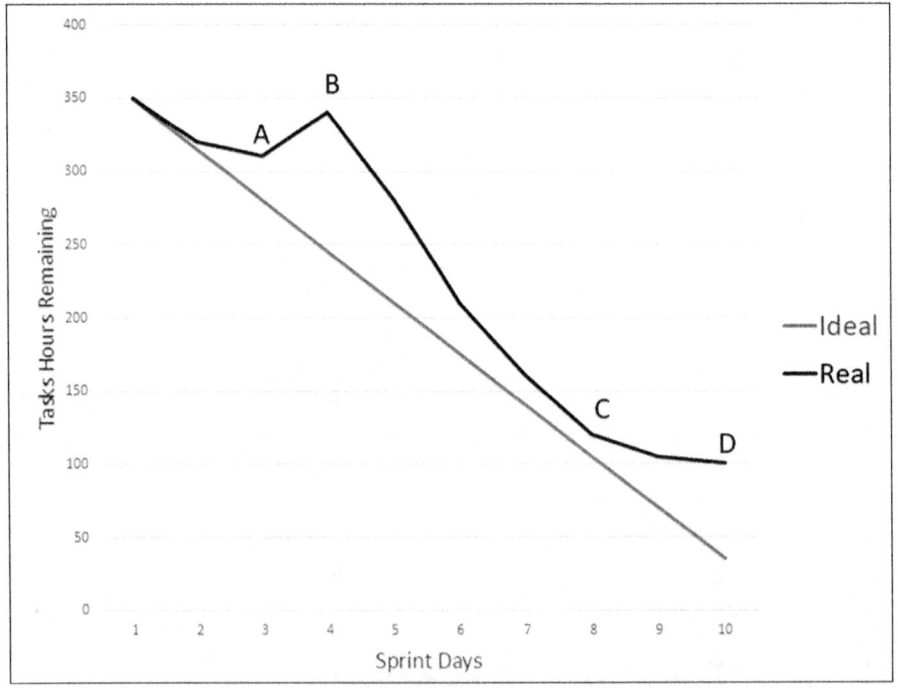

Figure 10.6: *Sprint burndown chart*

Every day, they are essentially reevaluating their tasks. They may realize the time needed to complete a task can be higher than they estimated. B is one such point on the curve. B takes the total hours remaining to be higher than the pending hours available in the sprint. The team can get an indication that some tasks spill over to the next sprint. With some better execution, they manage to bring the gap closer to the ideal at C, but again, some deficiencies prevent them from achieving the sprint objective at D. The hours spent are not an objective for a sprint burndown. Using that metric is not very helpful. The idea should be to align the actual time remaining to complete the task as close to the planned estimates.

Readiness Assessment

The release readiness is assessed again using the burndown philosophy but by evaluating the story points remaining. From the past experience, we know a team is capable of addressing 60 story points in a release of 6 sprints. The team is said to have a velocity of 10. Based on that, the team has the stories to fit in 60 story points. The remaining story points at the beginning of a sprint are shown.

In *Figure* 10.7, at A the team could not complete the stories. The stories went to the subsequent sprints.

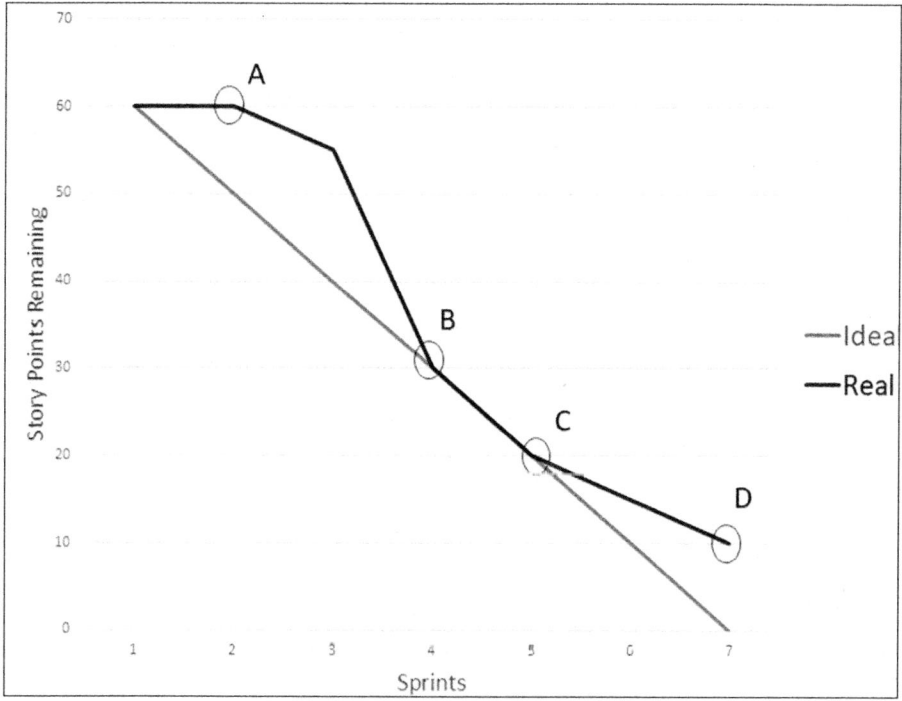

Figure 10.7: *Release burndown*

However, at sprint 3, they could complete stories and came to the ideal line at B. From B to C they maintained the ideal velocity. But, again at D, they missed the release as 10 story points could not be completed. The team probably should actively plan for 8 story points as the velocity and not 10.

The team can plan for a minimal product that can be released with a lower velocity. Since they have traditionally shown a higher velocity additional features can be added to the feature buffer.

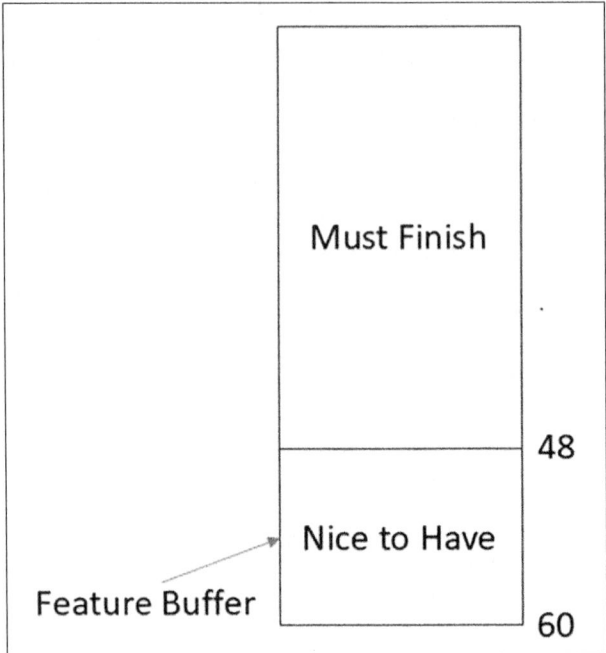

Figure 10.8: *Feature buffers in action*

If the team finishes the stories on time, they can pick up the nice-to-have items in the feature buffer.

Minimal Viable Product

The Minimum Viable Product (MVP) has three words:

- **Product**: We have discussed products in great length in *Chapter 1, The Practice of Product Management*.
- **Minimum**: It means there is just enough to have a stakeholder for the product development. The stakeholder is not always a customer.
- **Viable**: A context-sensitive term that shifts the product definition.

The current article is about such context and the associated viability of products. Viability can change with product and organization lifecycle. We will discuss the effect of context on viability here.

Concept Viability

Concept viability is the first phase of a project. A product based on just a concept is generally unfit for the market. An engineer with the concept puts together a running demo and presents it to a sponsor such as a product manager or BU head. A product manager can add a business case, a UI designer UI mockup, or a strategy consultant a business proposal with business viability. Based on the proposer, the MVP can change. It can be a working product, a prototype, or an artifact for the next step. Or, as a team, they create a pitch for an investor with all the right artifacts and components. There are some hypothetical customers or a few early adopters at this stage. The scope is clearly to get the mindshare of the investor and not to sell this product in the market.

Competition Viability

When you are David entering the market, the competition is a Goliath. Directly attacking the competition can be detrimental to your survival. The best option here is to slice and dice the market to the levels where you are the most prominent player vis-a-vis competition. Once you find your sweet spot, extend the product to pick up another adjacent market without significantly affecting the original market. A time comes when your market grows to a point where the original market looks miniscule. Apple introduced the iPhone to consumers, and they loved it. Microsoft and Blackberry selling into enterprises never saw the threat from Apple. At one point, the iPhone and Android took the market by storm, and the classic enterprise smartphone market could not compete and went out of business. iPhone 1.0 was a great MVP, multi-touch, internet-enabled browsing, integrated phone, and so on as discussed in *Chapter 2, Strategy* and *Chapter 3, Product Vision*.

Sales Viability

The products may be good, but the sales cycles take too long. In these cases, the product team can enable the sales team to sell by introducing some quick sales-enhancing features, such as creating demos for primary use cases, handling objections from customers, reviewing RFP questionnaires to identify feature gaps, and so on. Sales Ready Products (SRP)[24] is one such framework that claims to compress the sales cycles. While SRP helps in selling, the other non-functional needs of enterprise products have to be looked into as well.

Lifecycle Viability

There is a general feeling that MVPs are for new products. Do you need an MVP for version 2.0 of the product? Think of Adobe deciding to take Acrobat to the cloud. They

---

[24] Jim Goetz, The Templeton Compression and the Sales Ready Product, 12th July 2016, https://www.sequoiacap.com/article/the-templeton-compression/ accessed 21st Feb 2025.

had a base of millions of users on desktops, and they could not have asked everyone to work on PDFs from a browser-based software. Adobe's PDF document creation and manipulation (Acrobat or today, known as Document Cloud) has five parts.

1. Creating PDF documents
2. Reading PDF documents
3. Manipulations of PDF documents
4. Document workflows
5. Sharing of documents

Adobe Reader allows free reading of PDF documents. In 2008, Adobe made the PDF standard an ISO standard. So, they commoditized creation. The Acrobat product manipulates PDF documents and requires a lot of graphics and user manipulations, and moving that all to the browser may have been hard. Adobe took a step-by-step approach. Adobe Reader and Acrobat for PDF manipulation remained the desktop software. They introduced server products for PDF creation, workflows, and sharing documents. They introduced a small change for a group of customers while the larger audience remained unaffected by incremental changes. The user who sees a link in Adobe Reader to upload a Microsoft Word document to generate a PDF is not an Adobe Acrobat user. But if he clicks, he becomes a customer of Adobe Document Cloud. It does not affect the existing paying Adobe Acrobat customers. These incremental workflows and feature additions are MVP-like and test the market, and, in the long run, they could launch a full-fledged cloud product.

Go to Market

Small feature releases every three to six months do not work for marketing very well. There is no mechanism to announce a big splash or launch in the market. In reality, the product is on the market every quarter. In such cases, marketing teams prefer a solution approach to selling. They focus on a solution the organization is addressing and include all the product features that can align with the larger solution messaging. If you have such a feature in the sprint, find out if there are marketing activities for the solution, such that you can align the product release with a marketing event. The classic market message earlier was that this is a substantial product that does something better than every competition, even from its earlier version. So, adopt it. The message was a big splash for the buyers looking for these announcements. This kind of message has no meaning in the SaaS world. There is no new version migration. The messaging is becoming newsletter-kind, targeting users and not buying decision-makers. The message is becoming more like, Here is something you were not able to do earlier, but now we have heard you, and you can do it with our product. A product go-to-market strategy has to now look at both buyer and customer targets independently in its communications—one with solution marketing with every marketing launch event and the other with user newsletters with every product release.

Working in the Mixed Models

Some individuals have special skills that the team does not have. For example, documentation, legal, user experience, and so on may not be present in every scrum team. It may not be affordable to do so as there may not be that much activity over the years to keep the team busy. These people work on a Kanban model. Solving one task at a time which is placed on their queue. However, it is crucial to track their schedule with the sprint needs of the scrum teams. Their activities can be staggered across the team. For example, documentation tasks can be picked up as soon as a story is worked on rather than waiting for the completion of the release. These expert teams can be part of the scrum of scrum meetings to align their activities with the sprint timelines. Lastly, when so many moving parts are in a product, integration and deployment can be hard to manage. Some enterprises employ a full sprint to integrate, deploy, and test for this purpose. With the application of automation, such needs can be reduced but may not be eliminated.

Conclusion

In some organizations, a large part of a product management activity is spent with the agile team as a product owner. However, we believe a product manager can influence a lot more in an organization when the larger objectives of the roles are understood. Product managers acting as POs often look at the agile process as observers and provide valuable feedback enhancing the process. The processes are designed to achieve the agile manifesto and its principles. Ritualistic adherence to the processes cannot bring out the true spirits embedded in the process. We introduced the backlog management, estimation, planning, and execution of scrum practices with simple examples in this chapter. However, the knowledge and capabilities improve with experience, knowledge sharing, and working with the team regularly. The technology teams are not the only people product managers engage with. They engage across the organization with people having varying driving factors. Our next chapter will discuss some of these aspects of product management.

Questions

1. What are epics and user stories? Develop a feature as an epic and break it down into an implementable user story.

2. Why should you write a user story such that completion benefits the user? Why should they not be technical tasks?

3. How would you prioritize your backlog? What are the considerations you take for the same?

4. Why do you focus on relative estimates for backlogs and only conduct detailed estimates on tasks in sprint planning?

5. Scrum development is continuous; there is no break. How do you account for personal time off, training, or non-project activities?

CHAPTER 11
People

Introduction

We have understood the external forces that affect our business. We looked at the various functions that, if effectively worked on, can tame the external forces. We saw the benefits of the agile process model in orchestrating the functions. We realize the functions need the whole organization to come together. In this chapter, we will review how product managers interact with various organization teams to convey the vision and establish a coordinated effort to realize it. We will also look at the skills that PMs should gain in executing their craft with confidence.

Structure

In this chapter, we will cover the following topics:

- Internal Organization Interactions
    - Sales
    - Sales Engineering
    - Marketing
    - Support, Customer Success, and Training
    - Architects
    - Engineering and Delivery
    - Senior Management
- Management in Matrix Organization
- Managing Product Managers
    - Hiring and Team Composition
    - The Adult Mindset
    - Management by Objective
    - Negotiations

Internal Organization Interactions

Product management has the final responsibility for the product's success. However, the Product Managers (PMs) do not develop the product in isolation. They need to involve the whole organization in its success. Every product begins with a vision that requires clear communication with the internal teams. The internal teams a PM interacts with are shown in the following figure.

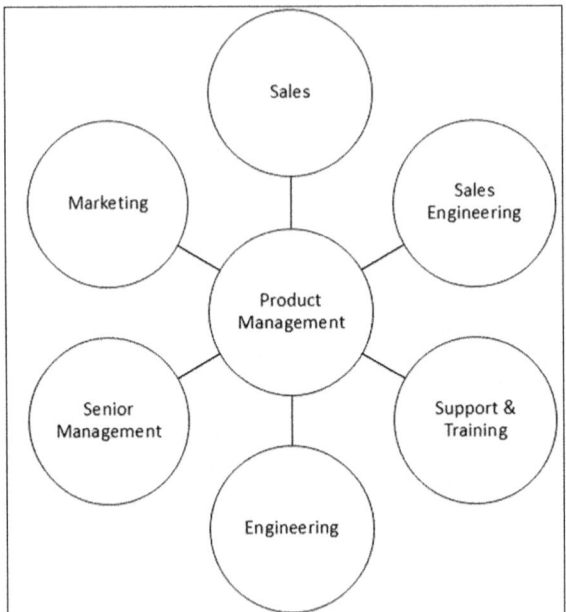

Figure 11.1: *Product management and the organization's interactions*

We will discuss how PMs need to understand the driving factors of the teams they deal with, how they bring the product vision into realization, and how they maintain a balance between the constituents of the organizations.

Sales

No product can succeed without the efforts and success of its salesforce. In *Chapter 4, Customer*, we discussed PM's interaction with the external teams, transitioning them from a buyer to a customer mindset. Before the relationship is established, the sales team engages with the potential buyers. In most cases, from earlier interactions and exchanges with these potential buyers from various industry forums, previous sales engagements, and so on, the sales teams try to create personal trust with these buyers. Some sales personnel would engage with the potential buyers socially, such as members of the same golf club, school alumni, neighbors, investors in similar ventures, and so on. The relationship is deeper than the product selling. When the product does not deliver the promise, the salesperson may feel like he is at the receiving end, as he has a strong relationship at stake. Sales jobs can be transitional, but they would not like to lose a relationship as they would like to utilize it later. For example, salespersons would resist customers using products with substantial perceived quality issues. A PM can see these in interactions with sales teams, particularly when the previous releases had quality issues.

A sales team is not a technology-driven team. They discuss the product in simple, use-case-driven slides, showcasing a catchy demo with minimal complexities and customer objections supported by ready-made solution articles. However, not all products are alike. Customers can understand some products easily, while others require a good bit of configuration before the customers can get to realize the value added. Some of these complex products need the help of sales or solution engineering. Since the sales teams are generally not technology-oriented, they take third-party perceptions of the products quite seriously. A product difficult to configure and showcase to a potential customer would not fly high in their minds. They also want to see sufficient marketing collateral and product information available through analysts. In short, they like to influence customers with information available in the market. Typically, organizations motivate the sales teams through commissions on sales. The sales teams are open to discounting to the extent that it may hurt the profitability of the products. PMs have to keep these motivators of the sales team into consideration.

Sales Engineering

Sales engineering, presales, and solution engineering, whatever the name may be, are the teams that work with the sales team to address customer objections in a sales process. They are shared resources across various projects and geographies, simultaneously meeting many engagements. Unlike the sales team, they do not have a compensation structure tied significantly to sales commission. They understand the product well and often become the conduit to communicate product capabilities to the sales team. They know the customers' environments, tools the customers use, customization needs for the product, and so on. Hence, they can be good resources to understand customer requirements. Often, they are the most significant proponents of the customers in the organization. They reply to the customers' queries and concerns, present demos to the customers, and integrate the product into the customer environment, showcasing the proof of concepts. Many PMs have served as sales and solutions engineers before transitioning into PM roles. There is a natural bond PMs establish with this team. However, being sales-focused, sales engineering teams prefer demos and PoCs over non-functional needs such as scalability and reliability of the product. Getting carried away by the sales engineering team's cool features or demo mindset should be moderated by product managers. Many product managers start their early careers in sales or solution engineering. However, sales or management perceptions of such PMs do not change with the change of roles. They look at them as an extension of their team in the product group. PMs get involved in sales discussions. It is natural for them to get involved in solution engineering. A PM should know where to draw a line, as it is fairly easy to get trapped in one customer engagement at the cost of the larger product.

Marketing

Traditionally, products are the value-creation part of the marketing function. However, in software management today, Product Management is a separate role. Hence, there will be some overlaps and clashes. We can split the value creation function into three aspects - build, perception, and realization. The PMs take requirements from the market. With the help of engineering, they build the product. The marketing teams want to develop the perception in the customer's minds so that the value is realized through a product sale. This value perception is also known as demand generation. Marketing teams are focused on events, conferences, and channels where they can meet prospects who need a solution, yet the need to demand conversion has not happened. At the end of the event, marketing teams pass on the generated leads to the sales teams to contact the prospects. The pipeline of spending on events to lead generation to actual conversion into sales is a metric a marketing team keeps on the radar.

Most events are expensive. A lack of conversion into sales from activities at such events reflects on the efficacy of marketing spending. In the classic software lifecycles, the marketing events were earmarked on the calendars, and products were launched in such events. Product champions like Steve Jobs would unbox the Mac or iPhone at an Apple Developer Conference and announce its arrival. Today, companies release SaaS products on a fortnightly basis. Existing users would like to know what is coming in this iteration and if they should renew their licenses next month, while the new customers are evaluating whether this is the right solution to invest in in the future. Traditional marketing campaigns are better tuned to target new customers. They reach out to forums where buyers will congregate and initiate the demand generation, while PMs focus on the releases and content for the releases. Customer success and retention are assigned to PMs in some organizations. In such cases, the content and communication needs for the existing customer, release notes, and what is new to keep the interest of the regular user are areas of interest for the PMs. Marketing teams do not get specific event coverage from PMs in such cases. In most cases, better planning and translation of product release content to marketing solution literature can target existing and new customers evenly.

Support, Customer Success, and Training

Understanding support and customer interaction can help a PM understand product operations well and enhance the customer experience. Ideally, a customer having to reach product support is an inefficiency in the system. The solution is not to push the support team further behind layers of chat or AI tools but to eliminate the need for the customer to reach them by improving the product. At the same time, an enabled support team who can understand the customer's problem as soon as the call reaches them and take remediation action is considered ideal. In the case of a Return Merchandise Authorization (RMA) of a cheap good, just sending the customer a replacement is better than tracking the goods, recovering the item, and delaying delivery. A product team would statistically quantify it in their planning rather than engaging a support team member. However, the problem has to be understood and the root cause analyzed so that the RMA does not become the norm. Organizations aggregate the support team across products. A frontline support team typically known as L1 and L2 is script-driven and can only solve simple repetitive tasks. Today, some of these get delivered through chatbots. The PMs should take cognizance of the workflows and ensure the customer is onboarding onto the flow when needed. However, the higher level of support teams L3 and L4 can be champion evangelists of the product. They work with the customers regularly. In the case of SaaS products, the customer data may not be exposed to the engineers who developed the product. The support team acts as a conduit to reproduce the customer problems or extract anonymized data from the customer environment for the engineering teams to work on. These engineers should have superlative product knowledge. Another area where a PM should look forward to engaging the support team is understanding the customer environment and cross-selling adjacent products. The users open up to support engineers and discuss adjacent problem areas in the product. They show inquisitiveness when knowing the product or if the product has a solution for their day-to-day problem. A well-connected PM can look for an opportunity to sell additional functionality or build additional features with the main product. However, the product vision should be well-ingrained in the support team. The PMs are responsible for keeping the support team engaged with the product vision.

Architects

Let us say we are laying vitrified tiles as flooring in a bathroom. Water has to flow down the tiles; Tile 1 will be at a higher elevation and 12 at the lowest elevation, and there is a gradual gradient in that direction. You may wonder why you cannot put the exit at the extreme corner of the bathroom. The water exit pipelines are already there before they start laying tiles. So, you cannot control their locations. After you lay the tiles, you will realize there is water logging at D, the right corner of Tile 12.

In *Figure 11.2*, we want point D to be raised and points A, E, and C to be made the lowest points. It can be achieved when we crack the tile along the line AC as shown in (e).

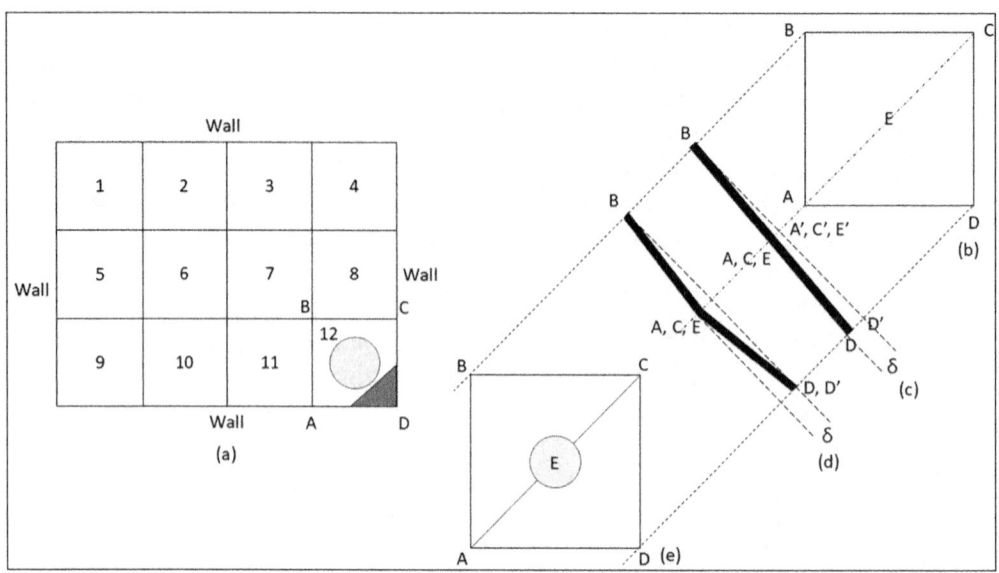

Figure 11.2: Floor sloping in a bathroom (a) Overall bathroom floor tile layout (b) The top view of Tile 12 (c) Side view of the tiles along the line AC. D is the lowest point. (d) Sloping modification to make A, C, and E the lowest points. (e) The top view of the tile shows the tile broken along the AC line

The sloping requirement is common sense, but the need to crack tile 12 for better gradients is a detail an expert can bring in. It is harder to explain and needs a complex engineering drawing. Standardized engineering practices can solve many such common-sense problems. The finer details require an expert to implement, document, and explain to people with a layman's understanding of the art. Adopting Docker and Kubernetes can solve the scalability and continuous deployment issues, but designing the workloads for orchestration to be effective for your service portfolio requires a lot of design considerations. You will need a good architect to understand these nuances and make the system design. Unfortunately, architects report to engineering management, which focuses on the volume of functional delivery, while the architect focuses on non-functional delivery aspects, such as quality, reliability, scalability, and so on. These detailed architectural considerations may seem esoteric and non-relevant to an average engineer. With a higher numeric strength, they may influence the management over the decisions of a handful of architects. As a PM, you may need to support the architects in justifying their focus on NFRs by providing the actual customer environments and why the scale is important for the product. The other issue is supportability. Software products are developed for long-term use. The underlying operating systems, third-party libraries, and connectivity architectures may change. A PM, with the help of an architect, should plan for updating them. The user stories for a release should consider the engineering debts from the previous releases.

Engineering and Delivery

Product management and engineering work closely, ensuring the release of the product. In the agile framework, product management acts as the product owner. For some, the overall product management responsibility is not apparent, leading to conflicts. PMs also look at engineering as one technical unit. In scrum, the ideal team should be able to address any technical challenge directed towards them. There are no developer or tester distinctions. In reality, the engineering teams are becoming highly specialized with deep yet limited exposure to one technology area. Some developers want to move into a broader set of skills called full-stack development. While respected in the community, only a few developers can develop on a varied full stack. For example, a front-end developer releases for iOS, Android, and Web. However, knowledge of all three platforms at an even level of complexity is hard to achieve. No single developer can be good at all the platforms. If we include all the backend technology frameworks in operations, it is a substantial uphill task to cover by one individual engineer.

Engineering understanding of the domain becomes a challenge for PMs. PMs struggle with technology, while engineering teams want detailed technical discussions. The user story is a middle ground through which a PM explains the customer benefit. However, engineers sometimes prefer the stories to be simple engineering tasks. For example, as a user, I would like to get the same values I entered in the form. For an engineer, it is a form that preserves data on a database. For testers, the user story approach is better as they can replicate the scenario easily in test cases. The engineers understand the user stories over several iterations and discussions. However, some PMs assume the engineers understood the story the way it is written. Even if the stories are understood, the vision requires regular reinforcement. There is regular communication between engineers and PMs; otherwise, apparent gaps can be left in the released product. PMs are entrusted with the responsibility of fostering innovation in an organization. However competent the PMs are, they can only succeed when the engineering teams are aligned and produce innovative solutions. The innovations have to align with a well-defined vision. We discussed how open-ended epics can enthuse the scrum teams to approach a problem through multiple possibilities. Many engineers aspire to challenging work and fulfillment in accomplishing tasks. PMs can use these opportunities to produce innovative features for the product and recognize the team. Lastly, a good working relationship does not always mean a friendly social association. It means the team will produce their best professional output, which benefits the product. As long as that is maintained, it is good for the organization.

Senior Management

In this chapter, we discuss several specific departments. Every department has its senior leadership PMs interact. However, when we collectively look at senior leadership, we are considering senior leaders across the organization who affect the strategy of the product. While the PMs are responsible for the product vision, the investments come from the organization's strategy. Here are some challenges that can be seen in organizations. The organization strategy does not keep the individual interests of BUs in mind. Since BUs are independent profit centers in their rights, they do not want to align with the larger organization strategy and work on the established product visions. In maintaining the revenues and profits over the year, the organizations do not question the BUs' decisions. In short, the impact of the strategy remains as a guiding principle rather than an enforceable order unless it is accompanied by restructuring and portfolio planning. The distinction between the BU and organization is relatively small in single-product companies. They look at the PM role as a function for requirements elicitation and maintaining the product backlog. They even involve product backlogs and prioritization into senior management roles.

The typical software product comes into existence when a few functions come together. A domain expert interacts with the industries and understands the product gaps. She explains the gaps to a technology-savvy friend. They start building the first product and make the product sale to the initial few customers. They realize functional challenges and induct the various roles the organization demands. However, the newer functional leadership and their understanding of the product do not match. Instead of driving the organization's strategy that produces a consistent product vision that is passed on to each functional team, the focus goes to managing each functional silo of the organization. However, when the organization reaches a size, the same principles of opportunistic market acquisition do not work. For example, larger customers would like your product in the analysts' discussions and forums. The small customers would like to see more self-service purchase and support options. Moreover, too many direct contact touchpoints for SMB customers drain the sales and support teams. The customers do not get access to the senior leadership now and complain about it. The 1-100 growth phase poses different challenges from the 0-1 phase of the organization that the founding leaders of the organization have addressed. A better understanding of each other's roles and responsibilities can make the PM function rewarding and beneficial to the overall organization. It may help senior leadership discuss and develop the product vision with the PMs and internalize it for the larger good of the organization and its investors.

Management in Matrix Organization

Product management roles interact across various departments. They have market insight and access to customers and users. Often, they have to wear multiple hats depending on the teams they interact with. It is unlikely that they will have the knowledge and understanding of the domains of the teams they interact with. Yet, they should be confident in leveraging the knowledge of all the constituent domain leaders. In short, they should be able to influence without authority.[1] The principles are summarized in these approaches:

- Assume all are potential allies
- Clarify your goals and priorities
- Diagnose the world of the other person
- Identify relevant currencies in theirs and your world
- Dealing with relationships
- Influence with give and take

While these principles are common sense, the applications can be challenging. We have the organization, department, and individual aspirations. Some interests can be conflicting. In the agile framework, the teams are almost unchanged. The focus is on the customer. The overall team's goals are beyond any other individual or department aspirations. It is where PMs need the help of strategies set forth by the senior leadership. PMs work one-on-one with some constituent teams and are exposed to an individual's interests and aspirations. For example, sales management is not able to pitch a product due to a lack of understanding of the domain in the assigned pre-sales staff. A PM can assist the sales manager in overcoming these hurdles by coaching or guiding the pre-salesperson. Engineering teams may find the development monotonous for some time. The PM can run a few parallel ideas open to everyone to contribute as hackathon events. Even some people can aspire to be PMs in their career progression and mentoring them in their larger goals can be fruitful. We highlighted some basic thoughts about currencies. However, PMs can learn better as they interact with the teams regularly. Being present in various team events and discussing challenges that a person faces is a good way to communicate and exchange ideas. Some challenges may not be associated with work and business at all and can be personal as well. Sometimes, hearing out may be helpful as well. PMs can become peers and gain more insights into people than supervisors of authority.

Managing Product Managers

When we started writing this book, some suggested we discuss product management careers. What are the skillsets needed at various levels of PM careers? We consciously avoided it as we wanted to keep the book to product management, not product managers. In the organization structures and processes, the processes are important. The structures needed to accomplish them are the flexibility an organization should work out based on the size and financial resources. Marketers in P&G carved out the product management role to one person to coordinate across functional teams and eliminate the bottlenecks to ensure smooth operations. Technically, PMs are outcome-

---

[1] Allan R. Cohen and David L. Bradford, Influence Without Authority, John Wiley & Sons, Inc., Hoboken, New Jersey. 2017

driven rather than persons of functional skills seen in other roles. Unlike functional roles, where managers spend substantial time building the right teams to set up a balanced team of skills—one member supporting the other—PMs do not get that much flexibility. Most of the time, PMs cannot choose their teams (you can hardly decide your customer), they are probably the first to explore the market (they cannot expect guidance or handholding), they are limited on resources (most exploratory projects are light on budget; hence almost no additional helping hand), and they are expected to be domain leaders (because they have tried to venture into the market). Why would someone engage in a profession like this? A large part of the answer lies in people's psychological makeup, interest, and ability to define their work and explore unknown business problems. In many organizations, there are no PM supervisors. They either report to the BU leaders or PM directors. Organizations struggle when they try to set up the same boundaries as they would for other functional organizations.

Hiring and Team Composition

The PMs come from all walks of life and graduate into these roles. Sometimes, you would find the least technically savvy person acting as a PM of one of the most complex technical products. The most diverse PM teams the author worked for had a product trainer, a sales engineer, a technical consultant, a research scientist, a documentation expert, a marketing manager, and so on as coworkers. While everyone had significant functional skills and expertise, they all had a great understanding of their customers and markets. Earlier organizations hired product managers from other functional roles where they saw strong business acumen in the individuals. Such people derive a natural trust and respect among their peers. However, a trend has emerged in the past decade to hire fresh MBA graduates as associate PMs. It has also led to the general question—an MBA is a requirement for a PM. Business acumen is a serious skill set needed for a product manager. In this book, we saw the need for business knowledge. Whether a person picks it up through experience or education is her prerogative.

In an outcome-driven role, often, the work allocation is delegatory. In a team of PMs, the individual product manager caters to her product independently. There is no intervention unless there is an exception or the PM requests help. PMs also delegate their activities to the scrum teams to expedite the process. For example, if a PM is not finding enough time to attend the scrum planning meeting, she can explain the stories to an individual in the team to represent her. They sometimes may ask sales engineers to present at a conference if the geographical presence makes it easier rather than the PM traveling. Sometimes, a PM may represent all the products of the BU in a business region to minimize travel costs. Openness to newer needs and challenges helps develop additional domain skills among the PMs. It also gives them the ability to delegate with ease rather than micromanaging.

The Adult Mindset

The nature of PM activities makes it easier for people with certain mindsets. In the transactional analysis,[2,3] individuals are classified into three mindsets: parent, child, and adult. A person with a child mindset likes to be guided, and a parent finds his duty to guide a child. The bonding develops quite naturally in such groups. However, many colloquial manager-subordinate relationships develop over such sentiments. As much as positive strokes develop a great working relationship, a negative stroke can shatter the child's faith in the parent. The adult mindset works independently. People with these mindsets look for cues and guidelines but no handholding. They would like to open themselves to new challenges. It comes with the possibility of failure. They are open to failure and start again rather than be prodded for failure. PMs land up in such challenges regularly—the product may not be liked by the customers, the quality may be lacking, the sales teams are not able to understand and sell the product, and so on. If you look deeper, in many of these, the PMs do not have a direct role in the problem, nor can they solve the problems independently. Yet, they become the last point of escalation for the product and are responsible for it. A useful tool in such cases is the Responsible-Accountable-Contributing-Informed (RACI) model. While the PM is responsible for the overall product, she should delegate the functional aspects to various stakeholders and make them accountable. The PM shall inform the BU leadership about the progress and challenges in delivering value to the customers.

Management by Objective

A PM role is outcome-driven. PMs should learn to define and act toward Specific, Measurable, Achievable, Realistic, and Time-bound (SMART) goals. The agile framework user stories are SMART goals the teams achieve. The specification of acceptance criteria, the consistent evaluation, and breaking down with the team involvement make the user stories achievable. The user stories are realistic user benefits. Moreover, the teams complete within a time-bound sprint cycle. The PMs also have to be evaluated using measurable goals. Suppose a BU has to raise its sales by 10% year-on-year (y-o-y). Not all products will be able to increase revenues at the same rate. The product in the growth phase or with a lesser initial base may have to grow at 20% y-o-y. It means the product should keep the renewals to the maximum, say 90% (some customers would not renew), while there will be 30% net new customers. The sales team has to have a pipeline of 150% (assuming 20% conversion). Customer retention is as important as getting net new customers to meet the annual revenue target for SaaS products. The PMs have a significant role in customer retention; it may be part of their objective for the year. It is a small example of how BU's objectives converge with the PM's annual objective. It would also mean the PM has to evaluate customer satisfaction (CSAT) and

---

[2] Eric Berne, Games People Play, 1964
[3] Thomas Harris, I'm OK – You are OK, 1967

work on cases where there are potential CSAT issues. Surveys are not the only ways to capture CSATs. They may have to contact the support teams, reach the troubled accounts, and add the features to immediate releases. From the new accounts, the PMs have to estimate the customers looking for specific features and align the releases so that the critical features are well within the deal-closing expectations from the sales team. A delay in product release can affect the revenue realization estimated for the year. We discussed a simple example of how to set a product objective aligned with the larger organizational objective. Generally, we try to keep Big-Hairy-Audacious-Goals (BHAG) for the organization or the North Star goals that keep us focused, yet they are hard to achieve. However, goals not achieved take away confidence from a team. The objectives and Key Results (OKRs) framework help maintain a base level of confidence in the team to achieve objectives. For every objective set, there is a minimum achievable key result. However, there is another set of higher-order results the PMs should achieve to ensure better-than-expected performance.

Negotiations

In *Chapter 4, Customer*, we discussed principled negotiation and BATNA.[4] Unlike the customers, where economics is the driving factor for determining the BATNA, there will be a different strategy for internal teams. As discussed in the influencing without authority framework, the currencies may not be all economics-driven. Some organizations have simple awards, such as thank-you awards, to recognize a person from another team when someone achieves something beyond the duties at work. When dealing with senior leadership, knowledge in the domain and statistics can be handy. Sales teams get excited when a catchy demo or tool is given to them to discuss in front of a customer. Even a good Fear-Uncertainty-Doubt (FUD) against a competitor's product can be a great talking point to sales engineering teams. Analysts can be impressed when your product features and decisions are in sync with their predictions. Engineering teams are excited when they are allowed to explore new ideas for the product. A well-defined vision can be the most important bargaining metric; when something is aligned with the shared vision, the mere statement of the intent becomes acceptable to everyone. However, visions have a slippery slope. Teams start missing it when not enforced time and again. Every communication and message that enforces the vision must clarify the intent. As much as PMs would like to positively reward the teams, there are situations where they have to take a negative posture. For example, a non-inclusion of a specific feature crucial for a product release should hold the release back. PMs would not approve of such a release. Similarly, when a product may not meet the compliance needs of a certain market, the PM may ask the sales team not to venture into the market rather than making non-substantive marketing claims.

---

[4] Better Alternative to the Negotiated Agreement, Roger Fisher and William Ury, Getting to Yes, 1981.

Conclusion

The product management role works with various organizational functions to make a product a reality. However, in most cases, they influence their decisions without having apparent authority. There are challenges, and the numerical strengths are always against the PMs. We looked at some of the techniques the PMs can use to overcome these limitations. Secondly, we looked at some aspects of managing product managers. Although we have kept the book focused on product management rather than product manager hierarchies, certain psychological traits, like the adult mindset, are apparent in PMs due to the very nature of the work they are involved in. While individuals can differ from the collective wisdom, awareness of transactional analysis (psychology) will help in managing product managers.

Questions

1. Consider a situation in your organization, where there is a conflict between engineering and PM. How are you addressing the conflict?

2. Does the senior management have conflicting viewpoints on the working of the product managers? If yes, how can you resolve the issues?

3. How are you apprising the field teams about your product releases? How are they getting to know about the product features?

4. What is the composition of product managers in your team? What were they working on before they became product managers?

CHAPTER 12
Epilogue

Our attempt to explore the product management processes and directions started with the paper Product Management at Crossroads.[1] We realized many product managers are trained in specific frameworks of product management, and they do not appreciate the rationale behind them. We wanted to change that thinking. We got back to the drawing board again. Thank you for joining us in that adventure. We started with defining the product and product mindset and how software products came into existence in the first place. Product managers are supposed to look outside the organization and bring in changes to the product based on what they see. Michael Porter helped us in making an objective evaluation of the outside. We realized the five forces, namely, industry rivalry, bargaining power of buyers, bargaining power of suppliers, new entrants, and substitutes, affect the sustained competitive advantage of our business. We tamed them using ten focused areas. In each chapter, we delved deeper into each of the processes and convinced ourselves why those processes are relevant to the success of a product.

We worked with the organization's leadership to align the **strategy** with our product. We developed a clear **product vision** and communicated it internally and externally, giving a clear market message. Our focus is clear, and our resolve to take on the competition head-on is part of that execution. We influenced our buyers to become our **customers**. They now see value in us and are ready to pay us an equitable **price**. We asked our customers to help us reach the users and create a compelling **user experience**. In doing so, we ensured our users became our cheerleaders, influencing our customers in the long run. We knew we could not meet our customer commitments alone; we needed suppliers with us all along. The suppliers are trying hard for us to become customers and not buyers. We want a long-term business relationship–documented and reviewed periodically with **contracts**. We developed our **intellectual properties**. They work as a moat, protecting our castle against new entrants. Over the years, we have been a compliant business, and any substitute in the market will not meet the regulatory **compliance** needs. Some early adopters of the substitutes will take risks, but most of our business is protected. We cannot do it all ourselves; we need **people** to work towards the vision and deliver. Our business processes have to be

---

[1] Dash, Sambit Kumar, Product Management at Crossroads (January 22, 2022). SPM Summit India, IIM Bangalore, 22nd January 2022, Available at SSRN: **https://ssrn.com/abstract=4195893**

Epilogue

agile to ensure changes in the business are identified early and acted on. That is what we would call the **Practice of Product Management**.

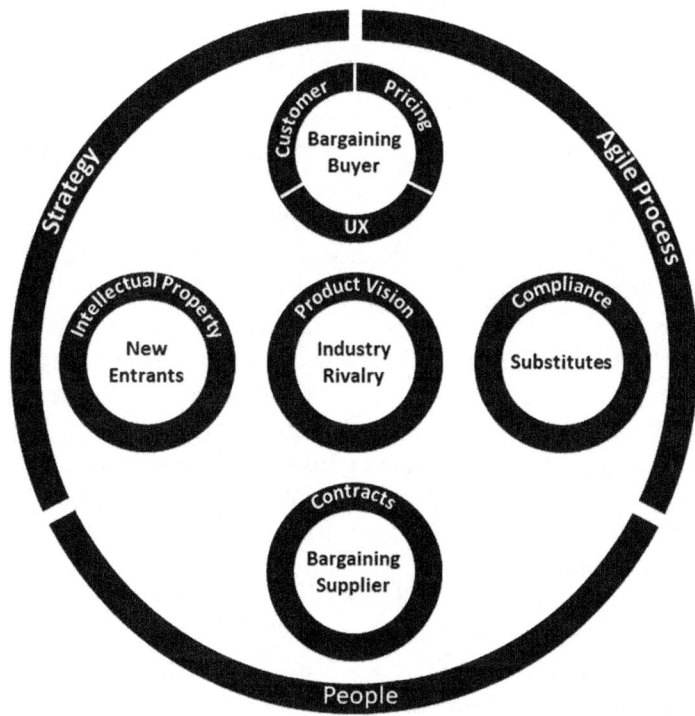

Figure 12.1: *The Practice of Product Management Framework*

The author introduced the practice of product management framework[2], suggesting what the product management function should be. The timing could not have been better. The number of product managers has increased substantially. Several management institutes have introduced MBA courses around product management. Moreover, people have started becoming disillusioned with product management. Some even have opined that product management is a dead field. They believe it is becoming bureaucratic[3] or AI will take away product management,[4] thus making the function irrelevant. When we started this book, some people suggested we discuss hierarchical competencies needed for various career levels of product managers.

---

[2] Ibid.
[3] Joe Procopio, Is It Time for the Tech Industry to Rethink Product Management? It shouldn't take 73 days to make a simple text change to an app, 25th November 2024, Inc., **https://www.inc.com/joe-procopio/is-it-time-for-the-tech-industry-to-rethink-product-management/91023511** accessed 30th December 2024
[4] Joe Procopio, The Untimely Death of Product Management, Tech execs ask: Why have product managers when you can just keep using AI? 22nd Oct. 2024, Inc., **https://www.inc.com/joe-procopio/the-untimely-death-of-product-management/90990600** accessed 30th December 2024

We consciously decided this to be a book on Product Management and not Product Managers. We do not even suggest all the functions we discussed be worked upon by a person with the designation of a product manager or any career level that fits. Can we build a product and sustain a competitive advantage without implementing the functions we discussed? We leave this question to the readers to reflect on.

Now, let us look at the impact of AI on a product manager's function. Let us look at a few activities from a product management perspective. A few years back, the PM would review the technology business press or analyst websites to find the percentage of devices or operating system versions in the market and decide the OS and device requirement for the release. Today, the information is available to the developers in Android Studio. If there is a policy that the application will be available on 80 percent of devices in the market, the developers can decide which platforms to choose. Every product manager would read general business news relevant to their domain to know what is happening in the market. Now, most PMs set a news alert notification on a few relevant keywords and get access to the information they need. Keyword-based text search was the AI probably 4-5 years ago. Today, AI has moved on. With OpenAI ChatGPT or Google Gemini, you can probably get deeper insights into data. However, is that insight enough? If you search for multi-factor authentication on G2,[5] you will get about 250+ SaaS-based solutions. Similarly, if you try to search for purchasing software, there will be another 150+ SaaS-based solutions. Even with such a list, you can hardly get actionable insight unless you target specific customer use cases and find that differentiating golden nugget. With the video summarization facility on web conferencing tools, you can access customer interviews for specific areas of interest. A PM does not have to be in every meeting but can train the client managers, support executives, and solution architects to solicit the user requirements. Only when there is confusion in the summary do PMs solicit additional interactions. The volume of data that is getting generated is making AI a necessity. If you look at a PM to summarize a customer interaction and write user stories, we would assume such jobs will not be there in the future. Here is an experiment the author tried with Google on the translation of user stories to acceptance criteria.

User Story: *As a content creator, I want to use an AI writing assistant to generate ideas and draft text quickly, so I can focus on refining and editing my work.*

Acceptance Criteria:

- **Idea Generation:** *The AI tool can generate a list of relevant content ideas based on a given topic or prompt within 5 seconds.*
- **Text Drafting:** *The AI can produce a coherent paragraph of text based on a user-provided prompt, including variations in tone (informative, persuasive, casual).*

---

[5] G2, Insights on Software Products, **https://www.g2.com/**

- **Customization:** Users can adjust the length and style of the generated text through parameters like formality level and target audience.
- **Accuracy:** The AI-generated text should be factually accurate and free from major grammatical errors.
- **Feedback Loop:** Users can provide feedback on generated text to improve the AI's future outputs.

Key points:

- Focus on the user's goal: to efficiently create content with AI assistance.
- Define clear, measurable criteria for quality and functionality.
- Ensure acceptance criteria are testable and can be used to validate the AI tool's performance.

It is impressive but still reads like a template. The PM has to intervene to make actionable criteria. The PM can start with this template—a copilot to speed up the activities. The PM can spend more time soliciting better requirements and reaching more customers. In the coming days, we will see lots of such tools, content-generation capabilities, and workflow automation, reducing our efforts. However, the PMs as final decision-makers will not be replaced so soon. We hope this book and the Practice of Product Management Framework can guide you in making better decisions.

Index

A

Agile Process 177
Agile Process, components
  Estimation 188, 189
  Iterations 192
  Requirements 182-184
  Retrospective 193
Agile Process,
     configuring 177-179
Agile Process, models
  Kanban 190
  SAFe 191
  Scrum 190
Agile Process,
     principles 179

B

BCG, application 27
BCG, categories
  Cow 26
  Pet 26
  Question Mark 26
  Star 26
Beneficial Relationship,
     preventing 60-64
Boston Consulting Group
     (BCG) 26
BTC, aspects
  Purchase Involvement 58
  Strategic Alignment 58
  Value Perception 58
BTC, configuring 59, 60
Buyer To Customer
     (BTC) 58
Buying Process,
     optimizing 54-56

C

Certificate Authority
     (CA) 161-163
Compliance 160
Compliance, importance 161
Contract 115
Contract,
     architecture 116, 117
Contract, parts
  Licensee Rights 129-132
  Licensor Rights 132, 133
  Service Provider
     Rights 134-136
Contract Performance,
     preventing 127
Contract, steps 117
Contract, terms
  Lawful Subject 121
  Parties 117-119
  Sale Of Goods 119, 120
  Tenders 121
Copyright 141
Copyright, configuring 141, 142
Copyright, highlights 142, 143
Corporation 19
Customer, identifying 51-54
Customer Value,
     establishing 64-66

D

Design Thinking 113
Design Thinking, process 113
DuPont 27, 28

E

Enforcement 126, 127

F

Framework 10
Framework, configuring 10-12

G

Graphical User Interface
    (GUI) 104
GUI, devices
  Desktop/Laptop 104
  Mobile Phones 104
  Tablets 104
GUI, fundamentals
  Accessibility 109
  Knowledge
      Dissemination 109
  Platform/API 106-108
  Screens/Devices 104
  Technology 105, 106

I

Implied/Express,
    comparing 122-124
Independent Software
    Vendors (ISV) 6
Intellectual Propertys
    (IPRs) 138-140
IPRs Application,
    process 154, 155
IPRs, incentivizing 157, 158
IPRs, innovation 157
IPRs, preventing 155, 156
IPRs, types
  Copyright 141
  Design 153
  Patents 149
  Trademarks 145

J

Jurisdiction 124
Jurisdiction, use cases 125

K

Key Factors Success (KFS) 24
KFS, domain 25

M

Matrix Organization 210, 211
Messaging 170
MVP, elements
  Competition Viability 199
  Concept Viability 199
  Lifecycle Viability 199
  Sales Viability 199

N

Negotiation 66, 67
Non-Compliance 163
Non-Compliance Cost,
    optimizing 168, 169
Non-Compliance Criteria,
    gating 167
Non-Compliance,
    guidelines 163

O

Open Source 156
Open Source, levels 156
Organization Interactions 204
Organization Interactions,
    points
  Architects 207, 208
  Customer Success/
      Training 206, 207
  Engineering/Delivery 209
  Marketing 206
  Sales 204, 205
  Sales Engineering 205
  Senior Management 209

P

Patents, elements
  Application/Continuation 152
  Complete Disclosure 151
  Industrial Application 150
  Infringement 152, 153
  Non-Obvious/Inventive
      Step 151
  Novelty 150
  Patentable Subject Matter 149

Porter Five Forces 20
Porter Five Forces, effects
  Buyer, bargaining 22
  Competitors, rivalry 21
  Entrants 23
  Substitutes 22
  Suppliers, bargaining 22
Pricing 70
Pricing, architecture 71-73
Pricing, factors
  Alternative 80, 81
  Demand 81, 82
  Supplier 78, 79
Pricing, implications 90-92
Pricing, principles
  Metering 76
  Software License 76, 77
Pricing, schemes
  Bundles/Suites 86, 87
  Enterprise Plans 90
  Tiered Pricing 88, 89
  Volume-Based Pricing 84, 85
Product Management 7
Product Management,
    architecture 8, 9
Product Management,
    areas 9
Product Managers 211
Product Managers, setup
  Adult Mindset 213
  Negotiations 214
  Objective Managing 213
  Team Composition 212
Product Release, tools
  Burndown 196, 197
  Go To Market 200
  Minimal Viable Product
    (MVP) 198
  Readiness
    Assessment 197, 198
Product Vision 37
Product Vision, advantages
  Development 38
  Evaluation Guides/
    Battle Cards 38
  Influencers/Reviewers 38

Product Vision, communication
  External 47, 48
  Internal 46, 47
Product Vision,
    ensuring 44, 45
Product Vision,
    preventing 32-36
Product Vision, steps
  Documentation 43
  Product Development 43
  Roadmap 39-42
  Workflows 42
Product Vision, strategy 45

Q

Qualitative/Quantitative,
    insights 29

R

Realization 48
Realization,
    optimizing 48, 49

S

SaaS, terms
  Licensing 174
  Open Source 172, 174
  Operations 171
SCA, tools
  Boston Consulting Group
    (BCG) 26
  DuPont 27
  Key Factors Success
    (KFS) 24
  Porter Five Forces 20
Scrum, sections
  Communication Across 195
  Product Owner
    (PO) 195
  Scrum Master 194
  Scrum Teams 194
Software Product 1
Software Product,
    architecture 2
Software Product Management 56

Software Product Management, reasons
  Delivery Channels 57
  Operative Environment 56
  User Sophistication 57
  Workflows 56
Software Product, terms
  Economics 3
  Engineering 4, 5
  Infrastructure 5, 6
  Sales/Marketing 3, 4
  Technology 6, 7
Strategy 13
Strategy, architecture 17-19
Strategy, scenarios 16
Supplier 78
Supplier, guidelines
  Breakdown Structure 79
  Currency, effects 80
  Direct Labor 79
  Direct Material 79
  Indirect Costs 79
  Profit Margin 79
Sustained Competitive Advantage (SCA) 14

T

Trademarks 145
Trademarks, configuring 146, 147
Trademarks, principles 146
Trademarks, types
  Devicemark 146
  Wordmark 145

U

Uniform Domain Registration Policy (UDRP) 148
User Experience (UX) 94, 95
User Interface 104
UX, elements
  Architecture 98, 99
  Configuration 99, 100
  Culture 103, 104
  Domains 102
  Permission/Roles 100
  User Persona/Profiles 101
  Views 97, 98
  Workflow 96, 97
UX, frameworks
  Figma 111
  Flutter 112
  Material Design 112

V

Value-Based Pricing (VBP) 82, 83

Printed in Dunstable, United Kingdom